Care Management in Practice for the Registered Manager Award NVQ 4

Andrew Thomas
Lynda Mason
Sharon Ford

Heinemann Educational Publishers
Halley Court, Jordan Hill, Oxford OX2 8EJ
Part of Harcourt Education Limited

Heinemann is the registered trademark of Harcourt Education Limited

First published in 2003

2007 2006 2005
10 9 8 7 6 5

A catalogue record for this book is available from the British Library on request.

10-digit ISBN: 0 435401 59 9
13-digit ISBN: 978 0 435401 59 7

Pages designed by Artistix, Thame, Oxon.

Typeset and illustrated by J&L Composition, Filey, North Yorkshire.

Cover photo: © Bubbles

Printed and bound in Great Britain by CPI Bath.

Tel: 01865 888058 www.heinemann.co.uk

Websites
Please note that the examples of websites suggested in this book were up to date at the time
of writing. It is essential for tutors to preview each site before using it to ensure that the
URL is still accurate and the content is appropriate. We suggest that tutors bookmark
useful sites and consider enabling students to access them through the school or college
intranet.

Contents

Acknowledgements

I would like to thank my family for their unconditional support. Thanks also to Nicola Clarke, my personal editor and lead audio typist, for whom nothing is impossible. To my support staff Amy, Beverley, Dorothy, Tracey, Mrs Jones and Mr Huffer. To my inspirational role model Val Laurence, to Phil, Shelagh and Sandra whose knowledge of library resources knows no bounds. To friend and mentor Fred Harvey. To Graham Williams, Phillip Orton and all the staff at Broad View Care Limited for their kind permission to reproduce materials to support this text. Thanks also to Mike Singh and Anju Kaur and all the staff at Appledore Lodge for their kind permission to reproduce material in this book. Finally, thanks go to Mary and Matt at Heinemann for their continued faith in me.

Andrew Thomas

I would like to thank a number of colleagues who have helped and supported me throughout the preparation of this book. They have demonstrated both enthusiasm and interest in the subject matter. In particular, I would like to thank Irene Sziler and Elaine Kemp for their professional knowledge and their continued banter during 'stress busting' early-evening runs. You have kept me sane! A very special word of thanks also needs to go to my very supportive husband, Stuart, who has learned to shop without a list during the production of this work.

And finally, thanks to the 'team' at Heinemann who, as ever, have proven themselves to be imaginative, responsive and, most of all, supportive.

Lynda Mason

Photo acknowledgements

The authors and publisher would like to thank the following individuals and organisations for permission to reproduce photographs:

Gareth Boden – page 105

Format Photographers/Brenda Prince – page 351

Sally & Richard Greenhill – page 12, 204, 301, 312

Help the Aged – page 53, 161, 210

SPL/Ron Sutherland – page 343

Andrew Thomas would like to thank Appledore Lodge and Broad View Care Limited for their kind permission to reproduce material in this book.

Introduction

A career in care management is one of the most rewarding opportunities available. Due to regulations introduced as a result of the Care Standards Act 2000, all people managing in the care sector are required to have a recognised management award. The NVQ 4 Registered Manager Award will be a popular route for care managers and this book has been written to provide you with a comprehensive resource that will help you gain your award. It includes complete coverage of the four mandatory units, and six of the most popular optional units, providing you with all of the necessary underpinning knowledge. Advice and support on the completion of your portfolio is also provided, together with case studies and activities to reinforce your learning.

About this book

This book contains everything you need to succeed in your Registered Manager Award qualification. The content of the units matches the specification and covers all of the core units as well as six of the optional units.

The four mandatory units are:

O3 Develop, maintain and evaluate systems and structures to promote the rights, responsibilities and diversity of people

RM1 Manage a service which achieves the best possible outcomes for the individual

B3 Manage the use of financial resources

C13 Manage the performance of team and individuals

The optional units included in this book are:

D4 Provide information to support decision making

C8 Select personnel for activities

D2 Facilitate meetings

RM2 Ensure individuals and groups are supported appropriately when experiencing significant life events

F3 Manage continuous quality improvement

SC15 Develop and sustain arrangements for joint working between workers and agencies

Features of the book

Throughout the text there are a number of features that are designed to encourage reflection and discussion and to help relate theory to practice in a care management context. The features are:

Learning outcomes	a list of the outcomes that you will have learnt by the end of the unit
Try it out	practical exercises to try out in the workplace with opportunities to analyse and evaluate the results
Think it over	thought-provoking questions and dilemmas that can be used for individual reflection or group discussion
Case studies	examples of 'real' situations taken from the care sector to help you link theory to practice followed by questions to check understanding and explore concepts and ideas
Keys to good management practice	suggestions for promoting good practice in care management
Evidence collection	a helpful guide to the evidence required for your portfolio

Terminology

The terms 'resident', 'service user', 'customer' and 'client' are used interchangeably throughout this book. The authors of this book are aware that current terminology changes from time to time and that different terms are used by different organizations. The authors believe that this reflects our mixed economy of care and have therefore chosen to use a range of terms rather than one.

A final word

The author team involved in the production of this book have contributed their expertise and extensive knowledge of the care environment to this book; their purpose in doing so is to support you in your chosen studies and to provide you with a firm foundation from which you can extend and develop your particular interests.

We do hope that you enjoy your NVQ 4 Registered Manager Award and wish you good luck and every success in achieving your qualification and in your future work.

03

Develop, Maintain and Evaluate Systems and Structures to Promote the Rights, Responsibilities and Diversity of People

This unit outlines the legislative framework to your work as a registered manager within health and social care. Certain legislation gives the individual rights and responsibilities. The unit explores how, at times, these rights can be threatened either by a lack of awareness on the part of staff or residents, or by competing demands made upon the organisation. It considers the part played by residents and others in upholding their rights. It reviews how workers and managers can promote the rights of vulnerable people, by creating, managing and evaluating systems and structures in the workplace. The unit also examines how you, as the manager, can balance the competing demands and tensions which exist between different people and the zones of responsibility.

The elements are:
- Develop, maintain and evaluate systems and structures to promote the rights and responsibilities of people.
- Develop, maintain and evaluate systems and structures to promote the equality and diversity of people.
- Develop, maintain and evaluate systems and structures to promote the confidentiality of information.

Learning outcomes

- You are familiar with legislation and policies relating to the promotion of rights and responsibilities, the promotion of equality and diversity, and the promotion of confidentiality (the 'care value base').
- You recognise and understand ways of developing and maintaining systems and structures to promote the care value base.
- You are aware of the pressure points in the management of systems and structures.
- You know what action to take at pressure points.
- You recognise and understand the importance of change in the workplace.

You are familiar with legislation and policies relating to the promotion of rights and responsibilities, the promotion of equality and diversity, and the promotion of confidentiality

Rights and responsibilities, equality and diversity, and confidentiality are together collectively referred to as the 'care value base'. A good starting point for you, as a manager, is to ensure that you are fully up to date with the legislation and policies relating to the care value base. The most important piece of legislation in this regard is the Care Standards Act 2000.

Care Standards Act 2000

The Care Standards Act is the foundation stone of service provision. It expands the regulation of services to include domiciliary care services, fostering services and family centres. These services were previously unregulated but are now drawn into a comprehensive monitoring system.

The Act created a new system for regulating health and social care provision. Until 2000, regulation was carried out by local councils and health authorities under the Registered Homes Act 1984. However, from

April 2002 this system was replaced by the National Care Standards Commission. This is an independent, non-governmental body with a national remit with regard to inspection and regulation (rather than localised inspection units with their own criteria, which existed previously). The Commission aims to increase consistency across the sector.

The Secretary of State has produced the National Minimum Standards of care, under section 23(1) of the Act. These apply to all homes (as defined in section 3) which provide accommodation and/or personal or nursing care for adults with:

- physical disabilities;
- sensory disabilities;
- learning disabilities;
- autistic spectrum disorders;
- mental health problems;
- alcohol or substance misuse;
- HIV/AIDS;
- dual and/or complex multiple disabilities, including those who are deaf or blind.

The standards were created following consultation with service providers, users and regulators. The standards acknowledge the uniqueness of individuals and place emphasis on holistic and person-centred packages of care. Separate standards have been issued for older people, children and younger adults. Each set of standards is underpinned by specific themes. For example, the National Minimum Standards for Younger Adults is underpinned by the following themes:

- *Focus on service users*. Evidence will be required to show that choice, inclusion and promotion of rights are central to service provision.
- *Fitness for purpose*. Homes will need to provide evidence that the stated aims and objectives are achieved.
- *Comprehensiveness*. Services need to consider how clients can receive a 'total package' of care through effective cross-service/cross-agency working.
- *Positive choice*. Regulators will look for evidence that those in care homes remain there out of choice.
- *Meeting assessed needs*. Evidence will be required that care planning acknowledges and acts upon assessed needs and that changing needs are addressed.
- *Quality services*. Evidence will be sought that providers are working towards constant improvement of the quality of life of service users.
- *Quality workforce*. Regulators will seek evidence that managers and staff are trained in line with TOPSS requirements. This includes the induction of new staff and NVQ training for all care sector staff.

The National Minimum Standards are set out in sections, each of which deals with a specific issue. For example, Standard 23.1 sets out the minimum standards for care homes for older people: 'The National Minimum Standards for Care Homes for Older People focus on achievable outcomes for service users – that is, the impact on the individual of the facilities and services of the home' (Department of Health, 2002). It applies to all care homes that provide accommodation with nursing or personal care for older people.

The standards are organised under the following headings:

- choice of home;
- health and personal care;
- daily life and social activities;
- complaints and protection;
- environment;
- staffing;
- management and administration.

As we have already said, the National Minimum Standards promote the rights of residents to high-quality services which in turn promote independence. Central to this is the provision of appropriately trained staff teams and management. The new system values the inclusion and participation of service users, and places an emphasis on reviewing and adapting services for their benefit. All of this affects you, the registered manager, because your home will be inspected under the new guidance.

Therefore, we can see that the Act as a whole focuses on the individuality, rights and responsibilities of residents, and the ways in which these are central to service provision.

Try it out

Obtain a copy of the National Minimum Standards and make yourself familiar with the contents and layout. How do you think they will affect you?

The role of the National Care Standards Commission

The National Care Standards Commission has responsibility for the registration of health and care homes and agencies under the Act. Successful registration will depend upon the degree of compliance with the National Minimum Standards. If your service does not meet the standards, registration will be withheld or withdrawn. It is worth remembering that the standards represent the minimum expectation. You can, of course, go beyond these, but never below.

Individual managers seeking registration will need to demonstrate to the Commission that they are 'fit' to carry out the role of manager within that organisation. The Commission will consider qualifications and experience, as well as criminal records.

Inspections carried out by the Commission will focus on outcomes for individual service users and inspectors will demand hard evidence from providers, not simply statements of goodwill. As the registered manager, you will be asked to demonstrate *how* the service meets the standards. Inspectors will make judgements based on observations carried out in the home or agency, discussions with service users, staff and families. They will also want to examine records. You will need to have a working knowledge of the Act so that the National Minimum Standards are maintained. It is significant that many of the standards begin with the phrase 'The registered person . . .'. As the registered manager, you are accountable for the activities of the home.

The Commission will also investigate any complaints received about service providers.

Select one of the headings from your copy of the National Minimum Standards and consider how far your current recording systems will allow you to provide evidence of meeting the requirements.

General Social Care Council

The General Social Care Council is responsible for the promotion of conduct and good practice and for high training standards for social care workers. Workers will be required to register with the Council and will need to be appropriately qualified. The Council will also keep a record of those considered unsuitable for positions in social care, which should lead to an improvement in protection procedures for vulnerable people.

Modernising Social Services (1998)

The Government White Paper *Modernising Social Services* was published in November 1998. Although it is not a piece of legislation, it is a good practice guide. You should therefore know and understand it. Although we have provided a brief résumé here, you should obtain a copy of the paper for your records.

The White Paper promotes three things:

- independence;
- protection for vulnerable people;
- raising the quality of services.

It emphasises respect for and the dignity of service users and the promotion of their independence. It advocates the philosophy that care can and should be provided to individuals without them losing control over their lives.

Individual needs and the value of partnerships between agencies and users are central to the White Paper. It also advocates the raising of standards through the use of educational programmes and qualifications for care workers at all levels. Table 1 summarises the content of the White Paper.

Table 1. Summary of *Modernising Social Services*

Difficulties to be addressed	Solutions identified
Concerns over standards of children's care services	The creation of the General Social Care Council to raise standards of social care staff through improved training
Inadequacies of community care for the mentally ill	The creation of the General Social Care Council to raise standards of social care staff through improved training
Young people leaving care facing unemployment, homelessness and having achieved little educationally	Establishment of 'Quality Protects', a programme to protect children and to enhance their opportunities
Lack of access and awareness for people needing support from social service departments	Increase awareness of services and make systems and policies more user-friendly
Poor provisions of hospital/residential care for the elderly and payment issues	New independent inspection services (under the Care Standards Act)
Concern about residential care provision and standards	Systems to enable adults to live in their own homes and to exert more choices about their care via direct payment schemes

Disability Discrimination Act 1995

The Disability Discrimination Act 1995 is an important piece of legislation for the care sector as, for the first time, all individuals (this includes both staff and residents) have received protection from discrimination as a result of disability.

The Act provides you with a useful definition of a disabled person. This is someone who has a 'physical or mental impairment which has a substantial and long term adverse effect on his ability to carry out normal day to day activities'. Because the definition is quite loose, it can and does include a whole range of impairments, including reduced mobility, sensory impairment, learning disability and recognised mental illnesses.

The Act considers discrimination in three areas:

- employment;
- goods;
- services.

If you have an employee with a disability (as defined under the Act) you should be willing to make 'reasonable adjustments' within the workplace to enable that person to carry out her or his duties. Employers can access funding if they carry out an assessment of the worker's needs within the first six weeks of employment.

The Act prohibits discrimination against disabled people in the provision of goods or services. This means that it is unlawful for a service provider to treat someone less favourably because of a disability. Again, the 'reasonable adjustment' clause is relevant and could include physical adaptations such as ramps and larger doorways.

This section of the Act is probably most relevant to you in terms of the services you provide to residents: you need to ensure that you do not discriminate against disabled people who use or wish to use your services. Additionally, you may have a role in enabling residents to gain their right to equal treatment in other situations.

As you are probably aware, discrimination can take two forms: direct and indirect. Direct discrimination means treating one person less favourably than another and is usually easily identified by the manager or other staff and residents. Indirect discrimination is more subtle but equally damaging. It involves the application of some sort of condition which has the effect of discriminating against a particular group or individual. Examples could include policy and procedures, or information given or requested in a particular format which excludes people from the process required. Indirect discrimination can be more difficult for the manager to isolate and deal with.

Case study — Discrimination

Malcolm is a profoundly deaf man working as a team leader in a residential home for deaf people. As part of his duties he should prepare reports but rarely does so. Although team meetings are high on the agenda of his manager, Malcolm rarely holds staff meetings. Members of his team often avoid using sign language when Malcolm is around. However, he gets on very well with the residents. His manager is often exasperated and is constantly passing him copies of the written procedures for the home in the hope that things will improve.

- What forms of discrimination may be in action here?
- How could you improve the situation?

It is important to remember that it is your role to protect people from discrimination, whether staff or residents. They have a right to expect this, although some of the people you work with may not be aware of their rights. You must think about how to change this.

The Disability Discrimination Act is supported in its aims by the Disability Rights Commission, a body set up by the introduction of the Disability Rights Act 1999. The Commission seeks to eliminate discrimination, promote equal opportunities and encourage good practice. The roles of the Commission cover advice, conciliation, investigation and research.

Try it out

Use the Internet to find out more about the Disability Rights Commission and its work. Are there any issues which you face that could be helped by communication with the Commission?

Data Protection Act 1998

The Data Protection Act applies to those records held on computers which are not a matter of public interest. The information held should be relevant to the purpose for which it is intended, kept to a minimum and kept no longer than necessary. Additionally, people have the right to access information held about them and should be made aware of this right.

You need to be aware of appropriate storage arrangements for case files. Workers should be encouraged to familiarise themselves with information but at all times respect this privilege by adhering to systems to protect the privacy of individuals. You need to review procedures, to take action to remedy any inadequacies in the system and to alert team members to any inappropriate practice.

Keys to good management practice

Data protection

- Assess your current practice in the light of the Data Protection Act 1998.
- Provide training and support to your staff team on how it affects their practice.
- Review at regular intervals the information which is held and take appropriate action to dispose of unnecessary documentation.

Think about what conflicts there may be for you in your day-to-day work when balancing the rights of individuals against those of a group. Using examples, discuss how you might ensure people's individual rights without interfering with the rights of the community.

Health and Safety Act 1974

The Health and Safety Act 1974 places responsibility on both employers and employees. For example, any employer with more than four employees must, by law, have a written safety policy. The Act places a responsibility on employers to make the working environment safe. This is a huge responsibility that will fall on your shoulders as the registered manager. (You may arrange for some support by delegating to a health and safety representative.) This must be a fully trained person who will be named a 'competent person'.

Try it out

Obtain a copy of the Health and Safety Act. Ensure that your responsibilities have been met.

In keeping with the care values, staff need to remember that their work environment is the residents' home. Every attempt should be made to acknowledge this by respecting privacy and choice. Decor and furnishings should reflect diversity rather than the provision of standard schemes for everyone. Nonetheless, in considering the health and safety of residents, some compromise is required. You must, for example, ensure that exits are clearly marked and that adequate fire-fighting equipment is provided around the home.

Duties for your employees include:

- taking reasonable care of their own health and safety, and that of others who may be affected by them;
- working in accordance with policy, procedure and training guidance given;
- reporting any concerns without delay.

Inspectors will visit your workplace to assess health and safety standards. This inspection will include making sure that the environment is healthy for your residents and staff (see Figure 1).

Figure 1. Aspects of a care home that will have a bearing upon health and safety.

You have a duty to report some injuries, diseases and dangerous incidents to the appropriate authority. This may be the local environmental health department or the Health and Safety Executive.

Try it out

Write a list of those diseases which you think are notifiable. Then, with a colleague, check your answers with the guidance provided by the Health and Safety Executive.

The care value base

It is the combination of legislation and policy discussed above that provides us with the care value base; that is, the right of residents and staff members to respect, non-discrimination, confidentiality, diversity and empowerment.

Respect

Each person has the right to be treated with respect. Team members and working practices need to respect the people receiving the service. This means taking account of their feelings and wishes.

Non-discrimination

Your residents have the right not to be discriminated against. You should be particularly concerned that they do not experience discrimination in their own home. Discrimination means unequal treatment. Unequal treatment dehumanises and devalues individuals. You must actively work to break down barriers to equality and advocate as necessary for residents.

Confidentiality

Article 8 of the Human Rights Act 1998 states that 'Everyone has the right to respect for his private family life, his home and his correspondence'. Clearly, this is one of the central issues for workers in social care. Residents have the right to be treated with respect and information held about them should also be treated with respect.

For unskilled workers, information gathering can become intrusive for both the residents and themselves. It is important therefore to give clear guidance and support to team members about the privilege and responsibilities of holding personal information.

It is the management of information which distinguishes a good system from a poor or ineffective one. Managers can provide additional protection to their residents by sensitively organising their records and sharing information only in accordance with the care value base.

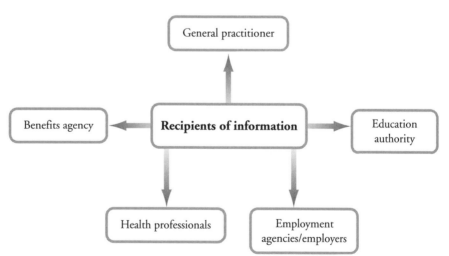

Figure 2. The agencies that most commonly 'have a need to know' about otherwise confidential information.

The agencies that most commonly will 'have a need to know' are shown in Figure 2, but in each case it is essential to think about the consequences of passing on the information and involving the resident in the decision to do so. You should be leading and directing this process through staff training and your monitoring systems. Again, the most vulnerable residents are often the least aware of their rights. The onus is thus most definitely on you and your staff to see that the residents' right to confidentiality is respected.

Think it over

Familiarise yourself with your organisation's confidentiality procedure. What recourse do your residents have if they feel that their confidentiality has been breached? Is the means of recourse accessible and sufficient?

Diversity

Diversity demands acknowledging the differences between people as well as those things which people may have in common. This could include religion, race, gender and sexual orientation. Rather than simply seeing diversity as an added difficulty, see it as an opportunity for new learning and development. You could instigate training for staff that is led by a resident.

Being different can be challenging – there can be comfort in fitting into the norm and being average. However, your residents are not the same. Each person is fundamentally different and has the right to be seen and treated as such. For example, each person comes to you with a different past, a different life experience. They may have different religious beliefs or may have developed their own communication system. In simple terms, this means not assuming that all older people like bingo or that all young men like football. Valuing the individual means taking the time to explore who they are.

Recognising the diversity of residents can provide an opportunity for learning and development.

Group services are especially at risk of losing sight of the individual and it is easy to slip into a group approach rather than an individual approach, not least because of pressure on time and resources. Stereotypes and generalised assumptions play a part in the depersonalisation of services and the dehumanisation of individuals. You need to be aware of this risk and prevent your team from treating people as a homogenous group. This is not necessarily deliberate or cruel – it may be the result of lack of awareness and the pressure of getting things done.

Empowerment

Few workers, if asked, would be opposed to empowerment as a philosophy. However, true empowerment and the participation which results can be rather more difficult to put into action.

Empowerment is a way of developing potential and acknowledging the strengths of individuals rather than the challenges. Power imbalances exist within care relationships. Carers are in a position of power and care receivers are vulnerable. Empowerment means a shift in this balance towards the person in receipt of care. Enabling residents to participate in their own lives gives them more control and a better quality of life.

You have a role in educating your team about the importance of empowerment and in developing ways of achieving empowerment. You also need to be aware that staff teams can feel disempowered by the systems within which they work. They, too, may experience feelings of powerlessness. A hierarchy can develop in which residents will be at the bottom of the power structure with staff a little above.

You must ensure that team members understand that their interventions have a huge impact on people's lives, be this positive or negative. Empowerment is about improving lives by sharing information, negotiating and remaining person centred. Remember that your residents have the right to be informed of and involved in decisions about their lives.

Social care workers need to be aware of the values which underpin their work. Managers have the role of advocating those values in the day-to-day work with service users. Your systems and structures will indicate how far you advocate these values. Strict regimes which consider groups rather than individuals are symptomatic of a workplace which does not value individuals or respect their rights.

Working practices which do not acknowledge and promote diversity need to be highlighted as oppressive and action taken to change them. As a manager, you will find that tensions stem from different sources and it is your job to balance them. In other words, you need to get the job done but be aware of the potential for compromise if care values become a lower priority than output.

There is a danger in categorising your residents as 'people who . . .' or 'people with . . .'. Labels gather people together into groups by those things which they have in common rather than their uniqueness. While recognising the competing demands, you must retain the centrality of the individual.

Labels tend to be given by those in a position of power and this includes care providers. You need to be alert to any tendency to describe people by their behaviour, for example as an 'attention seeker' or 'self-harmer'. This is the behaviour, not the identity of the person. Workers who fall into this trap are moving away from the care value base, are denying the value of the person and are missing an opportunity to find the meaning behind the behaviour. The rights to respect and equal treatment are not relinquished because an individual exhibits challenging behaviour.

Residents will be affected by the physical, emotional and psychological environments within which they are placed. Their experience is likely to be more negative if the environment is rigid and uniform. This is because their choices are limited and their power to influence their lives will be reduced. This illustrates the inherent vulnerability of residents and the comparative power of staff.

The care environment can be a stressful place. It is important to acknowledge the impact on your staff while retaining respect for and acceptance of residents. The residents of a care home will not necessarily be living together through choice. While a care home is 'home' and workplace, it must first and foremost be a home. Workers come into the space for a limited time. You have duties in terms of your staff's rights but also in terms of the rights of the residents. This will create conflicts for you.

Keys to good management practice

Legislation and policies

- Keep yourself up to date with the legislation relevant to your workplace.
- Implement appropriate systems to monitor compliance with legislation in your workplace.
- Know your residents' rights and support them in claiming those rights.
- Individuality is central to the new standards for vulnerable people: you need to demonstrate how you satisfy this requirement.
- Systems should be underpinned by the care value base.

You recognise and understand ways of developing and maintaining systems and structures to promote the care value base

A good starting point when thinking about systems is to consider why they exist and for whom they exist. Some of your systems of work or policies and procedures will be the result of external forces; others will be set out by your own service or organisation. You need to know what your duties are in relation to your workplace and it is your job to pass on this information to your team. This is important because it gives boundaries to your actions. You will delegate some tasks and responsibilities to your team, but they need to be clear where their discretion ends.

Your agency or organisation will have policies and procedures which provide the framework for your approaches. A policy is an *aim* in the area of work. A procedure indicates *how* to go about it. The relevant documents provide a good framework for you, your team, your residents and your purchasers. They will indicate your philosophy of care and are undoubtedly an excellent tool.

The basic question that you must ask is whether your systems are effective. The manager has a key role in the development, maintenance and evaluation of systems. It is crucial that the service is created around the people rather than the people being fitted into the service.

External systems

Some systems will be imposed as a result of regulation and inspection. These systems will largely exist so that services can be measured against standards and so that residents can be protected from risk. The Care Standards Act is an example of an external system put in place to maintain consistency and good practice. From the guidance relating to the Act, you will need to provide evidence of a range of systems, including: confidentiality, aims and objectives, complaints procedures, and systems for the recruitment and selection of staff.

Internal systems

Some systems and structures will be directly enforced by your agency or organisation. These will support the underlying philosophy of regulation and inspection and will highlight the individual expectations of workers in the organisation. The internal systems will relate to the practical tasks which facilitate the daily smooth running of the service. Examples include fire registers, medication procedures, access to finances and catering arrangements.

Systems for whom?

The systems used in your workplace will be set up for a range of purposes and some will be acknowledged as more important than others. For example, a fire procedure will rank high in terms of priority since it relates to the safety of residents. Fundamentally, systems and structures are set up from four different perspectives – those of:

- the carers;
- the care receivers;
- the organisation;
- the regulators.

Think it over

List the systems established in your workplace and then think about why and for whom each one exists in terms of the four different perspectives mentioned above.

Systems for staff

Systems and structures are means by which working practices can be measured against agreed standards. They also provide a framework within which to carry out tasks in an orderly way. In order to be effective and work to an expected standard, your staff need to be aware of and understand what systems and structures exist.

You must ensure that this process begins at induction and that ongoing support and guidance are provided. A good example of such support is the handover meeting. Handover meetings enable team members to understand what has occurred and what else needs to be achieved. They also provide workers with key pieces of information which may affect their working day. A handover is a useful tool for the team but also facilitates good care practice by highlighting what needs to be done. The written record provides evidence to employers and to outside agencies of work undertaken. It is useful to base these written records on a pro forma. A pro forma for a handover meeting would include the following elements:

- date;
- time;
- shift leader;
- staff on duty;
- issues raised in relation to residents;
- residents' appointments;
- residents' social activities.

Case study — Systems and procedures

Sarah is a new part-time member of the team. She has settled in well and is eager to please. One day, as she is leaving work, a resident asks her for a lift into town. Although she was not too familiar with the man's situation, she was aware that he goes out alone and readily agrees. She took the request at face value and did not stop to question whether her colleagues had been informed that he was going out.

There are several different issues in this case. Here are some examples:

- Sarah was about to leave and was not therefore in contact with her colleagues – they might have no indication of this resident's whereabouts or when to expect him back.
- They might be concerned about his safety and, in the event of a fire evacuation, might have to search for him needlessly.
- Is Sarah suitably insured? Is the vehicle roadworthy for carrying residents?
- Is there any reason why Sarah should not travel alone with this resident? She does not know his history. He may be prone to fits, for example – could she cope?

In summary, then, she has not followed any procedures, she has not passed on information and she has not considered her own safety or his. She may have caused the home to instigate the missing persons procedure. The home will probably have a fire procedure, a communication book, risk assessments, and guidance for staff on the use of private vehicles. However, the systems did not prevent Sarah from making an unwise decision.

- What could Sarah have done instead?
- How could the manager follow up this matter?
- What could the manager do?
- How could Sarah have been better informed about the boundaries of her workplace?
- What documentation might have supported Sarah's decision in this situation?

Good systems

Look at the case study on systems and procedures. What makes a good system? Three of the main features of a good system are:

- awareness;
- accessibility;
- accountability.

Awareness

The reality is that your systems will be effective only if they are used. They will be used only if they are known about. You need to make sure that there is awareness of your systems, not just on the part of the staff but also on the part of residents and external customers.

Accessibility

You will have many different systems and structures. Perhaps the most important issue to consider is access to them. It is crucial that residents have access, too: what use is a complaints procedure if it is inaccessible to the very people for whom it is intended?

To make systems accessible, information needs to be disseminated and you need to be creative in the way in which it is presented. A glossy procedures file written in jargon will not be effective because it will exclude anyone who struggles with official language. Your systems are a way in which you can actively promote equality and break down the causes of discrimination. You are accountable to regulatory bodies, your organisation/employer, and your staff and service users. Your systems need to provide protection and clarity of approach for each of these interested parties. Therefore your system must be robust enough to stand up to scrutiny.

Accountability

Your systems need to provide accountability for staff and residents. This means being clear about what is being done and being able to provide evidence of this. An example may be a record of accidents in the home: a clear record of an incident will show what occurred, action taken and will indicate a satisfactory conclusion.

Try it out

Get a copy of your complaints procedure. How accessible is it to your residents? Does it take account of the diversity of your residents and their right to complain? If not, rewrite the complaints procedure using the three main features of a good system.

Information

Information fulfils a coordinating role for you in providing care and potentially in working alongside other agencies. Information should also be shared with purchasers and residents.

Records are a way of making service providers accountable. For example, you will have records of work undertaken. This is a way in which actions and responses can be measured internally and externally.

When you are gathering information it is important that your system is not interrogative. This will evoke feelings of fear and people will be reluctant to participate. You will no doubt be delegating some responsibility to your team for gathering information. This means that you need to provide a framework for them. You will need to consider the purpose of the information being gathered, the impact for the user, and the skills and behaviour of the person doing the work.

Again, a pro forma can be a useful tool, in particular for new team members. Forms can act as guides and you are more likely to get the information required. However, because one of the aims is to treat people as individuals, the form could feel stifling. When there are boxes there can be a feeling that they need to be filled.

You will therefore need to consider which information is standard and will be required from everyone, for example, date of birth and next of kin. The basic information about residents could be recorded on a pro forma as follows:

- name;
- date of birth;
- National Insurance number;
- NHS number;
- address;
- next of kin;
- religion;
- health information;
- general practitioner;
- finances.

This form would give the basic details of an individual. It requires very factual information and does not leave much room for the individual to come through. For example, if the name Benjamin Brown is recorded for the first item on the list, you would not know the person's preferences with regard to being addressed – Benjamin, Ben, Mr Brown? What are his interests? The more sensitive and individual information could be collated differently to encourage participation and ownership by the resident.

Confidentiality

We have seen that confidentiality is important in the field of social care and that legislation such as Data Protection and the Human Rights Acts provide some protection to users of care services.

Many situations will arise in the course of your work that present you with a dilemma regarding confidentiality. There will be times when information needs to be shared with other agencies and you need to provide guidance on how this will be managed. In an extreme case you may be directed to release information as the result of as court order. We have already looked at the right to confidentiality and you should be clear that sensitivity and privacy are central to information management. Residents should be aware of the circumstances in which information about them will be shared.

The fundamental challenge which exists here is the balance between the right to privacy, and confidentiality and safety. If the withholding of information could result in harm, you will be faced with a difficult situation. Staff as well as residents need to be protected by your systems.

When a decision is made to disclose confidential information, the authenticity of the receiver needs to be verified and action taken to ensure that the information arrives securely. You may not know, for example, where the fax would be received. It may be into a communal office and this could compromise confidentiality. You need to check this before proceeding.

Confidential information must be stored securely in communal offices.

If discussions are at an initial stage, you need to proceed with some caution and seek advice before releasing personal information to a party who does not necessarily need it. You should gain agreement from interested parties – for example, the resident, family and social worker – about what to release, to whom and in what format. You should not make the decision entirely on your own.

If subsequently you were asked for additional information, you would once again negotiate with the interested parties before proceeding. Privacy and dignity need to be central to the process and the involvement of the resident should be sought wherever possible. If this is not possible, you should formally log the decision and the reason for it. You would also need to record what information was sent, to whom and when.

If you are unsure about the validity of a request or the protocol of passing on information, you should always seek advice from your manager or organisation before proceeding.

Case study — Sharing information

A recent case review recommended that James Gaskell should move to a more independent living situation. In response to this, several service providers have been approached and some key information has been provided in agreement with James and his social worker. You are the key worker and on arrival at work you have received a note asking for additional information to be provided. You have been asked to send the information by fax that afternoon to a lady called Jane.

▼

- What things would you consider in deciding on a course of action?
- From whom might you seek advice?
- What consideration would you give to the content of the information you send?
- How would you verify the identity of the person seeking the information?
- What records would you keep of the episode?
- How would you go about dealing with issues security at the other agency?
- How would you involve Mr Gaskell?

You need to be aware not only of the way in which information is gathered but also of how it is kept subsequently. Your duties in terms of confidentiality also affect storage. You need to provide adequate safe storage which can be locked. This is to protect residents from unnecessary intrusion and is an example of how you can respect the individual.

Information needs to be kept safely but at the same time must be accessible to staff and the residents concerned. Staff members need to appreciate that the records which they keep are open to residents. All records should be accurate and non-judgemental. Give clear information to your team about their access to information. Information held about residents should not be taken out of the workplace. Guidance on the keeping of information states that three years after the last contact, records should be destroyed.

Case study — Staff responsibility for confidentiality

Jean has worked in the office for many years. She is very proud of her organisational skills and has kept the resident and staff records throughout her employment. You have just discovered that she holds records from 12 years ago and that for convenience she is no longer storing all the records in the locked cupboard but has them in a cabinet by her desk.

- As the manager, what would your concerns be?
- What legislation is relevant to this case?
- Who could offer advice and support on this issue?
- Outline the key factors that an effective policy on record keeping would contain.

Communication

Communication will be the key to a system which is valued. Communication varies hugely from person to person and from situation to situation.

We have considered the differences or diversity of people earlier in the unit. It is crucial to effective communication that everyone is given an equal opportunity to participate. You will need to think about communication systems, including sign language, dialect and word usage. You could also consider pictorial systems which pick out the key messages.

What might affect the success of communication? The key factors may relate to:

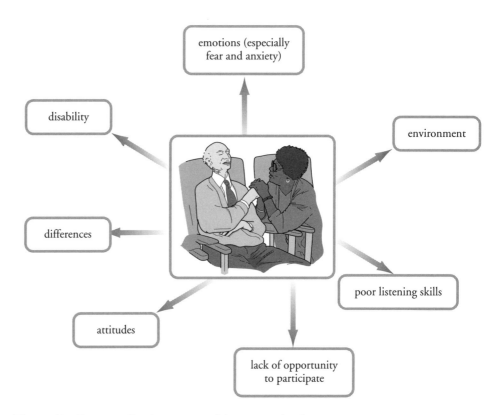

Figure 3. Factors affecting successful communication.

Underlying all of these issues is respect for individuals, irrespective of their situation or needs.

We have all experienced staff meetings or training sessions where one person dominates the discussion. This can have a stifling effect on other group members and will affect the outcome for the group. You need to be aware of this potential inequality within the team and encourage all team members to participate. Similarly, your team needs to be aware of who are the less confident residents and facilitate their involvement.

Once you have identified the barriers to effective communication, you can begin to address these. There may be practical issues to consider, such as the provision of a private place, the provision of an interpreter, or simply the physical presence and support of a staff member to encourage and advocate if necessary.

Feedback

Feedback will be one of the most important types of communication to you, as manager. How else will you find out whether your systems are effective, accessible and supportive? Being aware of the different viewpoints gives you and your team an opportunity to make changes to systems where necessary. Figure 4 shows some potential sources of feedback.

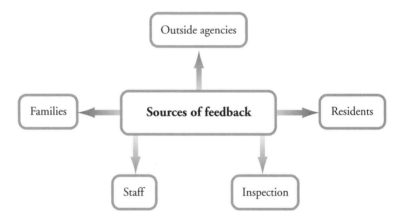

Figure 4. Potential sources of feedback: staff, residents, outside agencies, families, inspection.

Perhaps the most challenging feedback is that from residents. They are your front-line customers and are therefore an important source of feedback. There has been increased emphasis on the involvement and participation of residents and you need to think about how you can facilitate this. This is empowerment in practical terms. It is an opportunity to shift the power balance rather than merely talk about it as a concept.

Try it out

Check out the work of People First, an organisation set up by service users for service users. It is active in the promotion of involvement for service users and has groups around the world.

The barriers to gaining effective feedback from your residents may include a lack of any one of the following:

- awareness;
- resident forums;
- group discussions;

- understanding;
- advocacy;
- provision of information in a range of languages and media.

Most importantly, you must be clear that feedback and evaluation are valued by you. Your systems will not be effective if they not are accessible and open to change and review.

Think it over

What would you consider the main features of a user-friendly feedback system to be? Have a go at devising a form which would meet the needs of your resident group.

Keys to good management practice

Systems and procedures

- Make your systems enabling, not controlling.
- Regularly review the effectiveness of your systems.
- Ensure your systems serve people and that people don't serve the systems.

You are aware of the pressure points in the management of systems and structures

Pressures on managers, staff and residents

For you, as the manager, the main pressure is in balancing the expectations and demands of the different parties concerned with the provision of care, from legislators, regulators and inspectors to your own organisation and residents. You are the central reference point for each (Figure 5).

Figure 5. The manager is the central reference point for all the parties concerned in care provision. You will therefore have to balance a variety of pressures from each source.

For your team, the main source of pressure is likely to be time – it can be difficult to carry out job-related tasks while at the same time giving individual responses and attention to residents. Residents, too, will be under some pressure, to understand your systems and how they are affected by them, and how they can be involved in changes.

It is important to acknowledge that a system which is valued by the staff team may not be effective from the residents' point of view. Some degree of routine and order usually exists in the care environment. You must recognise that if this goes too far, there can be a negative outcome for residents. The system can stifle their individuality and fail to recognise their diversity and individual rights. You must be alert to this risk and take appropriate action to remedy the situation.

We have already looked at the dangers of seeing people as a group. You must be alert to this constant challenge and advocate holistic approaches which not only highlight but also celebrate the differences in people. Workers can become desensitised to the needs of those they care for. You can help prevent this through the use of mentoring and review. Workers will always be under pressure to get everything done in the most efficient way. The most efficient way, however, may not be the best way, as it may compromise the care value base.

It is important that you lead the team. You will need to acknowledge the complexity of their work and offer ideas and solutions. Communication needs to be specific and you need to offer ongoing support. It is your role to balance the tensions and make sure that all aspects of the system are addressed. Although systems exist for different groups, the underlying purpose of systems is the same: accountability. Accountability means being able to answer and explain.

You are accountable to residents, your organisation, inspectors and, increasingly, the profession. Competent registered managers will do what needs to be done and will understand why they are working in a certain way. Managers are accountable in a range of ways for their practice. They must strike a balance between the inherent tensions of the work.

Responsibility inevitably evokes feelings of vulnerability. You will experience this and so will your staff team. One of the challenges for providers of care is in striking the balance between protection and control. In protecting individuals there is a risk of infringing their rights. You have a duty to care, to assess risk and to keep people safe from harm. Harm could be physical, emotional, psychological or sexual. Empowerment and choice are about shifting the power to residents, but this must not be done without considering the wellbeing of the individual.

The pressures of managing an organisation

You may be presented with organisational policy and procedures for everything, including day-to-day issues, rather than developing them yourself. If this is the case, have the needs of your particular service been considered? It may be that the policy writer has little experience of direct care or the challenges of effective communication. It may well be based on the safety of workers and the plugging of issues dealt with in case law and less to do with language and understanding from the viewpoint of residents.

When considering inadequacies or gaps in the service it is also important to consider the impact for the service. Overcoming inadequacies in the service will have cost implications, it may involve increased levels of one-to-one staff time and it may demand more willingness on the part of individual team members to listen.

Honesty is important on the part of the manager when looking at whether a system is effective. Fear of change and of the burden of additional tasks should not override the need to move things on for the good of the residents. If current staffing arrangements cannot allow for the recognition of the care values, you need to look at levels of staffing and training, and to seek support from your own management.

The anxiety of staff members may manifest in what is sometimes called the 'yes, but' response. It is a way of avoiding the new and seeking problems rather than solutions. In a care setting, a staff member may say something like 'Well, we can't do that because he/she . . .'. The statement will then be followed with a list of difficulties rather than creative responses.

Staff members need to be updated on the external pressures of the care sector. In this way they can be given the opportunity to experience the layers of responsibility placed on the manager.

The pressure of managing systems

The biggest challenge is in turning a policy or procedure into a working document. In reality a policy works only once it is given life by those involved with it. Team members need to be involved, as do residents.

Think again about the complaints procedure: how accessible is it to residents (for whom it is intended)? If the complaints file is empty, are we to assume that the provision is so good that no one ever complains? Awareness and access are the ingredients which will bring the policy to life for the residents. You will play a key role in establishing and designing systems which work for residents. Services are different, as are the residents, and this means that approaches need to be different too.

Individual registered managers need to consider the most effective way of communicating information. For one practice setting this may mean the provision of pictorial information but in another this could appear patronising. The issue is access and the challenge is in achieving this for your particular service.

Try it out

Check out what information technology is available to support understanding for those with a learning disability or for whom English is not the first language. Is this an issue for your residents and would it be viable to incorporate such technology into your care home?

Policies and procedures provide protection for the service, the manager, the team and the residents. It is therefore important that there are contributions from all of these sources. You will no doubt have many different systems in operation, some of which will be more effective than others. Some may lose their value over time and it is important that systems are reviewed for their relevance at regular intervals.

It is not practical to have policy for the minutiae of day-to-day life. In any case, it is important for your staff to have some degree of autonomy. There is a balance to be struck here: some workers will embrace autonomy while others may feel daunted and resent it.

Policies which are inaccessible or simply not read will not support the work to be carried out. You need to find ways of promoting systems. The induction of new team members is an ideal opportunity to freshen up on procedures for all members of the team.

- Feature a particular system at each staff meeting and review its effectiveness and the staff's understanding of it.
- Set aside specific times for training sessions to refresh the knowledge of the team and to promote the ongoing development of systems.
- Network with other agencies to share ideas on good practice. Research what information is available to the team.

Systems can give order and structure; they may also stifle and control. You need to keep this to the fore and advocate empowering systems rather than those which have an institutional feel. Systems may be deemed oppressive by some people. Where this is acknowledged, action should be taken to counter it. You need to lead by example, acknowledge the challenge, seek ways of approaching difficult issues and offer support.

Try it out

Create a table with two columns. In first column list some of the challenges for you as a manager in setting up effective systems. Then in the second column, list the possible solutions and strategies.

Keys to good management practice

Pressure points in the management of systems

- Acknowledge the pressures: the rights of one person may conflict with those of another.
- Invite participation and feedback from a range of sources.
- Be honest about the efficacy of your systems.
- Support your team and keep good practice on the agenda.

You know what action to take at pressure points

Now that you know what difficulties can exist, you need to consider what you will do if you encounter them. The skills you will need relate to:

- being challenging;
- being assertive;
- being supportive;
- communication;
- decision making;
- reviewing.

Challenging

You have a crucial role in controlling the service provision for residents. It is important to keep an eye on detail and to assess how things are working. If things are not working as well as they should, you need to challenge your staff and organisation more widely to redress the inadequacies.

A significant part of your role is explaining what needs to be done and why. Your staff will then be more likely to work to the required standard. In the field of social care, it is not just what is done but the way in which it is done which affects people's lives. Mentoring and ongoing support will enable your team to understand why the integration of the care value base is so crucial.

Assertive

Even when you are aware of what you need from your team, it can be difficult to get it. One of the skills you will need is assertiveness. Assertiveness should not be confused with aggression or rudeness. It means being clear in stating what you need. You will see from the continuum shown in Figure 6 that assertiveness falls between passivity and aggression.

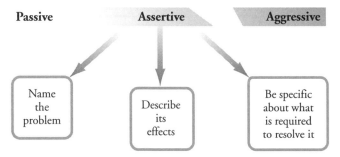

Figure 6. Assertiveness falls on a continuum halfway between passiveness and aggressiveness. To be assertive you need to be clear in stating what you need and why, without being rude or aggressive.

You need to be assertive because, if you are not specific, you will not get what you need. You will get either a half-hearted version of what you want or what you had before, because it is familiar. It is your job to give clear instruction. By being assertive you will be able to get the action you need without resentment and you will also be able to say 'no' when necessary.

Supportive

It is crucial that your team feels supported. This may involve you in a range of things, including formal supervision, listening, advising, training and development. You want and need the involvement of your team in the day-to-day running of the service. You need feedback and ideas for improvement. You need to know how members of your team are feeling. You may also want to make use of counselling skills, such as active listening, empathy and unconditional positive regard.

Communication

Effective communication is a vital element of managing situations. In your role as manager, you need to test how effective your communication is and what impact it has on those around you. In other words, does your message get through?

Your messages need to be both understood and accepted. You must check that this has occurred. If necessary, rephrase or clarify your messages. Be aware of the barriers which may exist. Just as with residents, members of your team may have different needs. You need to consider when, where and the way in which you communicate. Communication is a two-way process and you should to encourage your team to participate.

Decision making

Decision making is another skill you must master. Your team will look to you to make decisions – that is, for leadership and guidance.

You may need to take some time to make a decision. This can feel rather disempowering but is preferable to making the wrong decision because you feel under pressure. Taking time allows you to think through the advantages and disadvantages, and where necessary to consult with others. You may wish to seek advice from someone who has more experience of that particular issue. You may need to consult others because they will be affected by the decision.

Sometimes you will be faced with decisions for which you can draw on available or previous information. If you are in the process of reviewing a system you may want to test more than one option and then ask for feedback. In this way you would be involving others in the process and the outcome may prove more favourable.

You may not relish making difficult decisions. It can be daunting, especially when there is some sort of risk involved. However, if you do not manage actively, you may be faced with an undesired result. It is better to take some control of the situation.

You also need to communicate the decision to your team. You will want other people to accept that the decision is a good one. This is more likely if there is understanding about how the decision was reached, particularly if other people were involved. In other words, the process will be important to your team and to your residents.

How to make a decision

- Identify the presenting problem.
- Obtain all the information you can.
- Identify the options.
- Consult.
- Take into account the pros and cons.
- Make the decision.
- Review.

Reviewing

The review of systems is important in order for you to keep on top of any difficulties. If you have planned the change well, with a clear outcome, you will be able to measure your success. For example, if you change the complaints procedure because it is inaccessible to residents, one of your checks would be how to see they find the new system.

Your role is to test out the effectiveness of your systems. It can be disheartening to find that a system is not effective, and so there is a need for honesty at this stage. Communication with team members comes to the fore once again in looking for suitable adjustments. However, your system must meet the needs of your workplace and stand up to the scrutiny of the regulatory bodies.

Review and change in an atmosphere of involvement are important.

Keys to good management practice

Taking action

- Always look to develop your own leadership skills further – your skills will directly affect the results that you achieve.
- Strike a balance between support and clear management.

You recognise and understand the importance of change in the workplace

Change happens to all of us and in all aspects of our daily lives. At least in the short term, it signifies a loss of control and this evokes a range of emotions, including fear, anxiety, powerlessness and sadness.

Care as a profession is under constant change and review. The legislative changes detailed above are beyond your control. Change is not always a choice but you do have choice about the management of change.

You need to be aware of the impact of change on you, your staff and those for whom you provide care. You may feel afraid of change and may prefer to keep things as they are. Your position as a manager does not make you immune to the usual emotional responses. Allow yourself time to adjust.

Everyone has emotional needs. Individual team members may have a sense of being stuck and may become immobilised in the face of change. They are likely to meet change with a series of reactions:

- *Immobilisation*. This is the initial response to change or loss. People are shocked and become immobilised. There will be a feeling of powerlessness and hopelessness.
- *Minimisation*. This stage involves resistance. People may seek to lessen the impact of change by reacting as though something less extreme is happening than is actually the case.
- *Depression*. People may well experience the full emotion of the loss brought with the change and will mourn and feel depressed by it.
- *Bargaining*. People then become aware that the change is happening and seek to take some control of it. They cannot change it significantly but there is some room for making it more acceptable. This may be by seeing something positive in the change, by way of a payoff.
- *Acceptance*. People then move to acceptance of the situation and can look towards a new beginning. The new situation will become their new reality.

By understanding and anticipating the response of others you will be in a position to minimise the stress which can result from change. Avoidance of change is normal and should be expected. Workers may initially hide behind the idea that 'We've always done it like this . . .'.

Think about the admission or discharge processes within your organisation. In the form of a table, list the emotional responses you would expect a resident to experience and then consider ways in which you could make the transition easier.

Change is more effective if there is involvement at the initial stages of its introduction. It is important to give information about the need for change. Without this, those involved will have no context for the change, will have no ownership of the process and will feel powerless. The experience of powerlessness is the same for team members as for residents; it stifles, evokes feelings of low self-esteem and prevents participation. You have a duty of care to your staff, too, and to predict their needs. Once they are made aware of the need for change, the process of planning can begin and the impact of the change can be considered (Figure 7 shows the cycle of managing change). Those involved are able to ask questions and gain understanding. This planning stage will then lead more naturally into action.

Figure 7. The cycle of managing change.

Your team will look to you for guidance and reassurance and your personal preparation will enable you to feel more in control. It is important for you to have management skills in decision making but you must also encourage an atmosphere of participation. Staff may require additional training and support to carry out new elements of work. Seeing change as a positive opportunity and being receptive to the challenge can affect the experience of change for you, your team and your residents. Organisationally, change may be imposed as a result of increased competition for business.

Change

- Remember that change is inevitable.
- Acknowledge that change can be scary, and prepare.
- Remember that change will be more successful if it is understood.
- Look on change as an opportunity.

Evidence collection

This unit requires you to demonstrate your knowledge and understanding of the systems and structures that promote the rights and responsibilities and diversity of people. In order to do this you will need to refer closely to your NVQ standards and carry out secondary research into the relevant legislation, policies and guidelines that exist to support all parties involved; for example, The Disability Discrimination Act, Health and Safety etc..

You should then produce a report that outlines the impact of the legislation on your organisation and on you in your role as a care manager. This should include copies of organisational policies and guidelines that you have developed or worked with in order to ensure compliance with legislation and good practice. In addition, you should use real working examples to explain your roles and responsibilities in relation to good working practice and the maintenance of this across all aspects of your organization.

RM1

Manage a Service which Achieves the Best Possible Outcomes for the Individual

In this unit you will have the opportunity to consider in more depth the challenges raised by the promotion of residents' independence. We will look at the tensions between care and control, and the ways in which you can achieve a balance between freedom and safety via effective risk management. The unit will also consider how care planning can enhance the achievement of the best possible outcomes for residents. This will be seen in the context of the legislative framework and in light of the philosophy of the care value base.

The elements are:
- Ensure services are designed and reviewed to promote and maximise the achievement of the best possible outcomes for individual clients.
- Ensure the promotion of participation and independence in order to facilitate the achievement of the best possible outcomes.
- Manage and monitor systems for the assessment of risk of abuse, failure to protect and harm to self or others.
- Manage and monitor systems for the administration of medication.

Learning outcomes

- You understand how services are designed to promote the best possible outcome for residents.
- You are familiar with the legislation and policies that inform and guide care staff of the best possible outcomes for residents.
- You identify organisational factors relating to the achievement of the best possible outcomes for residents.
- You understand the importance of residents' participation in care planning and independence for facilitating best possible outcomes.
- You are able to identify ways of involving residents in care planning and daily living decisions.
- You are able to manage and monitor systems used for the assessment of risk.
- You are able to manage and monitor systems for administering medication.

You understand how services are designed to promote the best possible outcomes for residents

During the last 20 years there have been many changes and developments within the health and social care system. Many of these have focused upon bringing clients' needs, rights and choices to the forefront. For example, the NHS and Community Care Act 1990 developed a system of care that encouraged service users to exercise their rights and make choices about their health care. A further example is the Disability Discrimination Act 1998, which ensures service providers take positive action to meet the needs of clients with disabilities.

These changes have meant that services should centre on meeting the needs of clients. This in turn should ensure that the best possible outcomes are achieved in every case. As a care manager, you probably realise that this is more difficult to achieve than may first appear: there are tensions between service design, residents' rights and choices, and the achievement of the best possible outcomes. These tensions will be discussed below.

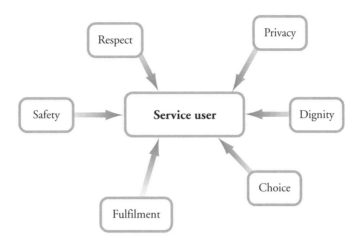

Figure 8. The care value base. *Privacy* means respecting people's right to be alone when they choose. It also means affording them the same right to personal privacy that anyone else would expect, for example in their personal care activities. To treat someone with *dignity* means to value them as an individual irrespective of their particular needs and challenges. It means valuing their uniqueness. *Choice* means the freedom to make an independent choice from a range of options. *Fulfilment* means the opportunity to realise personal goals and aspirations as part of daily life. Fulfilment leads to positive feelings of self-esteem, which enable the individual to feel valued. Whilst striving for the facilitation, the *safety* or security of the individual must not be compromised. *Respect* means that each individual is valued for who they are.

However, your organisation and team structures must be underpinned by the care values of social care. It is useful to recap on what we mean by care values at this point. They are indicated in Figure 8.

It is no coincidence that Figure 8 shows the service user centrally. Your practice must reflect a philosophy which advocates the user as the centre point of service provision. It is not sufficient to say that you, your staff and service are committed to the care value base – you need to show to inspectors evidence of how you incorporate these values into your day-to-day interactions with service users.

Think it over

Think about each of the care values listed and give three examples of how these are experienced in a real way by residents in your care.

You are familiar with the legislation and policies that inform and guide care staff of the best possible outcomes for residents

To put the resident at the centre of all your care practice is not always easy to achieve. However, help, advice and guidance are available through legislation and policies. For example, the Secretary of State has published the National Minimum Standards under section 23(1) of the Care Standards Act 2000. The standards apply to all care organisations (under section 3 of the Act) which provide accommodation with care.

You will find that the standards are split into several different categories:

- choice of home;
- lifestyle;
- individual needs and choices;
- personal and health care support;
- concerns, complaints and protection;
- environment;
- staffing;
- conduct and management of the home.

Each category contains a series of directives, which you, as a care manager, must adhere to. The National Care Standards Commission will judge your service on the way you follow the directives for each category. The central theme underpinning the standards is a focus on service users. This is a reflection of the recommendations of two Government White Papers *Modernising Social Services* (1998) and *Valuing People* (2001). The latter in particular encourages service providers and contractors to place the client at the centre of everything they do.

Try it out

Choose one of the categories of the National Minimum Standards and identify the directives attached to this. Does your own service meet the requirements or are changes required? You may like to work through the rest of the categories as you work towards completion of this unit. After all, you will be inspected on your organisation's compliance.

Human Rights Act 1998

Another piece of significant legislation underpinning best outcomes is the Human Rights Act 1998. The Act has given additional recourse to individuals within UK courts if they feel that their rights have been infringed. There are 16 rights contained in the Act, including the right to life, the right to liberty and security, and the right to a fair trial. You need to be aware of the Act and how it affects your work with vulnerable people. Every person has the same rights and you must ensure that these are not denied. You need to be conscious of the ways in which the rights of one person may affect those of another. You will no doubt have experienced this as it inevitably arises where a group of people live together.

You and your team need to be creative in finding ways to promote and maintain the rights of all your residents, irrespective of their particular needs.

Think it over

What might you need to do about the Human Rights Act? You need to think about promoting awareness of the Act within your team. You may need to review your practice and policies to ensure that they promote rather than undermine rights. You need to support residents in claiming their rights as equal citizens.

No Secrets

The guidance contained in *No Secrets*, a document issued by the Department of Health in 1999, builds on the philosophy of the Human Rights Act to protect and promote rights for everyone while aiming to make sure best outcomes are achieved for service users. The guidance is the result of concerns raised about crime against adults in care environments. It is a multi-agency strategy issued under section 7 of the Local Authority Social Services Act of 1970.

It advocates clear and transparent strategies for the prevention, management and resolution of cases of abuse, and supports inter-agency working. It is important for you to be aware of the contents of this guidance and the way it could affect your organisation. The guidance in *No Secrets* sets out the types of abuse which may occur in the care of vulnerable people. Types of abuse are identified as:

- *Physical.* This is the direct infliction of injuries on another person, for example by hitting, kicking, slapping, shaking or force feeding. Other forms include lack of food or drink and being left in soiled clothes or bedding.
- *Sexual.* This means unwelcome sexual acts – in fact any for which no consent has been given (full penetrative sex does not need to have taken place as abuse can involve, for example, inappropriate touching during personal care or simply 'flashing').
- *Psychological.* This can be just as damaging as physical abuse but often is more subtle. It often includes verbal abuse, which can result in a resident's loss of control and self-esteem. In a care setting, depriving

an individual of choice can be described as emotional psychological abuse.

- **Financial.** This is the dishonest use of another person's money or belongings. Vulnerable people can be abused financially because of their lack of awareness and a tendency to be too trusting.
- **Neglect.** A failure to provide a service that meets the holistic needs of a resident could be classed as neglect. Insufficient food and drink are obvious examples, but failure to promote medical health or social activities could also be classed as neglect.
- **Discrimination.** Treating people better or worse because of difference is not to be tolerated. Residents have the same rights and carers have the same responsibilities no matter what their race, creed or sex.

Think it over

Find out what local protocols in relation to vulnerable adults exist in your area and how they might affect your working practice. What changes do you need to make to your service to ensure that the protocols are reflected in your organisation?

You identify organisational factors relating to the achievement of the best possible outcomes for residents

There are many factors and tensions which have the potential to affect (positively or negatively) the achievement of the best outcomes for residents. When you are working towards outcomes for individuals, barriers and enablers will always exist. As the registered manager, you need to be alert to organisational risks and take action to minimise or remove them. Working in a group setting, the main tension is often one of balancing the needs of one person against those of the group. For example, staff time needs to be shared among the group, but this is not always easy to achieve if one person is more demanding than another.

Staffing ratios

It is important to have the right skill mix of staff to cope with the requirements of your organisation and your residents' needs. It will not be helpful to have all nurses on duty and no carers and neither will it be helpful to have two senior managers and a catering assistant.

Shift patterns

This can be a difficult one to handle, as you will have to balance 'continuity of care' with staff needs. Many staff will be unwilling to work irregular or antisocial hours and this is not always easy to spot at interview! Also, residents usually like to be able to establish normal routines and this may be difficult for them if they do not know which staff to expect and when.

Case study — Staffing issues

Abdul is an adult with Down's syndrome. He lives in a core and cluster home with support from key workers. He is gregarious and outgoing. He loves bowling and going to the pub. This has been easy to accommodate in the shift patterns of the organisation. However, he recently said he wanted to start going to nightclubs. His chosen venue does not close until 2.00 am and Abdul expressed his disappointment at being brought home at 10.00 pm because staff were due to go off duty.

- How would you handle this situation?
- What are the issues for Abdul and the care staff and the organisation?
- How could balance be achieved?

Staff training

Staff need to be trained and knowledgeable if they are to meet all the requirements of the job role allocated to them. Staff training could also cover teamwork and partnership working. Working in isolation is unlikely to result in the 'best outcomes' for residents.

Incompatibility of residents

Not all residents who live together will socialise positively. Unless there are some baseline commonalities between your residents, for example, similar age groups, people who need high levels of nursing care or people who are old and frail, compatibility will be difficult to achieve. Lack of this can result in tensions which may prove impossible to deal with successfully.

Crisis and chaos

Poor management skills can result in crisis management – that is, dealing with problems only on a day-to-day basis. While crises will always have the potential to surprise and cause confusion, they should not be part of everyday working life.

Organisational structure

The organisational structure should be clear in determining the required aims and objectives for both the service and the resident, and methods for achieving these outcomes. Without this, staff can be unfocused and uncertain in their roles and responsibilities and will be unable to measure progression for their residents.

Policies and procedures

Staff need to be clear about their boundaries: they need to know when to deal with issues and when to refer them on. It is only through the direction of policies and the procedures of your organisation that this will be achieved. Your role should be to interpret and implement the guidance received from policies.

Case study — Staffing problems

William is the care manager of a younger person's day centre. The centre is always understaffed, because of its lack of resources. Today his only qualified social carer has just called in sick. The two trainees cope very well with the daily tasks of caring for the clients but are less confident with report writing and recording the day's events. At the end of the day, William goes through the care plans for the clients and finds that they contain comments such as 'John is fine' and on Mary's records 'no problems'.

- How should William have managed the absence issue? What might you have done in this situation?
- How will the comments written on the care plans affect best outcomes for John and Mary?

Institutional discrimination

Another organisational factor which would hinder the achievement of best outcomes for residents is institutional discrimination. You will be familiar by now with the need to treat people equally and avoid discriminatory practice. When prompted about forms of discrimination you will probably think about issues of race and gender quite readily. As manager, you also need to be aware of the potential for 'institutional discrimination' in your workplace and the negative impact this can have on outcomes for residents.

Institutional discrimination is important because it can undermine any individual attempts to break down discrimination. You are the link between your organisation and the staff and users. Therefore you have a duty to consider whether any institutional discrimination exists, and if so to act.

Some typical forms of institutional discrimination include:

- communication methods which do not take account of residents' needs (consider the need for the provision of Braille, British Sign Language and translations for those who do not use English as their first language);
- staff complements which do not reflect the race, gender and age profile of the residents;
- lack of environmental support for those with a physical disability.

A service which does not advocate the care value base and hold these values central to the care of residents compromises quality care and would be considered guilty of institutional discrimination.

Acknowledging that there is an issue to be addressed is the first step, but it is important then to be active in the resolution of institutional discrimination. The outcomes for your residents could be directly influenced by institutional discrimination. If your complaint procedure is not readily accessible to residents, you must deal with this and locate the resources necessary to redress the situation.

In relation to institutional discrimination, you will need to know:

- the limitations of your role;
- how to refer issues on for action directly above you;
- what to do if you are not happy with the response obtained from your managers.

Know your residents

For the best possible outcome to be achieved, you need to work with and include residents in every stage of the care process. The desired outcomes will vary with the needs, aspirations and abilities of any given resident. Your challenge is to facilitate a process by which decisions can be made about this.

You need to demonstrate your processes both internally and externally. You are unlikely to achieve the best outcome if your team is not aware of the process or the desired result. Externally you will be judged on your ability to demonstrate how changing needs and goals are addressed.

There are four elements to the care process:

- *Identification*. What is it that you and the resident would like to achieve?
- *Barriers*. What factors may affect the success of the outcome and what compromises may be necessary and acceptable?
- *Action*. The process by which the outcome can be promoted and achieved.

- *Achievement*. There should be a clear means of determining whether the outcome has been achieved.

Case study — Four elements of the care process

Kate is 26 and has always been interested in trampolining. Despite this being well documented over several years, she has never tried it. Kate has only partial sight and trampolining has always been considered inappropriate for her. At the case review, Kate's key worker has agreed to raise the issue as an aspiration. Kate herself will be bringing a picture from a magazine to illustrate her message to the meeting.

Consider the following questions in the light of the process highlighted above.

- What would a realistic goal be with regard to Kate's aspirations?
- What barriers are there to Kate's wishes?
- What suggestions can you make in order to deal with the barriers?
- How would you go about dealing with conflict and disagreement at the case review about the most appropriate way forward?
- What sort of documentation would you keep regarding this issue?

Coping with tensions in the workplace

As you have probably realised, involving the resident in achieving best outcomes is likely to result in a range of tensions that you will have to deal with. For example, you will need to plan ahead and think about how staffing ratios and patterns of work may positively or negatively affect service provision. You also need to consider how staffing can be used flexibly to allow for additional one-off pieces of work to be carried out. Moreover, staff training and supervision can place pressure on the day-to-day delivery of services. There will also be unpredicted incidents such as an unplanned hospital admission or staff sickness at short notice. To an extent, these things need to be accepted as an unfortunate part of daily life and some compromise may need to be struck. It is your job, however, to minimise disruption to the service and outcomes by thinking and planning ahead with your team.

Evidence collection RM1.1 — Organisational policies and procedures

Collect together your organisational policies and procedures for staff training, resident access, risk management and so on, and systematically review their contents in the light of the Care Standards Act.

Circulate copies of these policies to staff and residents and others who are appropriate to collect their feedback and suggestions for change. Analyse their comments and then make recommendations for change.

You understand the importance of residents' participation in care planning and independence for facilitating best possible outcomes

In addition to organisational factors, the participation of residents in care planning and the maintenance of their independence also contribute to progress in the achievement of best outcomes. Residents' participation can be promoted by an effective care planning process. This is the central system for every resident. It is a written record of core needs and also indicates desired outcomes and how these will be achieved.

The crucial element of care planning is to consider the individual in the process. Although this process is certainly not new to the field of social care, over recent years there has been an increase in the value placed on resident involvement. The underlying philosophies of individuality and choice should be clearly seen within the care planning document. As the registered manager, you need to show that you are planning a service around the identified and agreed needs and desires of the individual rather than fitting a person into your service.

In order to achieve best outcomes, you will need to consider how to ensure the full involvement of the individual. It may be that an official care planning document will be threatening and at the every least inaccessible. For example, you may be supporting a deaf person who uses British Sign Language. You may need to consider a pictorial version or a translation into another language. You cannot have true participation if the individual cannot understand the content of the package of care.

Care plan documents vary and you do have some autonomy in terms of the design and content. However, it is important that you can clearly indicate the desired outcomes for the individual. There are many different aspects of daily living which may be included within an individual care plan. Some examples are shown in Figure 9.

You need to consider the desired outcomes in terms of all the relevant aspects of daily living for each individual resident. The process for the development of individual care plans should start by gathering information from key sources. These could include:

- residents (probably the most important source of information);
- significant others (generally family);
- social workers;
- community psychiatric nurses;
- current service providers;
- general practitioners;
- other health professionals (e.g. psychiatrists, psychologists, nutritionists).

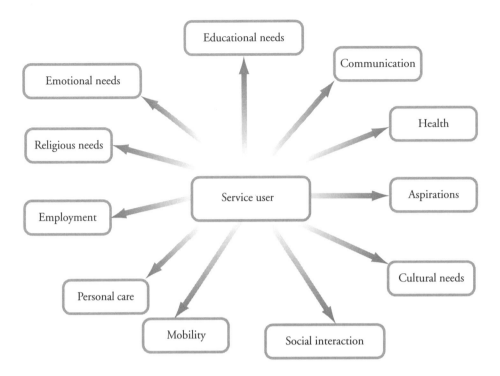

Figure 9. The different aspects of daily living which may be included within an individual care plan.

Your list will depend on the type of service you are providing and on the presenting needs of the resident. You may find that some overlaps exist but by seeking information from a range of sources you will form a fuller picture of the resident and therefore be more effective in developing an initial plan of care.

It is good practice to have the plan agreed by all relevant parties but in particular you must find ways of involving and informing residents in the process. It is, after all, their service to meet their needs.

The care planning process includes six stages:

1 *Initial assessment of need.* Involve the resident by agreeing dates and times, offering appropriate support, and explaining the process. Think about ways in which your staff can be supported to ensure the resident is fully involved from the earliest possible stage of the care planning process.

2 *Development of the care plan.* It is important to involve the resident throughout the development of the care plan. Your staff need to know how to gain agreement and ownership from the resident. The views of the resident must be included as well as aspirations, hopes and fears. Staff need to know how to check for the resident's understanding of the issues under discussion.

3 **_Intervention and support._** Once the goals or objectives have been agreed, you need to think about how to implement the plan. Your staff need to be aware of the need for ongoing negotiation with the resident so that outcomes will be more effectively achieved. Remember, initial motivation and enthusiasm are likely to diminish.

4 **_Monitoring and internal review._** Encourage your residents to participate in feedback sessions. You may need to think about effective strategies that your staff can employ to ensure residents take each available opportunity to feedback their views and opinions. At this stage it is also important to measure progress and to highlight areas of weakness.

5 **_Statutory review of the care package._** This more formal process usually involves outside agencies. The resident's view is an essential element. The staff member reporting on the resident should be only a part of the process. The resident's views and opinions need to be heard.

6 **_Agreement on goal setting._** When planning ahead for the next series of goals the resident should be encouraged to reflect on what has happened and what has been achieved to enable him or her to think about possible changes and new opportunities.

Your organisational systems need to reflect these stages and, furthermore, allow for clear recording of information to be made throughout. If your staff do not fully understand the issues at each stage, opportunities for resident participation and the achievement of best outcomes will be lost.

It is crucial to good practice that within the process there is opportunity for considering progress, what works and what does not. Internal monitoring will provide a forum within which the resident and the team can consider any changes to make for a more effective package of care.

If you do not provide an opportunity for problems to be raised, it is likely that at stages 5 and 6 things will be more difficult for everyone. Statutory reviewers may not have the evidence they require and agreement about goals and targets may not be achieved. You need to ensure that packages are effective throughout their lives and that residents are enabled to get the most from the package designed for and with them. In order to do this, you need to consider how to encourage constructive, ongoing feedback. You will gain a more balanced and useful picture if you invite feedback from a range of sources including:

- the resident;
- your team members;
- the resident's family;
- purchasers of the service;
- partners involved in the caring process.

Each package must be reviewed at least every six months and any changes made. You could do this in a range of ways. They would include:

- key worker meetings with residents to gather their views;
- internal review meetings;
- monthly update reports on progress and difficulties;
- staff meetings;
- the involvement of an advocate for a resident;
- consultation with others, for example, family members, counsellors, community psychiatric nurses and other professionals.

Case study — The care plan

Bob Small is living in residential care. He is profoundly deaf and has had to leave his part-time job because of stress-related illness. He is bored and feels isolated from the other residents. He enjoys creative activities but is self-harming due to frustration.

What would be the 'desired outcome' for this resident? Use the care plan below to identify the steps to be taken in achieving this. Fill in the columns to cover all aspects of his daily living. The first one has been done for you. Compare this to your own care plans. Are any changes required?

Individual plan of care

Name of resident:

Date of plan:

Goal or need	Desired outcome	Way of achieving it	Who is responsible	Timescale
Employment in sheltered workshop	Increased self-esteem	Partnership with Trinity Day Centre	Care manager	3 months

Date of review:

Care plan agreed by:

Key worker:

Local authority representative:

You are able to identify ways of involving residents in care planning and daily living decisions

There are many ways of involving the resident in care planning and other aspects of daily living. As the registered manager, your responsibility is to ensure that your staff use the most appropriate methods and strategies for ensuring effective and successful participation from residents. For many care settings, it will be useful to have a range of strategies available that can be called upon as the situation arises. Examples of useful strategies include **empowerment**, **advocacy** and **interpreters**.

Empowerment

In simple terms, empowerment means to have a voice and be heard. Empowerment is a way of developing potential and acknowledging the strengths of individuals rather than the challenges they face. An organisation that truly believes in empowering individuals in their everyday lives will use a range of strategies to ensure that their voices are heard and their wishes acted upon.

Empowerment means a shift in the balance of control from service provider to service user. This in turn enables users to gain control and an increased quality of life. You will have a role in educating your team about the importance of empowerment and in developing ways of achieving empowerment of residents.

Empowerment is absolutely about improving lives by sharing information, negotiating and remaining person centred. Remember your residents have the right to be informed of and involved in decisions about their lives. An empowering organisation may well find itself using external services to promote the empowerment of their clients.

Advocacy

Although it may involve quite a commitment in terms of time, liaison and even training, there are real benefits to be had from using advocacy – for both your service and those who use it.

Advocates help people to have a voice and to gain recognition of their needs and wants when they, for whatever reason, are not able to speak for themselves. Advocacy is an important form of empowerment by which some of the more marginalised members of society can effect change in the traditionally powerful elements of our society. Advocacy focuses on the inadequacies of the system. Discrimination rather than the individual is seen as the cause of the power imbalance. The role of advocacy has been heightened over recent years and, in response to this, there are many agencies offering advocacy on a professional basis. That is, people are employed as advocates. In addition, there are examples of voluntary advocacy, where non-professional citizens take on the role.

More recently, *self-advocacy*, where people speak for themselves rather than having a separate advocate, has become more prevalent. Arguably, self-advocacy offers more potential for personal development because it actively encourages the individual to gather information, and so gain skills, confidence and self-esteem. Self-advocacy often stems from a support group where facilitators are employed, and it can therefore be difficult at times to distinguish between advocacy and self-advocacy.

One of the best-known advocacy groups is People First, run by people with learning disabilities. People First has groups all over the world and campaigns about the need for equality for all.

Try it out

Find out what advocacy services are available in your locality. In what ways could they meet the needs of your residents? What might be the considerations for you as the care manager in engaging these services?

Advocacy is one of a number of ways in which you can raise the profile of residents and empower them within your service. It decentralises the control of managers and staff and places power in the hands of the residents. They may then comment and effect change where necessary.

You need to proceed with some caution, as advocacy may well be unfamiliar to your residents and they will need information and reassurance that there will not be repercussions from any feedback they give. You could think of different ways to introduce the idea to your workplace. This means considering the residents and the staff team. The arrival of advocates can feel threatening to staff because they may feel that their practice is being challenged rather than seeing the outcome for the resident.

The following steps represent one way in which an advocacy service could be introduced into your practice setting.

- *Network with other agencies*. Find out what has and has not worked locally. Introduce other users who have used advocacy services before. Approach an advocacy service directly and arrange workshops.

- **Develop a user forum.** Start the process with a few confident users and ask them to be active in the cascading of information to others.
- **Group meetings.** Introduce the topic of advocacy at meetings and provide supporting written information. Give people time to think about the proposal and then discuss advantages and disadvantages.
- **Example issue.** Use a current presenting issue to introduce an advocate and then build up a rapport with staff, residents and the advocate.

Interpreters

Communication is central to everyday interaction but its effectiveness can be compromised by barriers. Often access is the barrier and this may manifest itself in a range of ways. You need to consider what barriers may exist in your workplace and take action to counter them. For example, information needs to be presented in a format which is accessible to those for whom it is intended. This could mean different languages, large print, videos, Braille or the use of interpreters.

The use of an interpreter is a practical way in which you can help residents to access information and to be more involved in their care. As with advocacy, the central issue is that of independence. The interpreter's role is to facilitate participation of the resident in the caring process. By providing interpretation services you are directly increasing the levels of participation and independence for residents (Figure 10).

Working with an interpreter for the first time can be quite daunting, particularly for a resident. Some discussion needs to take place about the management of difficulties within the interaction. You can pre-empt some of these by effective planning, for example, good lighting and freedom from environmental distractions such as telephones.

When there is a need for an interpreter, you need to plan in order to minimise any anxiety for the resident and to ensure that the best possible outcome is achieved. Good rapport needs to be established between resident and interpreter and therefore, before any official business is dealt

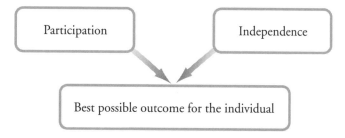

Figure 10. By providing interpretation services you are directly increasing the levels of participation and independence for residents.

with, some time needs to be set aside for their familiarisation. You may also need to reassure the resident that the interpreter is both independent and subject to confidentiality. In a sensitive situation the presence of a stranger could feel uncomfortable. (This may be a situation when you need both an interpreter and an advocate.)

Interpreting can be very demanding and it is therefore important to allow time for breaks. It is good practice to speak with the interpreter beforehand to agree the ground rules for the proceedings. It is also important to explain the purpose of the interaction and the desired outcome.

When arranging an interpreter, you should also consider the comfort and confidence of the resident. The gender or age of the interpreter could be a problem. You should be sensitive to these issues and minimise the likelihood of a failed interaction.

Finally, debriefing with both the resident and the interpreter can be a very useful tool for future reference.

Evidence collection RM1.2 — Resident participation

Obtain a copy of your care planning policies and procedures. Check them to see whether resident participation is explicitly indicated at each stage of the care process. Does the policy include suggestions for encouraging participation? If not, you need to amend and update your policy to bring it in line with national requirements.

RM1.3 You are able to manage and monitor systems used for the assessment of risk

Risk taking can be very frightening, not only for the person directly involved, but also for those on the periphery, in particular, family members, who may have been very protective in the past. Nonetheless, the National Minimum Standard relating to risk states: 'Service users are supported to take risks as part of an independent lifestyle.' It goes on to recommend 'responsible risks' – decisions being made within a framework of forethought and consideration. By following a clear process and indicating how risk can be both measured and minimised, responsible risk taking can be achieved.

Before we can consider the management of risk we need to understand some of the issues involved. These include:

- the benefits of risk management;
- the reasons for risk assessments;
- the types of risks your residents may be exposed to;

- when and how to carry out a risk assessment;
- ways of recording the risk assessment;
- review of the risk assessment and the overall process.

A good understanding of each of these aspects will help you to manage and monitor the whole process of risk assessment in your own organisation.

The benefits of risk management

Resident-centred benefits

As you already know, empowerment is one of the values which underpins social care work. You may miss out on opportunities to empower your residents through fear of being criticised if things go wrong. Effective risk management provides an opportunity to find a balance. However, records of activities need to be clear, concise and up to date in order to ensure accountability is evident.

The benefits to residents of effective risk management include:

- the development of new skills;
- increased independence;
- increased self-esteem;
- more participation;
- an increased sense of citizenship.

It is important to provide opportunities for residents to maintain an independent lifestyle.

Benefits to the organisation

A proactive approach to safe risk taking and assessment rather than a reactive one will promote a culture of safety in your workplace. It will bring to life the written policies and procedures, and enable staff to have living documents rather than pieces of paper which remain unread in a file.

Risk assessment enables you:

- to monitor and evaluate services;
- to have accountability for the activities of the home;
- to provide a framework within which to make informed decisions;
- to work actively towards achieving the best possible outcomes for residents.

The reasons for risk assessments

There are many reasons to carry out risk assessments. Here are just some of the more frequent issues that may affect your decision to carry out risk assessments on certain activities:

- *Age*. Age can bring about physical and mental deterioration, which may require you to think about the risk attached to everyday activities. On the other hand, you may need to think about age in terms of competence and mental development.
- *Disability*. The physical, emotional and intellectual needs of residents can render them particularly vulnerable to risk. Risk assessment is essential to ensure safety with participation.
- *Experience*. New experiences for a resident may also need a risk assessment. This will give everyone involved more confidence and a willingness to experiment.
- *Competence*. This relates to the level of ability required for the activity. For example, crossing a busy road may need testing and the knowledge (pelican crossings, look left etc.) required for safe crossing must be established.
- *Specific illness*. Certain conditions can increase the risks associated with an activity. For example, flashing lights have a trigger effect for people with epilepsy. Therefore, assessments need to relate to the 'trigger factors'.

You need to think about the ways your residents could be considered to be at risk and vulnerable. This is not to reduce their choices and autonomy but to ensure that there is awareness and appropriate action to minimise any distress or harm that may occur. You will no doubt note that it is those who are the least equipped to cope who are at the highest risk in our society.

Residents are at risk from a wide variety of situations. These include exactly the same situations as are faced by many people in society. The difference and difficulties relating to the handling of risk, and therefore safety issues, are often due to lack of understanding and awareness of danger. The two principal categories of risk residents may face are **abuse** and **failure to protect**.

Abuse

The prevention of abuse in any form is a key role for social care professionals. Abuse usually takes place in a relationship where there is a power imbalance. This could be the result of gender, physical strength or status. As the registered manager you need to be aware of the power imbalance between staff and residents and, indeed, between residents, and the potential this raises for abuse.

Research has shown that abuse occurs between service users within care provision. You need to be aware of this possibility and take this into account when thinking about prevention and protection. You need to think about compatibility of the group and include any concerns within your risk assessment processes. This may also mean additional resources to manage the risk effectively. For example, you would need to think about support networks for the victim and for the perpetrator. One of the central considerations would be the extent to which perpetrators understand that they have done something wrong. You would also need to consider whether this was an isolated incident or whether there is an ongoing issue. Here, once again, risk management comes into play.

Abuse, whether between residents or between staff and residents, can take many different forms, and some are more obvious than others (Figure 11). However, the harm done by abuse of any kind should not be underestimated.

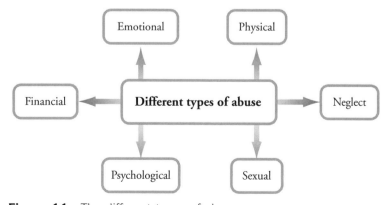

Figure 11. The different types of abuse.

Finding evidence of abuse is not always easy, which is why you need clear systems and procedures for monitoring risk in the workplace.

Case study — Power imbalance and neglect

Arthur is a member of staff who appears to work hard. Today he has been short of one of his team members and has had to carry out additional tasks, which has irritated him. He is glad to finish and get off home at 5.00 pm. At the medication round in the evening, the nurse realises that a particular resident has not had her epilepsy-controlling drugs at all that day. This is the third time that this has happened while Arthur was on duty.

- How would you react to this situation?
- Has abuse occurred?
- How could you find out?
- What action would you take with Arthur?

You need to have a clear policy statement about the protection of those in your care so that any concerns will be raised at an early stage and any necessary action taken. It is difficult for an individual staff member to speak out about concerns but they are more likely to do so if they understand how these issues will be dealt with. This process is commonly known as whistleblowing (see page 57).

Failure to protect

You need to have a clear policy on the protection of residents from harm. Your risk assessment process forms part of this policy.

Perhaps your greatest form of protection is the awareness which you and your team have of the potential for harm or abuse. Your policies must outline to staff and purchasers the philosophy of the service regarding prevention, recognition and management of risk and potential for abuse. Your procedures need to give your team the tools to deal with any issues when they arise.

It is crucial for the protection of residents that you are clear that every team member has a duty to report any concerns about risk taking and or abusive behaviour (see Whistleblowing, below). You, as the manager, must respond with appropriate action and ensure that support is available to the staff. This means that you need to be aware of the factors which can precipitate risk taking and abusive situations. These can be categorised as follows:

- *Medical.* Medical issues can exacerbate an individual's vulnerability to risk and abuse. For example, people who suffer from confusion or forgetfulness may well be considered an unreliable source of information. This unfortunately creates a cover for any perpetrator of abuse. The particular communication needs of an individual can also affect the incidence of risk taking and abuse. If people cannot verbalise their story or their needs, the vulnerability to risk is heightened.

- **Familial.** Pressures within the family could exacerbate the risk of abuse. When care is being given to a family member, the physical and emotional strain on the carer could be a precipitating factor for abuse due to sheer exhaustion. Exhaustion and stress, as well as feelings of guilt, may damage the relationship between the carer and the vulnerable person and resentment may build up. A key element of prevention here is often sufficient external support available to the family.

- **Environmental.** Lack of resources and the pressure this brings can also be a trigger that leads to 'risky' situations and events. You need to be aware of the pressure placed on your staff team. If they are over-stretched, feelings of powerlessness and exhaustion may affect their performance. Equipment and activities that are not sufficiently resourced place both residents and staff at risk from potential harm.

- **Institutional.** This is particularly relevant to your role as a registered manager. You need to be aware of the need for good working conditions for your staff. It is important that your team has regular supervision and ongoing training. Their awareness of good practice and what to do if problems arise can directly affect the care of residents. Cooperation and positive attitudes within the staff team are likely to increase the quality of your provision. In this way, you have a central role in ensuring that your environment is conducive to teamwork and that communication is clear and effective.

Whistleblowing

It is extremely challenging for any worker to whistleblow. Even when there is serious concern about service or individual practice, there can often be ambivalence about the process and the outcome. Although initially concern will be for the victim, other factors may come into play. For example, staff members are likely to ask questions such as:

- What if I am wrong?
- Will there be recriminations?
- What about my safety and acceptance as a team member?
- What about the perpetrator?

It can be particularly difficult for workers who feel they have limited status in the establishment, for example, a new worker, a part-time worker or a casual worker. They may observe something untoward from a more senior person and feel uncomfortable about challenging that person. They may fear for their own job security or just be afraid of official action being taken against them.

As the registered manager, you need to give clear guidance on the organisational philosophy and the process of raising concerns, both internally and externally. This should begin at induction and needs to be reinforced regularly. It is crucial that there is confidence in the reporting system and that there is clarity about how to report any concerns. You also need to ensure that a staff care policy is in place to manage the aftermath for the whistleblower.

When an issue needs to be reported externally, you will have limited authority to deal with the matter. It will be your role to report the matter to the National Care Standards Commission and then vulnerable adult or child protection procedures will be instigated.

Remember, you will be asked about your whistleblowing policy at inspection.

When and how to carry out a risk assessment

Risk assessment and management present major challenges for care professionals. Residents are vulnerable and you need to be very aware of your duty to protect those in your care. However, you must also strive to balance this by empowering residents through the offer of new, albeit often ordinary, opportunities.

You need to have a clear policy on risk taking for the care setting, which can then be shared with relevant people. These may include:

- residents;
- family and other carers;
- staff;
- social workers;
- community psychiatric nurses or other professionals (depending on your resident group).

What then makes for successful risk management? Certainly, every risk management exercise should have, as the absolute minimum, the following aspects included:

- centrality of the residents' wishes;
- resident participation in the process;
- clarity about what risk exists;
- the recording of potential harm and benefits;
- the agreement of review dates;
- the recording of decisions made.

The timing of risk assessment is also of major importance. There are times when risk assessment clearly needs to be carried out with a resident. For example:

- before entry into care;
- at entry into care;
- at ongoing planned reviews;
- at emergency (unplanned) reviews.

When is risk assessment carried out in your organisation? Does the timing match the list presented here? If there are differences, are they due to good or poor practice? Do you need to implement any changes?

Once the timing is established, you need to think about ways of recording this in your policy and procedures for risk management in your organisation.

Ways of recording the risk assessment

Your risk management systems and procedures must enable you to record recommendations and actions. Throughout this section we have seen evidence of the kind of information you must hold in written form. The assessment itself forms part of the written 'evidence'.

A good risk assessment tool needs to be comprehensive yet user-friendly – a lengthy document will tend to sit unread in a file. An example of a suitable pro forma for the recording of the assessment is shown in Table 2.

Table 2. An example of a suitable pro forma for the recording of the assessment
Name:
Date:
Identified hazard:
Who is at risk (e.g. resident, staff, community)?
Likelihood of risk (1 equals very low and 5 equals very high)   1 2 3 4 5
Severity of risk (1 equals very low and 5 equals very high)   1 2 3 4 5
Total risk score (multiply likelihood and severity scores) (high = 17–25, medium = 9–16, low = 1–8)
Action to reduce and manage the risk:
Conclusion/recommendation:
Risk assessment undertaken by:
Review date:

Take note of the middle section of Table 1, which scores the risk. This is a way for you to define what level of risk is being managed so that appropriate responses are made: 1 equals very low and 5 equals very high. When the two scores are multiplied, you have the total risk score (e.g. a likelihood of 3 and severity of 4 gives a total risk score of 12). You then need to identify whether the risk is high (a score of 17–25), medium (a score of 9–16) or low (a score of 1–8).

All of this information must be kept on record. Your records need to be:

- detailed;
- clear;
- timely;

- appropriate;
- relevant;
- accurate.

Review of the risk assessment and the overall process

Review is a crucial part of risk assessment and should be agreed at the point of the initial assessment. You will need to make a judgement about when and with whom to review the assessment and this will depend on the activity and the potential harm posed.

You need to be particularly alert to anything which may call for a risk assessment before your recorded review date (see Figure 12):

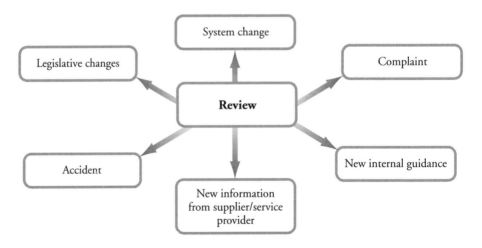

Figure 12. Reasons to perform a risk assessment before the formal review date.

Again, the review of the risk assessment and any necessary action must be recorded, and in sufficient detail.

Case study — Risk assessment

Miriam McCullough has been a resident at Oakfield Care Home for three months. Her care plan was developed with her sister, social worker, physiotherapist and occupational therapist. Mrs McCullough did not participate fully at the time, as she had had a stroke and did not feel well enough. She chose to ignore the care planning process from the outset. She is now feeling much better and is demanding to have 'a say' in her care package. She has asked for a review to take place immediately as she intends to leave the care setting.

- What are the implications of this situation?
- How could Mrs McCullough's care needs be met while still balancing the needs of the services involved?
- What should be the outcome of this situation?

Evidence collection RM1.3 — Risk

Obtain a copy of your risk assessment policy. Compare the information contained in it with that required by national policies. Find ways of involving your staff in the development and updating of your risk assessment policy.

Carry out an analysis of staff knowledge and training requirements relating to abuse or protection that could arise in your organisation. Plan and implement training activities to ensure staff are knowledgeable and empowered to take action if necessary.

RM1.4 — You are able to manage and monitor systems for administering medication

The management of medication is one of the most important and potentially dangerous activities for the social care worker. You need to be alert to the risks involved and ensure that you design, monitor and develop your systems to minimise any risk of harm to your residents through medication. In doing so, you must also face the challenge of finding a balance between the risks related to medication and the need to increase the independence of your residents.

As you might expect, medication is subject to the National Minimum Standards. Standard 20.1 states:

The registered manager and staff encourage and support service users to retain, administer and control their own medication, within a risk management framework, and comply with the home's policy and procedure for the receipt, recording, storage, handling, administration and disposal of medicines.

You need to think about how you and your home are responding to these requirements.

Think it over

How do you encourage residents to administer and control their own medication? What issues arise from the National Minimum Standard (20.1) in relation to both staff and residents? How confident are you in the systems, policies and procedures that your organisation has for managing medication?

The handling of medication follows a process which is traced by the Standard:

- receipt;
- recording;
- storage;
- handling;
- administration;
- disposal.

You need to think about each of these areas when establishing and reviewing your systems and policies for medication.

Try it out

Obtain a copy of the Care Standards Act and read Standard 20 in full. Compare the requirements of the Act with your internal policy and procedure and make a note of any gaps which currently exist. Now you need to review your policy.

Receipt

You should begin by ascertaining what is required by each resident and then obtain the required medication. In order to do this effectively, you need a clear ordering system. You will need to liaise effectively with your GP, pharmacist and other relevant professionals. There is no place for confusion. You must ensure that your system is clear and that communication is effective and complete. It is good practice to regularly review your system and update it as necessary.

You need to think about who will make and record the order and with what frequency. You will also need to keep accurate records of orders made and record the types and numbers of medications coming into your practice setting.

The manager has asked Lillian to make a list of the drugs required to restock the medicine chest. Lillian has examined all the bottles and tubes stored in the chest and ordered anything that looked like it was 'half empty'. She has written the name of the medication required on an old envelope and passed this to her colleague to write out in 'best writing' and then to send the order to the supplier.

- What are the issues relating to this procedure?
- What would you do if you found the same scenario occurring in your workplace?
- What are the implications for the organisation and for the residents?

Recording

In order to account accurately for the medication that is given to residents, you need to have clear records. If you use a 'pre-packaged' system your pharmacist will provide the relevant paperwork to you. This will be an official document on which to record all activities relating to medication.

A typical form for recording of information relating to medication would cover:

Physical needs	Intellectual needs	Emotional needs	Social needs

You need to consider confidentiality here. There is personal information which must be treated with respect. You must ensure that your records meet the requirements of the Data Protection Act and the National Minimum Standards.

Storage

You must think carefully about the ways you store medication. You are required to provide a lockable metal cabinet. Medication should be removed only when required and returned to the cabinet immediately after dispensation. If you have controlled drugs in the establishment, you need to provide a locked cabinet within a second cabinet.

Try it out

Do you know which drugs come under the category 'controlled drugs'? Check to see whether your home is managing any of these drugs and then ensure that you are following the guidance appropriately.

Some medications may require special treatment, for example, storage in a refrigerator. Others may need to be kept in their original packaging until dispensed. Your pharmacist will be happy to provide advice on these matters.

If any residents are administering their medications to themselves, they must be provided with lockable storage. This provides protection for the individual as well as those who share the home. If medication is to be kept in a private bedroom there is a risk that another person could take the medication. In creating more independence for one person you must not expose others to additional risk.

Handling/administering

You need to have an effective system for handling and administering medication. Safety is an important issue. Drugs should be locked away at all times. Staff need to be aware of the risk posed by unattended drugs. When administering drugs, the crucial factor is in checking that the correct dose and type of drug is being given to the right person. Your system needs to be clear, legible and up to date. Any changes to medication should be made immediately and your team alerted. Remember that your service user has a right to know what they are taking and why.

Disposal

You have a duty to ensure that any damaged or unneeded medication is disposed of safely. This means being able to account for the medication. You must not dispose of any medication yourself – you must return it to the pharmacist. You should also keep records of all returns. A form for this purpose would comprise sections to complete on:

- date;
- medication;
- reason for disposal (e.g. damaged, medication changed, death of resident);
- staff member signature;
- counter-signed by (pharmacist).

If any controlled drugs are kept within the organisation, you must keep a separate disposal register for them. You must also log exactly how many of these drugs you hold and keep a log of how they are dispensed and disposed of.

Communicating policy and practice

You must ensure that every member of your team is aware of the medication policy and procedure and, in particular, what to do if a discrepancy is discovered.

Your medication procedure is, in the main, a tool for your establishment. You may, however, need to communicate with a range of other people about your systems. These may include:

- residents;
- family members and other carers;
- other professionals (e.g. general practitioners or community psychiatric nurses);
- team members;
- purchasers;
- regulators and inspectors.

At first glance you may be surprised by the list. Let us look at how each of them may have a part to play.

Residents

Depending upon their level of independence, individual residents may wish to clarify what systems are used in the home. They may wish to administer their medications to themselves and seek reassurance that the system is easy to follow. They may be concerned about how and where the medication is kept or be concerned that their medication will be mixed up with that of another resident.

Family members and other carers

It is often difficult for a family member to give over the care of their loved one to professionals. Reassurance about safety and competence with the handling of medication is likely to be high on their agenda. You need to be able to explain and show the practice of the home.

Team members

Your team members will be dealing with medication first hand. They are also likely to be dealing first hand with any concerns or discrepancies. It is therefore crucial that they understand and implement fully the policy and procedure of the home in order to prevent problems.

Other professionals

Your pharmacist will want to be sure that your systems are working effectively. A community psychiatric nurse, health visitor or general practitioner may want to raise the possibility of a service user working towards self-medicating. Within the context of risk assessment, the National Minimum Standards also encourage this empowerment.

Purchasers

Potential purchasers may ask you about your medication procedure at the point of referral or contracting. You may be asked to provide evidence of your policies and procedures as well as staff training in this area.

Regulators and inspectors

At inspection you will be asked about the management of medication in your service. Your systems must be able to stand up to scrutiny. It is your job to make sure that your systems comply with all the necessary regulations and guidelines, and therefore provide the necessary support and protection for residents.

Staff training

Your systems should provide a good framework for practice and ensure consistency for residents. However, perhaps most important is the training and awareness of the staff team. Initial training is crucial if staff are to understand, not only the process, but the reasons for managing medication in the prescribed way. This is usually best done at induction. However, it is important to keep this on the agenda for your team. It is easy to become complacent and this is an area of potential high risk.

The National Minimum Standards emphasise the need for training to be accredited. It also emphasises that the content of such training should include the way in which medication is used, the problems which can arise and the principles which have informed the policy on the management of medication.

Self-medication

The National Minimum Standards advocate self-medicating whenever possible within a risk assessment framework. This does not mean that all residents should self-medicate; rather, it means that you should work proactively towards achieving this.

In order to make a judgement on this issue, you need to carry out a risk assessment. As we already know, risk assessment is not about preventing people from doing things; it is about looking at how to carry out activities safely and successfully to achieve the best outcome for the resident. A consultation approach with the team, service user and other relevant professionals often works best. You need to balance the safety of your service users with their wishes. Effective risk assessment will help to minimise any conflict here.

Case study — Self-medication

Jean Barlow is 36 years old and has recently been discharged from hospital after seven weeks. Before her hospitalisation she had managed her own medication for over three years. Although she had, on the whole, managed well, just before her admission she had been having difficulty sleeping and had at times been forgetful. It is very important to Jean that she retains her independence; even though her confidence has been shaken by her stay in hospital, she is anxious to prove her skills in this area.

- What are the presenting factors which might affect the decision to self-medicate?
- What measures could be introduced to minimise the risk?
- What would you consider to be the advantages and disadvantages of Jean's self-medication?
- Do you think that Jean should be encouraged to self-medicate at this time? Give reasons for your decision.

Reviewing medication policies and procedures

As you use your systems and procedures, you will no doubt pick up new ideas and highlight inadequacies. Rather than seeing this process as negative, you need to see 'gaps' as an opportunity to review and improve systems.

It is important that you gather information from a range of sources. The main ones are likely to be:

- training forums;
- staff meetings;
- resident group feedback;
- review of records;
- networking with others.

Your team is a good resource to use when reviewing day-to-day systems which affect residents. Often the practical experience of using a system raises positive suggestions for change.

You need to ensure that feedback and suggestions are part of your meeting and communication processes so that you can constantly be reviewing and improving your system for medication (or any other system or policy for that matter).

Making changes to systems and procedures needs careful thought. You need to be sure that any changes will bring benefits. This means that you must monitor changes implemented so that intervention can take place immediately if required.

Try it out

Think about the information each source can provide you with in relation to medication policies and procedures. Make notes of the main points. Which of these sources could be left out of the consulting process without adversely affecting the larger picture?

Evidence collection RM1.4 — Medication

Obtain a copy of your organisational policy for the use of medication. Review the contents and make recommendations for change if necessary. Consult with staff and residents on the process currently used and ask for recommendations for change that will lead to an improved system. Compare your own views with those of residents and staff, make notes of the recommendations and update your organisational policy as appropriate.

Keys to good management practice

Achieving best possible outcomes

- Always place residents at the centre of everything you do.
- Know your staff and organisation inside out.
- Understand and implement the guidance and legislation which underpins your service.
- Recognise that nothing is perfect and change can bring about many benefits.
- Listen to residents and others for examples of improvements that could be implemented.
- Use risk assessments at all times and be willing to review as necessary.
- Keep accurate and detailed records of everything your organisation is involved in.
- Involve residents in everything possible.
- Start and finish with your residents in mind!

B3 Manage the Use of Financial Resources

This unit is about making sure you use financial resources in the most efficient way possible. It covers making recommendations for the use of financial resources and controlling expenditure against budgets.

The elements are:
- Make recommendations for expenditure.
- Control expenditure against budgets.

Learning outcomes

- You give opportunities to relevant people to make suggestions for future expenditure.
- Your recommendations take account of past experience, trends, developments and other factors likely to affect future expenditure.
- You clearly state the expected benefits from the recommended expenditure, and any potential negative consequences.
- Where you have considered alternative options for expenditure, you provide valid reasons why you have rejected them.
- You provide sufficient, valid information for relevant people to make a decision on your recommendations.
- Your recommendations for expenditure are consistent with your organisation's plans and objectives.
- You present your recommendations to relevant people in an appropriate format and at an appropriate time.

You give opportunities to relevant people to make suggestions for future expenditure

In order for relevant people to make suggestions, the manager is required:

- to identify the relevant people;
- to communicate with them;
- to provide opportunities for them to make suggestions in the formulation of a service plan. A service plan is your plan of existing and future services which you would seek to develop within each financial year, costed appropriately to ensure that it complies with available expenditure.

Think it over

Who are your relevant people to include? Do you include residents as 'relevant people'? The involvement of a variety of relevant people is crucial and worthy of the time taken.

It will be important to refer to Standard 34 of the Department of Health document, *Care Homes for Older People*, which directs that there be a business and financial plan for the establishment, and that it is open to inspection and reviewed annually (34.5). Of equal importance, if you have chosen not *directly* to involve residents in your group of relevant people, you are still obliged by Standard 33 to obtain feedback on your ideas from residents and carers; and they equally have a right to challenge your ideas under Standards 16 and 17, which stipulate the right to complain and to have legal rights protected.

Think about the different ways in which you may communicate with your relevant people, both to recruit them and later by which they may suggest ideas that directly benefit your practice setting. Examples include official meetings, newsletters, bulletins and informal channels.

In your planning, take into account the advantages and disadvantages of your communication style, specifically, whether it is formal or informal. A formal style will ensure that the relevant people are aware of the boundaries in which they are operating. For example, you may choose to show them the budget allocation for the year and to make it clear that they must operate within it. An informal approach may allow previously unconsidered ideas to gain momentum, and in the same situation, there may be a suggestion to form a group to raise money from statutory or charitable sources to supplement the budget

As manager you will need to consider ways in which you can motivate your relevant people to become involved and to remain so.

Try it out

Identify your relevant people and consider how to communicate with them in order to allow them to be involved, and remain involved, in the business of planning the budget priorities.

Case study — Consultation on expenditure

It is the first meeting of a consultation group and you have provided group members with budget details on the overhead projector. On looking at the information, one of the carers instantly raises an objection that refurbishment costs are twice the amount allocated to special interests for residents, and she feels that her elderly father has been incorrectly advised about his choice of home. She demands that the group deal with the matter there and then.

- As manager, how would you respond?
- More importantly, how will you manage the process of consultation?

As may be seen, this first stage – consulting with and obtaining suggestions from relevant people – is crucial to the financial planning cycle, and while your finance officer and external auditor are available to guide you, your people skills will need to be to the fore in this vital stage of the financial planning process.

In terms of future expenditure, you will need to find out about development plans for other homes and present this information to your relevant people with your plans for future expenditure. Do you wish to improve the physical dimensions of your practice setting? If so, you will need to include in your recommendations an external description of the construction work, as well as an internal description, covering, for example, floor levels, lifts/stairs, room ratio, room sizes and staff accommodation. When presenting your recommendations you may consider including photographs of the practice setting, and drawing attention to particular features and areas for future development.

Your recommendations take account of past experience, trends, developments and other factors likely to affect future expenditure

Why do we need to look back in order to identify factors likely to affect the future? It is clear that your practice setting's financial plan, reviewed annually, will need to be evaluated before the new budget is agreed. By looking back over past results, the manager may best plan for the future.

The 1998 Government White Paper, *Modern Local Government in Touch with the People*, indicates that continuous improvements in services, in terms of both quality and cost, will be the basis of service delivery, and that there will be a duty to secure 'best value'. As manager, you will need to understand the principles of best value, and you will need to demonstrate that you employ the most effective, economical and efficient means available to meet residents' needs. The key principles of best practice are:

- challenge;
- compare;
- consult;
- competition.

Try it out

How will you analyse expenditure in the past and use the results to make recommendations for the more effective use of financial resources in the future?

The service or business plan for your practice setting should be regularly reviewed, kept up to date and be available for scrutiny. While looking back and planning for the following year, always consult your relevant people.

It is vital that you know what it costs your practice setting to provide one hour of care. This will allow you to compare this unit cost with those of other practice settings, as you need to be competitive in accordance with the principles of best value.

Consider, through looking back, whether you will be able to reduce your overhead costs, that is, those running costs which do not affect residents' care, such as lighting, heating in unnecessary rooms, office space unused, and so on.

As manager, you may decide to invest in a financial information system, which would monitor your budget and provide details of cheaper alternatives for your forward-looking plan. While looking back to plan for the coming year, there must be sufficient stability to allow current functions to continue, but also sufficient flexibility to incorporate value-for-money initiatives.

In conclusion, the need to reflect on the year that is over, before moving onto the plan for the future, is directly in line with the government's monitoring agenda and is set out clearly in the Care Standards Act. The manager must be able show the written policies which lead you to use the budget in certain ways and equally to demonstrate your analysis of unit costs. This analysis should be open to both resident scrutiny and comment and external inspection.

Case study — Budgetary changes to promote competitiveness

You are aware that to attract new residents you must remain attractive and competitive in your service provision, and you have to make some changes to your budget. You distribute your unit costings to your residents and set a deadline for feedback on cost-effectiveness and changes to service provision. Most people have complaints about the service they currently receive and others see no reason to make changes.

- How can you make changes while retaining the goodwill of existing residents?
- How will you demonstrate the benefits of change?
- At what pace should changes be implemented?
- How can you involve your relevant people?

Looking back allows you not only to learn what was positive, but also to forecast demand and equip the practice setting to remain competitive and viable (see Figure 13). By looking back, you are able to gather information from a variety of people and ask them what will motivate them in the future. Remember that planning is about residents, carers and providers and that it should not be assumed that 'more of the same' will meet residents' needs. Basically, we see the emergence of a budgeting cycle to complement the business plan. Performance evaluation is crucial. Use the looking back model below as part of the budgetary preparation and evaluate your results against budgetary goals.

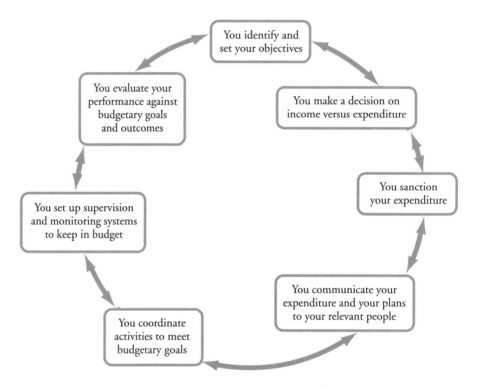

Figure 13. 'Looking back' in action.

You clearly state the expected benefits from the recommended expenditure, and any potential negative consequences

As manager, you will need constantly to analyse and to provide feedback on the budget, as well as on the positive and negative consequences of the recommendations for expenditure. There is no place for leaving things to chance.

Your practice setting may operate alone or as part of similar settings operating to a larger business plan, and feeding into it. Either way, your financial planning should follow a strategic path. One is shown in Figure 14.

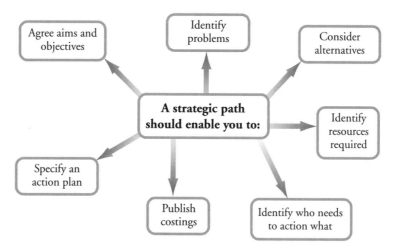

Figure 14. Strategic path for financial planning.

A report describing the strategic path is the place in which to state the expected benefits of expenditure. This is the second phase of the financial cycle (following the consultation phase). The business strategy involves describing the reasons for choosing the particular path, the resources needed and any possible change in contracted services (e.g. food suppliers, laundry, etc.). The potential positive and negative consequences need to be carefully explored and explained.

Try it out

Consider how you may best show residents your recommendations for expenditure, and the possible positive and negative outcomes.

Remember, reports must be updated regularly and it is generally viewed as better to adapt an existing report than to create a new one. Your eye, as manager, must always be on the future, and your analysis of what has gone before is worthwhile only if it illustrates a clearer set of choices for the future.

Your explanation of the positive and negative consequences of future expenditure needs to be simple. You should not devise reports which have to be reworked, as this wastes time and is not likely to interest residents. You need to show costs to your residents and look at continuous ways to improve what is provided on the basis of reduced costs. Residents will not want to see your practice setting improving while the direct care afforded to them deteriorates. Therefore, good communication and knowledge of motivation need to underpin this part of financial planning.

Case study — Cost versus quality

As manager, you are aware that some of the options for residents are helpful to your budget but may not be immediately attractive to them in terms of the quality of service they receive.

- What courses of action are open to you?

You are already aware that some of your established residents are resistant to change, while others are keen to try something new and to look on residential care as a new beginning.

- How would you seek to reconcile both standpoints and build positive attitudes towards the necessary goals?

Where you have considered alternative options for expenditure, you provide valid reasons for why you have rejected them

As manager, you may well be asked to account publicly for your reasons for rejecting alternative options, and your reasons will need to be robust and measured against proven 'best value' initiatives. Your considerations for expenditure come within the forecasting phase of financial planning, in which you will need to predict likely future demand by considering whether what has gone before will continue. You will need to judge how likely it is that the trends in demand will continue. If they are likely to change, in what manner might this be?

At all times your choices for expenditure must be based upon the long-term success of your practice setting. Thus your choices should be set in the context of your long-term objectives and your residents' needs. You will need to remember the value-for-money ethos of the modernising Government White Paper, and use this message to underpin your expenditure choices.

Think it over

How do you go about considering different viable options for expenditure to meet your organisational requirements?

The budgetary evaluation of Appledore Lodge is provided in the Appendix to this chapter as an example not only of a method of identifying unit costs but also of evaluating those costs, and presenting the possible outcomes of change in simple table form. It represents an example of best practice when considering alternative options for expenditure.

You may decide to undertake a budgetary evaluation for each of your overheads and publish the outcomes for consultation.

You provide sufficient, valid information for relevant people to make a decision on your recommendations

Try it out

Consider an eye-catching means of providing valid information to relevant people which encompasses confidentiality. What is sufficient and valid? Have you discussed and decided on a method of presenting valid information to relevant people at agreed times? How might this be done in a way which is cost-effective?

A history of the practice setting could be presented to residents and relevant people in brochure form. It could begin, for example:

> This property was purchased 16 years ago and began as a residential home for 10 residents. It was extended and then re-registered for the current occupancy of 23 residents.

Historical accounts

Obtain if possible the accounts of the unit from previous years.

Marketing

Do you understand advertising? What types of advertising are available, and what do they cost?

Market analysis and planning

The types of market analysis and planning available to you are simple, realistic and achievable. Your analysis, based on either research of **primary** or **secondary** data, should inform you of the demand for accommodation (residential or day care). Equally, your own research identifying actual and potential competition from inside and external to the care service sector will support the former criteria and help you. The former criteria is representative of your own analysis of primary and secondary data and its influence and inter-relationship to competing factors within the care service sector which will assist you in drawing up a competitive market plan.

Your market analysis should be able to assist the development of your market plan. This plan must demonstrate the distinctive features of your residential services. It will influence the way you unit cost and charge for care. It must focus on the way you advertise formally and informally to promote your residential setting, as well as demonstrate to actual or future residents how your care will be delivered in an individualised way.

In this way, your market analysis focuses on potential residents and future demand, your internal and external audit of market share, market size and trends in both. Your potential use of **time series analysis**, to obtain a correlation of recorded and evidenced take-up of care over a set period of time, will assist in identifying patterns or cyclical demands for care, which you must meet and provide for.

Your analysis and planning should give you accurate, quantitative information to share with your relevant people, which will essentially inform you of what fees potential residents can realistically afford, your potential market share and the nature of your participation in a contracting or expanding market.

Clearly, the enforcement of the Care Standards Act on 1 April 2002, which led to the closure of thousands of private residential care homes, has produced a shortfall in the number of care beds assessed to the new standards. Current estimates indicate a current national demand for some 10,000 places and further growth could be enormous.

The information from your market analysis and plan can be shared with your relevant people in order that decision making is based upon informed recommendations and research of market trends.

Then consider and breakdown the following:

- *Fees and services.* What do the current fees include? What services may residents choose?
- *Activities.* Are there organised trips? What is the extent of the residents' choice in the activities they participate in?
- *Menu.* Again, what is the range of choice?

What other information would you consider to be valid as a standard item available for updating at each evaluation stage? You may consider such headings as management, registration requirements, qualifications and training, staff turnover, holidays and benefits, staff rota, and staff costs.

You may choose to show this as a summary (see, for example, the staff summary for Appledore Lodge, in the Appendix), which could be incorporated simply into a software system for your practice setting.

Think it over

Consider the forms of market analysis and market planning you need to undertake with your relevant people in order to provide sufficient information to assist decision making based on your recommendations. Give examples.

Involving your relevant people in market planning remains an essential key to good management practice. Ownership of what ways, for example, your care/nursing home might be marketed and taking on board different perspectives can become a team approach to market analysis (the wider picture). Market planning is very rarely the sole responsibility of one person, 'the manager'; instead, a team approach made up of your relevant people is preferred and actively practiced throughout the care service sector.

Case study

You are aware of the massive shortfall in bed capacity in your local area, caused by home closure as an outcome of the enforcement of the Care Standards Act 2000. What types of information do you need to research and to provide to your relevant people in order that they can make decisions to increase your practice setting's market share, based on your recommendations?

- What types of market analysis and planning will you engage in to provide sufficient information to assist decision making by your relevant people? Prioritise these.
- In what way(s) will your market analysis take into account future demand?
- Why employ internal or external auditing or time service analysis to identify potential growth?
- How might you involve your relevant people in this process?
- With the information collated and quantified, what checks might you undertake to ensure that the final information given to your relevant people is both sufficient and valid to assist their decision making, based on your informed recommendation? Give examples.

Your recommendations for expenditure are consistent with your organisation's plans and objectives

Your practice setting is required to have a service plan which sets out your aims, the demand for places for residents and your capacity to meet that demand, both from your own resources and working in partnership with other agencies.

First, your recommendations will need to reflect your analysis of previous expenditure and the success of what has gone before. You will need to have carried out a review in order to maintain and increase satisfaction levels for residents and staff. Your recommendations need to highlight the best means of achieving your service delivery targets at the lowest cost; thus you must show how your expenditure meets your service plan objectives.

Of paramount importance is that you meet residents' needs by gathering evidence of value for money without wastage. Remember that residents are quick to perceive deteriorating standards in quality and you should not seek to change your advertised objectives, as this visible loss of trust in what you provide will not endear you to present or future residents.

Case study — Information provision at Appledore Lodge

When residents come to view a particular home, they look at two key issues:

- value for money;
- services offered (including, for example, atmosphere and décor, in addition to more direct services).

Residents must see they are getting value for money. This could be assessed in terms of the services you provide and whether residents are receiving individual care to meet their needs. This could range from the simple things, such as choice at mealtimes, to meeting personal care needs, such as dressing and washing. Residents will be looking for the services which are incorporated within their weekly fee and those which are available but chargeable.

Appledore Lodge provides the following information to potential residents. It caters for all its residents on the ground floor. It is wheelchair friendly, in that it has no split levels throughout the home, and only two ramps: one at the front entrance and one at the rear for access to the gardens; it also has wide corridors to enable wheelchair users to manoeuvre around the home. The services which are incorporated within the residents' weekly fees at Appledore Lodge include:

- single-storey building;
- en-suite facility;
- friendly staff;
- good décor;

▼

- one-month trial to allow the resident time to settle;
- day-to-day menu;
- the meeting of care needs;
- external entertainment;
- daily laundry;
- outings.

The services which are available but chargeable include:

- hairdressing;
- chiropodist;
- dry cleaning;
- transport;
- shopping trips;
- opticians;
- dentist.

As manager:

- Consider the services offered by your practice setting.
- How do they show value for money?

You present your recommendations to relevant people in an appropriate format and at an appropriate time

The concept of timeliness returns at this point, as it is of no value to present information too late, when competitors have used suppliers and materials and attracted residents in numbers, and so made your service non-viable. Your past expenditure will need to be recorded and presented accurately, and you will need to include your research into your forecasts for future expenditure, to allow others to make decisions on expenditure and equally check that the information is valid. You may choose to show how you gathered your information, the basis on which you rejected alternative options, and reports on the validity of the information you have used.

Your relevant people will expect to see that you adhere to your financial planning cycle, that you regularly review it, and that your record keeping is comprehensive, with parallel systems to ensure that each record relates to its predecessor and is not a stand-alone document. Remember that your records will be open to inspection and may be used at any time when a complaint arises.

Consider also that you may print off simplified reports to share at team meetings or meetings with residents and carers, and thus your presentations should be concise and easy to understand.

The presentation of your recommendations is likely to cover:

- Background considerations (i.e. an update from what has gone before).
- Human resource planning.
- Recruitment and selection. Are you getting value for money? How do you know that staff members are performing to their optimum? Have you looked at your current contracts? Have you analysed value for money and looked at alternatives?
- What percentage of total costs goes on salaries?
- Are training costs and outcomes identified? Does training complement your service plan and financial plan?
- What are the market trends and results of feedback from residents, in respect of service delivery?
- Are you competitive and providing value for money?
- Will you need to provide the same level of service next year? In five years' time?

Case study — Budget format

Consider the budget format illustrated for Appledore Lodge in the Appendix.

- What information would you need to gather to construct the profit and loss forecast?
- At what points in the financial planning cycle would you evaluate future needs?
- How would you communicate this to residents and staff?

Evidence collection B3.1 — Make recommendations for expenditure

You must prove that you make recommendations for expenditure to the National Occupational Standard of competence.

Your evidence must be the result of real work activities undertaken by yourself, and must show that you involve at least two of the following types of relevant people: team members, colleagues working at the same level, higher-level managers or sponsors and financial specialists. This can be obtained by giving opportunities to your relevant people to make suggestions for future expenditure, and communicating with them via newsletters, bulletins, official meetings and informal channels/networking.

You must also show evidence that your recommendations cover at least two of the following types of expenditure: supplies, people, overhead expenses and capital equipment. This can be found within exemplified profit and loss forecasts and your recommendations of past expenditure versus trends of future expenditure. Forecasting trends remains the key to solvency in the competitive world of a mixed economy of care.

Learning outcomes

- You give team members clear and consistent advice on how they can help to control expenditure.
- You give team members opportunities to take individual responsibility for monitoring and controlling expenditure.
- Your methods of monitoring expenditure are reliable and comply with organisational requirements.
- You monitor expenditure against agreed budgets at appropriate intervals.
- You control expenditure in line with budgets and organisational requirements.
- The corrective action you take in response to actual or potential significant variations from budget is prompt and complies with organisational requirements.
- You refer requests for expenditure outside your responsibility promptly to the appropriate people.
- Your records of expenditure are complete, accurate and available to authorised people only.

You give team members clear and consistent advice on how they can help to control expenditure

Let us look at why it is important to give team members clear and consistent advice on their role in controlling expenditure. What is the background to this? It may be helpful to provide the legal backdrop to the team's function in controlling expenditure, by reference to the Government White Paper *Introducing Social Services*.

In November 1998, the Government published its White Paper on modernising social services. Its aim was to create services to protect vulnerable people and raise the standard of care they received, while promoting their independence. The proposals rested on national guidance on charging for services and the devising of eligibility criteria for services, and publication of the rights of people who use care services. The White Paper also gave advice on improving partnerships and pooling budgets, the prevention of unnecessary admissions to care and improvements to service delivery, and set out standards for care providers. Residents' rights to protection were also included and are clearly outlined within the Care Standards Act 2000.

Standard 34 of that Act stipulates that suitable accounting and financial procedures are adapted to demonstrate financial viability and to ensure there is effective and efficient management of the business. Staff need to be aware of the financial plan of their practice setting and need clear guidelines on their role in controlling expenditure.

Try it out

As manager, what budgets will your staff be able to assess? What training will you need to put in place to ensure that financial control is followed by everyone? Have you allowed for day-to-day expenses and set limits on what amounts staff may use?

You may consider holding petty cash as a convenient way of paying for small items. Staff should not mix income or their own money with petty cash. They must be advised to obtain receipts for anything they claim from petty cash and they will need a standard form on which to make their claim. You, as budget holder, should check and approve each claim, unless you are making a claim, in which case it should be your superior. As manager, you will need to know how to locate your financial officer and your auditors. You must report any problems directly. If you hold amenity or private funds, you must record them and check the requirements of your auditors.

As manager, you are responsible for advising staff about the handling of individual resident's money and possessions. Standard 35.6 is specific in this regard: 'Records and receipts are kept of possessions handed over for safe keeping'.

Case study — Meeting Standard 35 (residents' money)

One of your residents, who has mobility problems and is unable to go out, leaves a member of staff some money in an envelope, to buy a present for his daughter. He does not remember how much is in the envelope, and says it doesn't matter as you can put any change left in a charity collection of your choice.

- What steps will you advise staff to take to ensure that expenditure is controlled, their own expenses are met and Standard 35 is adhered to?

Finally, having given consistent advice about the control of expenditure, you will need to feedback to staff at regular intervals on progress of services against budgets. Staff will benefit from knowing whether their expenditure control is providing value for money for the practice setting, themselves, residents and carers. A fun component may arise from searching for continuous improvement within the budget while not exceeding it. Your consistent feedback and motivation will be crucial here.

You give team members opportunities to take individual responsibility for monitoring and controlling expenditure

As manager, you will need a cash control manual which sets out your organisation's rules for collecting, moving and controlling cash. Cash includes coins, notes, postal orders and any other money orders. In order for your staff to take individual responsibility and be protected from accusations of stealing, you must have basic rules on the handling of cash, which your finance department can assist with. It is your responsibility to ensure that all your staff know the procedures they must follow. You must also make clear arrangements for receiving, saving and banking. Such procedures will be the prerequisite for team members to have opportunities to be responsible for monitoring and controlling expenditure. This is encompassed by Standard 32.5 of the Care Standards Act, which calls upon the manager to encourage 'Innovation, creativity and development'.

You may decide to provide some training, initially to all staff, in order that they are clear about the responsibilities of people who either manage budgets or who handle cash. From this it will emerge that some members of your staff group may have a special interest in the management of a particular budget, which they can take responsibility for devising, agreeing with the finance department and residents, and reporting on at regular intervals. Clearly, staff involvement in monitoring expenditure can be seen as part of the manager's wider role for ensuring that staff enjoy continuous learning and improve in their jobs, in order to motivate themselves and be of direct benefit to the practice setting.

Financial management is often viewed as complex and thus best left to managers outside your own setting. The disadvantage of this is that the business of the practice setting is conducted by individuals unconnected to its daily life and aspirations.

You hold a number of budgets which you would like staff to manage on behalf of the establishment. Some team members express an interest and ask for some basic training to equip them to manage and teach others, in order that all staff who wish to be trained can do so. Unfortunately, no staff are able to work outside their specified hours to attend the training, which is available some distance away.

- How can the task be accomplished?
- What system needs to be put into place to review progress?
- What is your role as manager?

Remember that, while you may delegate some aspects of budget control, you remain ultimately responsible. Thus you will need to consider the necessary safeguards around practice for staff ready to adopt this role.

Your methods of monitoring expenditure are reliable and comply with organisational requirements

Have you noted in your service plan how you will monitor expenditure? Have you explained this to staff and residents? It may assist residents and staff alike to know where monitoring fits in the financial management process. Any explanation given of how the monitoring of expenditure meets and complies with organisational requirements, to meet changing residents' needs, must be kept simple and understandable. Figure 15 should assist you in this process.

First, as manager, and with your relevant people, you identify and set your expenditure objectives over the next financial year. Setting objectives provides the opportunity, secondly, to plan proactively and to take account of unexpected sequential variants, such as staffing costs, utilities or under-capacity. To underestimate this potential outstanding expenditure can negatively influence your overall budget and your forecasts for profit and loss. So planning remains a key component within the monitoring process. The third step must be to set and align your budget against your proposed expenditure.

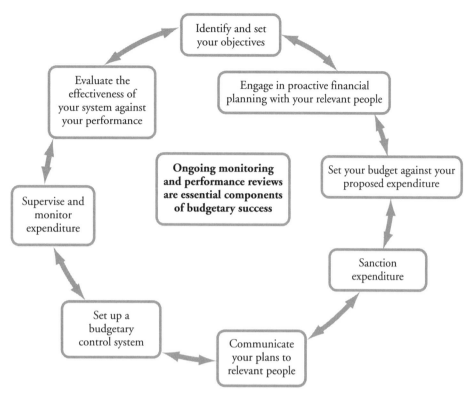

Figure 15. A monitoring system of expenditure that complies with organisational requirements.

The fourth step is to bite the bullet and sanction your proposed expenditure. Communication at all levels during this process remains essential to ensure that residents, carers and staff understand the planning as it relates to expenditure within the unit's actual budget. Such communication promotes a sense of honesty and involvement in the overall process, and being receptive to feedback provides additional information, which you may require to make adjustments to expenditure.

The next step, as part of your monitoring role, is to set up a budgetary control system to prevent any overspending. In tandem with this you must, with your relevant people, supervise and monitor expenditure on a weekly, monthly and quarterly cycle. By recording and monitoring costs you will have a better understanding of your overheads and will therefore more readily appreciate, for example, where you may need to make savings and where you need to invest more capital to meet residents' and organisational needs.

Ultimately, the acid test of your monitoring system is to engage in regular (quarterly) performance reviews of effectiveness. The performance review must examine each component of expenditure within your budget, evaluate the efficiency of your monitoring, supervision and budgetary control system(s), and ensure that planned and desired outcomes can be met. In any financial year, performance reviews of your expenditure and monitoring, on an ongoing basis, will seek to ensure that your organisational requirements, and ultimately your residents' needs, are met continuously.

What other methods of monitoring expenditure might you suggest to meet your specific organisational requirements? Jot down your thoughts.

Case study — Monitoring effectively

As manager, you have become aware that your existing methods of monitoring expenditure for budgetary control require updating, to meet changing demands upon your organisation.

- Will you identify and set objectives for the financial year or do you possess alternatives? If so, what are they?
- Does planning feature in your monitoring of expenditure? If so, give examples of what this might involve.
- How will you set your budget? Will it be to meet your objectives or to cover available expenditure? Explain your priorities.
- What kinds of communication systems, formal and informal, will you organise to engage residents and staff in this process?

You monitor expenditure against agreed budgets at appropriate intervals

As manager, you will need to know what budgets you control and what the appropriate intervals are at which to monitor them.

Budgets

As the nominated budget holder you must:

- manage your budget so that you do not spend more than you are given;
- keep on top of your budget and identify areas where you are not keeping within your budget;
- take action to bring these areas back within the budget.

You are responsible to your chief officer for the way you manage your budget. You should build up a good relationship with your finance officer, who will be able help you to monitor expenditure and income. You will need to make sure that what you have spent so far, together with your ensuing commitments, is less than your budget. You also need to check that you have received the monies that you planned to receive. If you invest in a computerised financial ledger system you will be able to view your budget position online.

If at any time you are concerned about the state of your budget, you should seek advice from your relevant people and your finance officer.

The monitoring of expenditure against budgets is a specified task entitled 'budget control'. You will need to publish **budget control indicators** at appropriate intervals to allow your relevant people to comment upon and question the control of the financial plan. Indicators represent areas of expenditure which are published within the financial plan.

You control expenditure in line with budgets and organisational requirements

To control your expenditure you must develop a budgetary action plan with appropriate monitoring controls. In this way, expenditure can be explained diagrammatically as a sequential process, as in Figure 16.

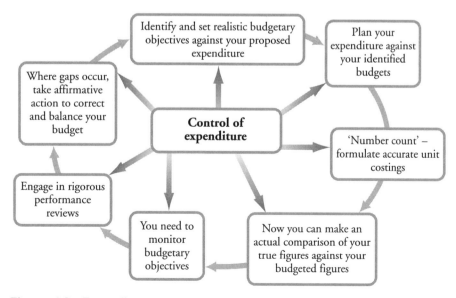

Figure 16. Expenditure as a sequential process.

Your budgetary action plan can be as explained above and translated into your overall financial plan. The danger arises when you construct a detailed budget for 12 months only and discount the subsequent years in your financial plan. Your expenditure control depends on accurate budget setting for each financial year. In this way, your budget is broken down into accurate unit costs. Where there are seasonal vacancies, extended staff absences due to sickness, overtime costs, fixed-term contractual positions (bank/agency staff), these can be built into the actual budget. Similarly, costs for essential utilities and food supplies will appear in your budget, which allows you to compare costs. Ensure appropriate financial controls through performance reviews to meet your expenditure objectives, which should prevent overspending. However, your overall expenditure budget will allow you to plan and take corrective action.

List the key questions you need to consider before you spend money:

- Are the goods needed?
- Do I have sufficient money in the budget?
- Do I need the goods?
- Am I getting value for money?

You should spend the money only if you find a positive answer to all of these questions. Even then, it is important to consider your options with other contractors.

Are the goods needed?

How do you engage in proactive financial planning which controls expenditure in line with your organisational requirements?

The following steps will form the basis for proactive financial planning:

- Identify your objectives.
- Identify what you actually need to achieve them.
- Identify time scales for their achievement.
- Identify resource provision and the reasons for that provision.
- Identify how you will provide your resources in a way which satisfies your residents' needs.

Try it out

Identify the process you go through to engage in proactive financial planning to control your expenditure, for example, with staffing costs.

How do you maintain your financial information system as a means of controlling expenditure?

Consider the following questions:

- Does your information system have accurate records of spending and income?
- Does your information system differentiate between spending (outgoing costs) and income earned?
- Does your information system have accurate budgetary information involving all the areas already discussed with residents, their families and your relevant people?
- Does your information system have the capacity to provide financial reports at regular intervals to relevant people?
- Does your information system contribute to both the production and auditing of end-of-year financial reports, which will be published in your advertising material?

Think it over

How would you develop a financial information system which addresses, for example, (a) records of spending versus income, and (b) outgoing costs versus money earned, and provides you with the means of control of actual expenditure?

What should your budgetary information systems consist of? Consider the following questions:

- What monies have been spent and on what?
- What monies remain in the budget?
- What budget provision is there for ring fencing?
- Where are there particular budget pressures? How can they be managed?
- What of itemised billing? Is there sufficient information?
- Does your budgetary information advise you of financial targets being met and expenditure being controlled in accordance with your financial plan?

Proactive financial planning, supported by accurate and quantifiable information and budgetary control systems, should enable you to control your capital expenditure despite the diverse sources of budgetary pressure, which are the norms for any residential care home.

Case study — Staffing costs

Your residential unit is experiencing a high turnover of staff. In order to retain staff and reduce workload stress, you are required to employ fixed-term agency staff on a temporary basis. This additional cost places your budget under strain.

- Does your budget allow for this contingency in the short, medium or long term?
- How will you develop a budgetary action plan to ensure sufficient monies for this contingency?
- What kinds of financial planning will you need to engage in?
- What kinds of financial and budgetary information do you possess to assist your planning?
- What improvements in this sequential process do you need to make in order to control expenditure but still employ additional staff?

The corrective action you take in response to actual or potential significant variations from budget is prompt and complies with organisational requirements

As manager, if your budget is not within its limitations you will need to establish the reasons for this. It may be due to spending more than you have planned or because the income you actually received is lower than you predicted. Look for such things as prices for goods or services being higher than you estimated. You may have had more or fewer residents than you budgeted for. More residents means increased costs, but fewer may mean less income. You may have been charged for an item which should have been charged elsewhere. Some of your income may have been added to a different budget.

Remember to look at under-spend as well as overspend. If you have under-spent, you may be retaining money which could be used to bolster another budget.

Requests for expenditure outside your responsibility

A simple procedure will help you manage your own budgets and assist staff and residents to know where to access monies not within your control.

Your records of expenditure are complete, accurate and available to authorised people only

Record keeping

As manager, whether new in post or experienced, you will be required to record your expenditure and ensure it is available to authorised people only, in a clear format.

A key effective practice is to keep an inventory of the valuable items on the premises. For each item, this should record:

- what the item is, with its serial number if possible;
- where it is located;
- when it was purchased;
- its worth;
- when and how it was disposed of.

Your records should clearly show what your unit has and who has what. From this type of basic accounting, all your other records should stem. As your inventory keeps track of valuable items, and records assets for insurance purposes, so your prepared reports account for your general expenditure against your practice setting plan.

You should always use an official order form, even if your suppliers provide their own, or you order by phone. Generally you will need to itemise:

- what is needed,
- in what quantity,
- where it should be sent,
- its cost (from the contract),
- the budget from which the amount is to be paid (identified usually by a number),
- the central contract number.

Think it over

What key information do you need when placing an order? What should your records look like and who can see them?

You should then send the top copy of the order form to the supplier and retain the bottom copy. If you have a third copy, you should send it to your finance officer. You, or your authorised person, must sign the order form.

You must also have separate records of goods ordered and received and services similarly. More than one person should be responsible for receiving and paying for goods, but you as manager have ultimate responsibility.

You will need to become familiar with the documents used by your practice setting to record expenditure. They are likely to be:

- purchase order forms;
- delivery notes;
- invoices;
- receipts;
- statements of accounts;
- bank statements.

Your records of expenditure and your accounts need to be part of a system of accounting which can be viewed by authorised people. There is a wealth of published information to assist you with constructing accounts and keeping accurate records.

As manager, you should focus on working with a simple balance sheet for each of your accounts, and explain your reasons for spending against the account, such as lack of upkeep, wear and tear, the age of the items and their need to be replaced. You could, of course, decide to spend some of your budget on a computerised accounting system, which can produce reports quickly and provide an instant view of how the practice setting is progressing.

Your budgetary report should contain:

- a statement of the cost of running the establishment, broken down into separate cost areas;
- a forecast of profit and loss;
- the value of contracts;
- the cost of private suppliers;
- insurance costs;
- targets;
- planned-for business;
- known business (from looking back);
- longer-term aims and objectives.

This record keeping will also need to be complemented by records about residents, and training employee budget costs, arising from accidents.

The records you keep, whether on paper or on computer, must comply with the Data Protection Act 1984 and the Personal Protection Act 1989, all consolidated in the Data Protection Act 1998, which stipulates how information held about people may be recorded, stored, retrieved and used.

Your records of objective setting must follow the pattern shown in Figure 17.

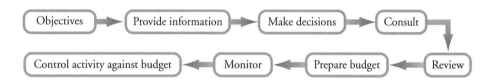

Figure 17. Objective setting.

Try it out

Look at the total cost of operating your practice setting. Break down the cost into specific budget allocations. Then, using your business plan, devise a simple chart to explain to authorised people the breakdown of your budget.

Your underlying budget cycle is essential to determine income and expenditure. Your budget must build in incremental costs for inflation as well as **developmental costings**. Projected income from growth or diversification into day care or community care might increase your overall profit margins. Projected earnings represent targets to be worked towards.

Remember, your budget does not remain static and you must prepare and allow for unforeseen eventualities. Incremental budgeting gives you the opportunity to forecast with caution, yet allows you the flexibility to plan for growth and to evaluate indirect costs, which can be inflationary or developmentally linked. A three-year cycle should focus upon growth and build in security for incremental costs that you forecast.

Your budgetary information should be kept as simple as possible and be kept confidential. For example, you must not name your residents directly and you must not allow your personal records to be accessed internally or externally without authorisation.

Case study — Records of expenditure versus cyclical budgetary expenditure

A recent external audit of your budget reveals that you have underestimated your developmental costs. Additionally, you are aware that too many of your staff can easily gain access to this material, as it is on paper in an office shared by five senior staff. How do you proceed to ensure that your financial records show your true developmental costs, and are available to authorised people only?

- Will you begin by breaking down the operating costs (your overheads) of every area within your practice setting?
- Will you itemise expenditure against income generation in order to obtain an accurate picture and begin the planning process?
- Will you develop an incremental budgetary system, perhaps over a three-year period, to provide the financial evidence you will need to forecast with caution?
- What measures will you take to restrict access to authorised people only? Will you consider storage in a locked cabinet or transference to computer data accessible electronically only via a password?
- Will you identify who has access to this material and give reasons for this?

Evidence collection B3.2 — Control expenditure against budgets

You must prove that you control expenditure against budgets by showing evidence of examining written information and financial data, and of referring to your actual expenditure against set budgets. You must also present the results of your expenditure control, together with corrective action you might have taken.

You must show evidence that you control at least two of the following types of expenditure: supplies, people, overhead expenses, capital equipment. You must also show evidence of two types of corrective action: altering activities, rescheduling expenditure, altering budget allocations within the limits of your responsibility, or renegotiating budgets.

Appendix: Budgetary evaluation of Appledore Lodge

This budgetary evaluation is provided with the kind permission of Appledore Lodge, a private residential home for older persons within the city of Coventry. It is an example not only of a method of identifying unit costs but also of evaluating those costs, and presenting the possible outcomes of change in simple table form. It represents an example of best practice when considering alternative options for expenditure.

You may decide to undertake a budgetary evaluation for each of your overheads and publish the outcomes for consultation.

Charges for prospective residents

Appledore has a base rate of £285.00. Residents are assessed to see if they require any additional services. If they do, the base rate is adjusted accordingly and residents are advised of this. If a prospective client is in hospital, two senior members of staff will go and visit the client to assess whether the home is able to fulfill their care needs.

Profit and loss forecast

This is set out in simple table form.

Appledore Lodge residential home for the elderly: profit and loss forecast

	Sep-01 £	Oct-01 £	Nov-01 £	Dec-01 £	Jan-02 £	Feb-02 £	Mar-02 £	Apr-02 £	May-02 £	Jun-02 £	Jul-02 £	Aug-02 £	Total £
INCOME													
Fees	25000	25000	25000	25000	25000	25000	25000	25000	25000	25000	25000	25000	**300000**
OVERHEADS													
Wages	11750	11750	11750	11750	11750	11750	11750	11750	11750	11750	11750	11750	**141000**
Food	1800	1800	1800	1800	1800	1800	1800	1800	1800	1800	1800	1800	**21600**
Finance	4000	4000	4000	4000	4000	4000	4000	4000	4000	4000	4000	4000	**48000**
Cleaning and sundry expenses	750	750	750	750	750	750	750	750	750	750	750	750	**9000**
Newspapers	100	100	100	100	100	100	100	100	100	100	100	100	**1200**
Residents' disbursements	75	75	75	75	75	75	75	75	75	75	75	75	**900**
Repairs and renewals	500	500	500	500	500	500	500	500	500	500	500	500	**6000**
Lighting and heating	500	500	500	500	500	500	500	500	500	500	500	500	**6000**
Telephone	200	200	200	200	200	200	200	200	200	200	200	200	**2400**
Rates	250	250	250	250	250	250	250	250	250	250	250	250	**3000**
Insurance	200	200	200	200	200	200	200	200	200	200	200	200	**2400**
Bank charges	100	100	100	100	100	100	100	100	100	100	100	100	**1200**
Registration fee	100	100	100	100	100	100	100	100	100	100	100	100	**1200**
Accountancy	150	150	150	150	150	150	150	150	150	150	150	150	**1800**
Postage and advertising	50	50	50	50	50	50	50	50	50	50	50	50	**600**
Motor expenses	200	200	200	200	200	200	200	200	200	200	200	200	**2400**
	20725	20725	20725	20725	20725	20725	20725	20725	20725	20725	20725	20725	**248700**
Operating profits	4275	4275	4275	4275	4275	4275	4275	4275	4275	4275	4275	4275	**51300**

Hourly income and expenditure

Cost of running the home per hour

Total cost as per budget	£248,700
No. of hours in the year	24 × 365 = 8,760
Total cost/no. of hours in a year	248,700/8,760 = £28.39

Income of the home per hour

Total income as per budget	£300,000
No. of hours in the year	24 × 365 = 8,760
Total income/no. of hours in a year	300,000/8,760 = £34.25

Appledore Lodge proposed staff summary

Care staff	Total no. of hours per week	Average hourly rate	Weekly cost
Manager	30	7.50	225.00
Senior care assistants	84	4.60	386.40
Care assistants	160	4.30	688.00
Trainee care assistants	22	4.00	88.00
Shift leaders (night)	90	5.00	450.00
Care assistants (night)	60	4.60	276.00
Total	446		2113.40
Ancillary staff			
Cook	50	5.50	275.00
Domestic	25	4.20	105.00
Total	75		380.00

Weekly wage cost: £2,493.40

Annual wage cost (allowing for holiday pay, weekend supplement etc., where applicable): £141,000.00

Annual wage cost as a percentage of income (£300,000): 47.0%

Budgetary evaluation

As can be seen from the calculations, the balance of providing good quality care for the right price requires close monitoring of budgets.

Accommodating change

If the cost of a particular product or service were to increase, it would in turn increase the overall unit cost for Appledon Lodge. In order for the manager to maintain costs within budget, one of the following would have to be done:

- Increase the fee to residents.
- Renegotiate with current suppliers for a better price, without compromising quality.
- Source a new supplier who will meet the budgetary requirements.

It is important to involve residents and their carers in any negotiations which such changes demand.

Profit and loss forecast — revised to assess expansion

The following budget is prepared making the following assumptions.

- A 12-bed extension is made, to increase the number of beds to 35.
- In order to provide the continued quality of service, extra staffing is required, which is reflected in the overheads for wages.
- The remainder of the costs are proportional to the increase in service users.
- There is an increase in interest rates and further finance is required to extend the premises.

Appledore Lodge residential home for the elderly: profit and loss forecast

Forecast assumes that a planned extension of an extra 12 rooms is carried out, bringing the total number of beds to 35, of which 33 rooms are occupied all year.

	Sep-02 £	Oct-02 £	Nov-02 £	Dec-02 £	Jan-03 £	Feb-03 £	Mar-03 £	Apr-03 £	May-03 £	Jun-03 £	Jul-03 £	Aug-03 £	Total £
INCOME													
Fees	40755	40755	40755	40755	40755	40755	40755	40755	40755	40755	40755	40755	**489060**
OVERHEADS													
Wages	17000	17000	17000	17000	17000	17000	17000	17000	17000	17000	17000	17000	**204000**
Food	2700	2700	2700	2700	2700	2700	2700	2700	2700	2700	2700	2700	**32400**
Finance	5500	5500	5500	5500	5500	5500	5500	5500	5500	5500	5500	5500	**66000**
Cleaning and sundry expenses	1200	1200	1200	1200	1200	1200	1200	1200	1200	1200	1200	1200	**14400**
Newspapers	130	130	130	130	130	130	130	130	130	130	130	130	**1560**
Residents' disbursements	100	100	100	100	100	100	100	100	100	100	100	100	**1200**
Repairs and renewals	650	650	650	650	650	650	650	650	650	650	650	650	**7800**
Lighting and heating	650	650	650	650	650	650	650	650	650	650	650	650	**7800**
Telephone	200	200	200	200	200	200	200	200	200	200	200	200	**2400**
Rates	300	300	300	300	300	300	300	300	300	300	300	300	**3600**
Insurance	250	250	250	250	250	250	250	250	250	250	250	250	**3000**
Bank charges	130	130	130	130	130	130	130	130	130	130	130	130	**1560**
Registration fee	150	150	150	150	150	150	150	150	150	150	150	150	**1800**
Accountancy	180	180	180	180	180	180	180	180	180	180	180	180	**2160**
Postage and advertising	60	60	60	60	60	60	60	60	60	60	60	60	**720**
Motor expenses	250	250	250	250	250	250	250	250	250	250	250	250	**3000**
	29450	29450	29450	29450	29450	29450	29450	29450	29450	29450	29450	29450	**353400**
Operating profits	11305	11305	11305	11305	11305	11305	11305	11305	11305	11305	11305	11305	**135600**

C13 Manage the Performance of Teams and Individuals

This unit contains four elements which focus upon how to make the most productive use of your team and its members in order that they can achieve your organisation's objectives. It covers allocating work and agreeing objectives, as well as the setting out of plans and methods of working. It reviews the monitoring and evaluation of work undertaken by your team as well as the provision of feedback on their performance.

The elements are:

- Allocate work to teams and individuals.
- Agree objectives and work plans with teams and individuals.
- Assess the performance of teams and individuals.
- Provide feedback to teams and individuals on their performance.

Learning outcomes

- You give opportunities to your team members to recommend how you should allocate work within the team.
- Your allocation of work makes the best use of your team's resources and the abilities of all its members.
- Your allocation of work provides your team members with suitable learning opportunities to meet their personal development objectives.
- Your allocation is consistent with your team's objectives, and the objectives, policies and values of your organisation.
- You clearly define the responsibilities of your team and its individual members and the limits of their authority.
- You provide sufficient information on your allocation of work in a manner and at a level and pace appropriate to the individuals concerned.
- You confirm team and individual understanding of, and commitment to, work allocations at appropriate intervals.
- Where team resources are insufficient, you reach agreement with relevant people on the prioritisation of objectives or reallocation of resources.
- You inform your team and its members of changes to work allocations in a way which minimises the impact on time, cost and inconvenience.

You give opportunities to your team members to recommend how you should allocate work within the team

As manager, you must identify appropriate forums which will provide opportunities to team members to make their own recommendations on how you should allocate work fairly within the team. These forums include:

- informal supervision;
- formal supervision;
- team meetings;
- weekly case allocation meetings.

Within informal supervision, which represents a non-structured format for ongoing professional development, team members can be enabled to identify new areas of learning through joint work. Thus work allocation is encouraged in an informal way to come from individual staff members. Equally, it must contribute to their continuing professional development. Examples may be as simple as learning new skills in managing challenging behaviour, pressure sore management, report writing, or working with physical and learning disability in a residential or day care setting.

Formal supervision is a pre-planned, regular activity, structured with mutual agenda setting and prioritisation. There are agreed ground rules for both behaviour and feedback. A team member may make a voluntary request to be engaging in different roles and tasks for professional development purposes. Competency needs to be both managed and measured through practice observation and written evidence of work undertaken.

There should be planned, regular team meetings. Any member should be able to contribute to setting the agenda for these meetings and the chair should be rotated among them in order to promote the development of their leadership skills. Within this forum, team members should be able to make recommendations regarding how you allocate work. There must therefore be an agreed way of raising ideas in a non-discriminatory way which facilitates individual participation and development. Information must be shared with individuals in advance, in order that they understand what the team priorities are. Additionally, team members must be allowed to set their own priorities within the existing framework. Practice examples can include joint work to learn skills in report writing, recording of daily assessment, monitoring and cultural diversity.

Regular team meetings allow team members to contribute ideas and share information.

How do your team meetings inhibit members from making recommendations regarding the allocation of work?

The weekly case allocation meetings can also provide a forum in which team members are able to recommend how you should allocate work within the team. How? Undertake a collective review of all existing cases. Jointly set and agree priorities of ongoing work. Agree and set review dates to ensure assessed and presenting needs are met. Set new priorities for new admissions and agree collectively their allocation with respect to their urgency and importance, and team member skills.

As manager, you must identify particular residents' needs and prioritise these against the skills and resources of team members. The case allocation meeting provides ideal opportunities for individual team members to make recommendations and develop their own learning. For example, there is a new admission of an older, frail, female resident, who is physically disabled and also has communication problems following a recent stroke. One member of staff has just completed an external course in stroke management and so she volunteers to take on the essential key worker role with this resident, so that she may translate learned theory into practice.

Case study — Case allocation meetings

The Courtyard residential home provides spacious accommodation and care to 36 older residents with a diversity of physical and cultural needs. This week there are two new admissions for a six-week block of respite care (to allow full-time external carers to be given a rest).

- How do you provide the information about these new residents and their needs?
- How do you assess residents' wishes and preferences, and encourage team responses for these to be met?
- Establish the reason for the respite care: is it for the resident or the carer?
- Prioritise what the resident wants from the respite care.
- How do you enable the care team to meet a written care plan within this defined timescale?
- How is the care plan to be reviewed and changed?
- Establish ground rules for residents' complaints, particularly if their needs are not being met, so they might be speedily addressed.
- How do you demonstrate your active listening skills to take on board the views of individual team members?
- How do you decide as manager which team members are best qualified to be the key workers for those residents? What priorities would you set?
- What practical methods might you use to encourage individual recommendations for the allocation of work?
- How do you differentiate between team members' professional development and residents' needs?

Your allocation of work makes the best use of your team's resources and the abilities of all its members

You will have developed an understanding – gained through supervision, observing practice and feedback from residents and their carers – of the strengths and weaknesses of both individuals and the whole team. In order to allocate work appropriately you must prioritise residents' needs against existing individual and team performance. You must also take into account what your staff need in terms of skills-based learning and progression.

Allocation of most kinds of work, with the exception of child protection and approved social work practice, will lead in residential care to less experienced staff either managing or key working a resident. This must be undertaken with sensitive but structured supervision and appropriate mentoring for personal/professional development.

Additionally, you must identify the collective skills of the whole team and regularly assess how they, as a group, can work together to meet existing and new allocated work.

Think it over

How do you allocate a new case where the team is lacking in experience of meeting, not only the basic, but also the essential cultural needs of an Asian resident who has been referred by social services as an emergency admission?

Where you identify individual and group weaknesses you must address them immediately. Consider using an internal or external mentor to work alongside team members to give practical advice, guidance and support. Employing internal members with special skills gives them appropriate recognition and allows for greater job satisfaction. It also facilitates professional development and will help to overcome feelings of stagnation among the most experienced staff members. Experienced staff are hard to recruit, so examine this delegated role carefully as a means of staff retention. There is also a cost factor, in that internal mentors are less expensive than external ones, and your organisation's budgetary requirements must always be given a special priority.

External mentors may be drawn either from different areas of your own organisation or from elsewhere. For example, district nurses involved in the care of your residents will be able to advise on catheter care, pressure sore management and so on. Social service disability enablers can assist with aids and adaptations. Also, professionally qualified RoSPA trainers, whether drawn from the disability teams or freestanding facilitators, can provide the statutory knowledge, training and skills required in assistance and movement. However, you must remember that external mentors, while providing a professional and neutral service, can also be expensive, particularly as their presence, as with internal mentoring, will be on going. It is advised that a careful balance of internal and external mentoring is used according to assessed resident and staff needs, as well as budgetary requirements and restrictions.

Case study — Using your team's resources and abilities

An existing resident named Dorothy Clarke presents with changed physical needs following a recent hip replacement. She is also visually impaired and finds mobility without assistance difficult. Due to her additional needs, much greater effort from the team is required to improve her quality of life.

- How do you begin to identify the knowledge and skills of individual staff members to meet Dorothy's needs?
- What particular skills exist within the team collectively to meet Dorothy's needs?
- How might these collective skills, once identified, be used to develop team members and equally improve Dorothy's quality of life?
- How do you facilitate team sharing of both knowledge and skills to assist with this task?
- How would you formulate action plans and reviews with the team to meet Dorothy's changed needs?

Your allocation of work provides your team members with suitable learning opportunities to meet their personal development objectives

As manager, ensure that you give consideration to learning opportunities when allocating work to team members. Such learning will contribute to personal development as well as task achievement. Learning opportunities in relation to residents' needs must be different as well as challenging. They will increase individual and team resources in terms of new knowledge and skills.

In order to ensure that allocated work provides suitable learning opportunities, you must first assess the developmental needs of your staff group. So how do you identify individual learning needs? These will be weaknesses or limitations in relation to service delivery.

- *Gather information* pertaining to staff members' training and retraining.
- *Explore and assess* your team's training history.
- *Compare* your findings (if you have more than one team), to build up a picture of actual and future training needs.
- *Consult* residents as to the quality of their care and how it might be improved. (How would they like to be involved in this process?)
- *Review* all job descriptions. Differentiate between expected and actual performance based on your observations.
- Build up a *profile* of each member of staff, focusing on current skills and knowledge.

Try it out

Request all staff to produce a list of any training they have undertaken in the last two years. Identify any gaps and suggest a new programme of training for each member of staff.

Adult learning

Once you have an overall picture of what your team needs to learn, you will be able to allocate work more efficiently and effectively. However, in order for your team members to improve their knowledge or skills base, you need to understand those features which influence adult learning and enable that learning to be effective in actual practice.

Adults engaged in learning need:

- an environment which is non-threatening and where anxiety is kept to a minimum;
- to know that their previous life or work experiences are valid, relevant and are transferable to different roles;
- to recognise their new learning is relevant to a newly allocated work role;
- to feel a certainty that their learning is being managed and phased into achievable parts, ensuring that any allocated work can be completed competently;
- fear of failure to be eliminated – a clear balance needs to be drawn between learning objectives and elements of newly allocated work;
- supervision of newly allocated work relevant to the learning;
- clear, constructive feedback which enables the team members to discern personal strengths and weaknesses and to see directions for further development;
- opportunities for self-assessment;
- increasing opportunities, as appropriate, to plan their own learning and evaluate that learning in relation to allocated work.

You must remember that new learning is often difficult, so you must be prepared to support and encourage team members engaged in this process.

Consider what other elements than above might influence adult learning. List them below and explain their relevance to the learning process.

ELEMENT	RELEVANCE TO ADULT LEARNING
1	
2	
3	
4	

On both sides of the Atlantic, since the mid-1970s, a great deal of research has been focused upon how adults learn. Of the main theorists, three stand out, namely David Hobb (1974, 1984) and Alan Mumford and Peter Honey (1986), who suggest that four learning styles categorise the learning process. These can be identified as:

- *Activists*. These are staff who enjoy the challenges and opportunities of working with change, or equally working with conflict in teams. They thrive on new experiences.
- *Reflectors*. These are staff who will observe people, data and situations before taking a step forward. They will not be harassed into making a decision that is not first carefully thought through.
- *Theorists*. These are staff who learn at their best when faced with a theoretical problem or issue. Their learning decreases if they fail to see any intrinsic value in the activity.
- *Pragmatists*. These are staff who learn best when they can apply their learning to their current role and test out their assumptions. Their learning decreases if they are unable to apply it to actual practice because of organisational apathy or where there is little relationship between what they have learned and what they are required to do, particularly with newly allocated work.

It is your responsibility to identify team members' preferred learning styles. It is unlikely that any team will prefer only one style. The training plan should therefore incorporate an eclectic approach to meeting a team's learning needs.

This exercise is designed to help the manager determine the learning style of their staff team, and to make effective use of learning opportunities within allocated work.

- Give the team written examples of the four learning styles.
- Ask them to identify their preferred learning style and explain why.
- Then ask them how their intended training would be assisted or hindered by this style.
- The collective responses will offer the manager an in-depth insight into how their team members prefer to learn and how training might be developed around the types of work allocation required of them to meet residents' needs.

The training plan

When developing a team training plan, what does the manager have to consider? Figure 18 serves to focus attention upon the key areas that require particular consideration before training begins.

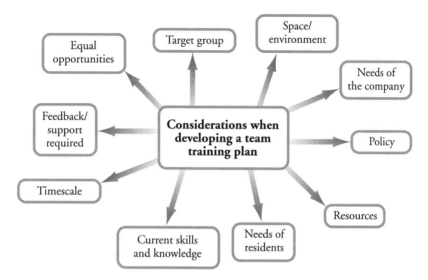

Figure 18. Key areas that require consideration before training begins.

Even though training will focus on team members' needs, it will be necessary to retain a focus on residents throughout. This will be a challenging task for a manager. It is here that you will need to exercise care to ensure that all training relates to both the team's and the residents' needs. For example, a demotivated team can be re-energised through phased learning with a view to improving the care they are able to provide to residents. Indeed, resident satisfaction is probably the best endorsement of the relevance of the training.

Practice example 1. Dementia

- *Type of allocated work.* Working with residents in the early stages of dementia.
- *Learning opportunities.* Dementia management.

The learning plan could be developed as follows:

- Introduce this topic at a weekly case allocation meeting and follow it up within team meetings and supervision.
- Assess the current situation from both a statistical and a subjective perspective (identify what individuals and the team are worried about).
- Consider with the team what new methods of therapeutic care individuals or the whole team need to learn. ▼

Before accepting referred residents, develop a four-week in-house training plan:

- **Aim**. To teach elements of therapeutic care.
- **Objectives**. To show that both care and control are achievable without upsetting the sensitivities of the existing resident group.
- **Time requirement**. One hour per week.
- **Cost**. This is £80 per week $\times$ 4 weeks $\times$ 8 members of staff.
- **Other considerations**. Consider using therapeutic enablers from your local NHS trust hospital or independent facilitators.

Follow up the progress of training with individual and group supervision of the team, as well as with residents during weekly review meetings.

- **Monitor**. Weekly, during and after each session.
- **Evaluate**. At the end of the four-week training period, with team and residents collectively. Test out whether training has been relevant, has met original identified needs and continues to meet these needs as they present to the team and residents. Ensure that the training has made a genuine impact upon individual learning and behaviour.
- **Supervision/resident review and weekly meetings**. Follow up through use of formal supervision and resident meetings that this training continues to have benefits. If new issues arise, such as residents wandering, consider further training.

Practice example 2. Challenging behaviour

- **Type of allocated work**. Managing challenging resident behaviour.
- **Learning opportunities**. Minimise risks of aggression.

The learning plan could be developed as follows:

- Introduce topic at both team and resident meetings.
- Assess the current situation. Take on board the concerns of team members and residents.
- Consider whether staff need to learn new methods of resident friendly control.
- Identify current limitations as well as new learning which needs to take place.

Develop a six-week in-house training plan:

- **Aim**. To minimise risks of violent behaviour.
- **Objectives**. To allay fears of both staff and residents of violence within the practice setting.
- **Time requirements**. One hour per week.
- **Cost**. This is £90 per week $\times$ 6 weeks $\times$ 10 members of staff.
- **Other considerations**. Consider using external trainers for specified areas, such as the police for reasonable restraint. ▼

Follow up the progress of training with individual and group supervision of staff, as well as with residents during weekly review meetings.

- **_Monitor._** Weekly, during and after each session.
- **_Evaluate._** At the end of the training period with both team and residents collectively. Test out whether training has been relevant, has met original identified needs and continues to meet those needs as they present to the team and residents. Ensure that the training has made a genuine impact upon individual learning and behaviour. Establish joint working between key worker roles for residents who are known to present with aggressive behaviours. Set accredited guidelines agreed with police, residents, carers and staff, as to how to handle aggressive and violent behaviour.
- **_Supervision/resident review and weekly meeting._** Follow up during formal supervision and resident meetings that this training continues to have benefits. If new issues arise, consider further training.

Think it over

Consider a piece of allocated work. Identify the learning opportunities and then design a training plan to meet that need through negotiation with your staff and resident group.

Evaluation of work allocation in relation to team members' learning and development

- Establish that learning, be it new knowledge or skills, has taken place. This can be via observation of practice, individual supervision or feedback from residents as well as team members.
- Establish the impact upon the team members' contractual roles and how their behaviour has changed or been modified.
- The setting of clear objectives before, during and after work allocation will help to ensure desired outcomes are met.
- Standards setting is key to effective work allocation. The final endorsement will come from residents and their external carers if standards improve.
- Establish whether the work allocation has assisted in meeting organisational goals or not.
- Evaluation can be continued in forums such as supervision and appraisal meetings; ensure that your allocated work has genuinely met identified developmental needs.

The object of this exercise is to improve what should be the proactive role of evaluation within the process of specified work allocation to meet the developmental needs of your team. Simply list the ways in which a recent piece of work allocation was evaluated and the ways in which it might have been evaluated to improve your developmental needs.

HOW WAS YOUR WORK EVALUATED?	HOW MIGHT IT HAVE BEEN EVALUATED TO IMPROVE YOUR DEVELOPMENTAL NEEDS?
1	
2	
3	
4	

Proactive evaluation should help you to understand and realise the benefits of work allocation and thereby to meet the developmental needs of your team members. However, the benefits should be recognisable to the resident, the team member and the organisation.

Benefits to residents include:

- improved service delivery;
- improved standards of care;
- greater control over the level of care they receive;
- participation at all levels of decision-making regarding their case;
- their opinions are valued, and sensitively responded to.

Benefits to team members include:
- increased opportunities to improve knowledge and skills;
- improved self-confidence and increased self-esteem;
- increased self-motivation;
- enhanced job satisfaction;
- greater diversity of work (which can increase opportunities for occupational mobility).

Benefits to the organisation include:

- increased flexibility in work allocation;
- staff with the required calibre of knowledge, skills and sensitivity to respond to residents' needs;
- more motivation to work towards higher standards of care;
- a greater focus on resident care and the way that care is defined;
- all-round improved performance, with a greater desire to meet the needs of a multicultural resident group with humility, skills and sensitivity.

At a weekly allocation meeting you are required to identify two or more carers to work with a newly referred resident who has mobility difficulties. He suffers from diabetes, the effects of which resulted in both the amputation of his left leg and the impairment of his sight. He is aged 78 and is very frail after his surgery. Assistance with both movement and care via multiple carers is now necessary. The managed work allocation programme for this particular resident should offer potential carers a variety of new and specialised skills.

- How do you identify the specific learning and developmental needs of team members?
- How do you develop your understanding of adult learning?
- How do you distinguish the different learning styles of your team members and match them with the work allocation you wish to give to the most appropriate person or persons in your employment?
- When considering a team training plan (a natural outcome of allocated work) what would you prioritise as the most important of this resident's needs?
- How could you evaluate the effects of individual team member learning on allocated work?

Your allocation of work is consistent with your team's objectives, and the objectives, policies and values of your organisation

For your allocation of work to be consistent with the team's objectives, it is helpful to draw up a service plan for the team. You must:

- make sure both you and the members of the team understand your service plan and its objectives;
- publicise the team's service plan to residents and other providers.

To meet the objectives, policies and values of your organisation, it is helpful to write, in partnership with your team, a team mission statement which outlines the ways in which they intend to deliver their daily services. You must:

- publicise this mission statement using a variety of media to ensure comprehension on the part of both residents and carers;
- obtain feedback from residents and carers to ensure that the language used accurately communicates the ethos of your plan;
- identify team values within the mission statement and decide how to communicate these values to your residents;

- reflect the organisation's objectives in the mission statement and detail how your team can transfer these into actual practice;
- ensure that residents and carers are involved in the writing of the mission statement and that their preferences and needs are included;
- make sure that the mission statement is followed up by third-party feedback, to ensure its accuracy, validity and independent credibility.

How might you draw up this mission statement with your team?

- Discuss with the team the value and purpose of the mission statement.
- Identify the different ways in which the statement could be produced. Who is going to write it – will it be one person, a pair or triad? A collective decision must be made.
- Ensure the views of all team members are included in what becomes a collective response that reinforces personal ownership and accountability.
- The statement must accurately describe the ways in which the team, on behalf of the organisation, can reasonably deliver its services in a non-discriminatory manner.

Think it over

Consider the value of a mission statement which reflects the work your team undertakes.

Try it out

Write a mission statement in partnership with your team which accurately reflects the services your team can deliver. Though consultations with your residents, ensure that it is relevant to their needs.

Example of a mission statement

Princethorpe Way is a charitable sheltered housing scheme offering assisted accommodation to 48 individuals or couples irrespective of their disability. Its mission statement includes the following:

> The team will seek to provide affordable and accessible accommodation to all its residents irrespective of their race, gender, culture, sexual orientation and religion.

Having written and published this statement, as manager you must then obtain resident feedback in relation to their comprehension. This must be tested and sampled as widely as possible. You will be expected both to inform and to clarify with residents and their carers of any use of jargon and how your service provision will meet their individual needs. You will be expected to find different ways of communicating to potential or actual residents who cannot read, speak or hear, or for whom English is a second language.

The mission statement must reflect the combined values of both the organisation and the team. Additionally, the work allocation must be consistent with the statement, as must any policies or plans. In this way, work allocation in accordance with the mission statement becomes value-based. However, if the statement is to be considered realistic, it must be regularly reviewed to ensure that it continues to meet residents' needs within the area of specialism that your team and organisation practise.

Case study — John Harker

Within your residential setting you have a male resident whose name is John Harker, aged 89, who suffers from arthritis. He has mobility needs and is not able to care for himself fully. However, despite his physical difficulties, Mr Harker wishes to return home to live with his wife.

- Can Mr Harker return home?
- What are his civil rights in this matter?
- Who can act as an advocate for him?
- How does the allocated staff member working with him assist in resolving his situation, such that his needs and preferences are recognised and met?
- How does the establishment's mission statement live up to enabling Mr Harker to meet his needs?

You clearly define the responsibilities of your team and its individual members and the limits of their authority

As manager, you must fully understand what your team's responsibilities are, and the limits of authority you would apply. Having done this, you must then communicate this in a manner, level and pace appropriate to all team members. Communication should be both verbal and non-verbal (written down) so that team members can read, reflect and comment.

Your team's responsibilities will depend on the nature, the size, the specialism and the philosophy/traditions of the organisation in which you work. Nonetheless, those responsibilities will, in essence, be to meet the residents' basic human needs. These have been defined by Maslow (1954), in his text *Motivation and Personality*, as physical, emotional, intellectual and social needs ('PIES'):

Physical

- A balanced diet and fluid intake.
- Warmth.
- Accommodation appropriate to needs.
- Security and feelings of safety.
- A hygienic environment.
- Access to own clothing at all times.
- Access to own money for any purpose.
- Appropriate physical contact.

Emotional

- Professional caring relationships.
- Company and support.
- Privacy.
- Freedom and autonomy.
- Dignity and self-respect.
- Acceptance and respect as a unique individual.

Intellectual

- Opportunities to think for oneself and make one's own life decisions.
- Assistance in realising one's own potential in whatever capacity one may choose.
- Assistance in developing the creative use of both personality and intellect.
- Access to a choice of reading materials.
- Access, opportunities and freedom to pursue religious needs with a dedicated prayer/sanctuary room of multicultural design.

Social

- Opportunities to engage in personal pleasure and fun.
- Opportunities to mix in company of one's own preference (in terms of race, language, culture and gender).
- Freedom of choice.
- Opportunities to enjoy the alternative – a day out or holidays of one's own choosing, individually, in pairs, small groups or collectively.

How would you begin to assess the PIES needs of your residents? What methods would you use to meet them?

The team has the responsibility to identify and assist in meeting the above needs. Once the needs have been identified, the team must apply fundamental principles of acceptance, being non-judgemental and respecting each resident's right to self-determination. Once a relationship of unconditional trust has been established, the team must assist all residents to find fulfilment. It is always a matter of resident choice first. The work that goes into promoting that choice will determine whether resident needs at basic or identified level are met or unmet.

The team must assess whether residents' needs are being met. This assessment can either be formal or informal, written (e.g. questionnaires, tick-charts or review forms) or verbal (e.g. an interview). It must link into the resident's care plan. Equally, monitoring is required, as presenting needs change, recede or expand. This may take the form of frequent reviews undertaken with the resident and carers. Monitoring can show whether the care plan has met the needs and preferences of the resident.

The team has the responsibility to ensure the continuity and consistency of this monitoring process by reporting accurate information to the immediate manager. This communication within the organisation's hierarchy would usually begin with a senior carer reporting the detailed content of and achievement of the teamwork to the care manager, who would pass this information up the hierarchy to the establishment manager. Feedback to all levels of the hierarchy then becomes essential, as it will motivate staff and further the principle of responsible teamwork. It is important to give constructive advice about forward planning and the promotion of residents' welfare, and to include contributions from the team in what remains a collective partnership between team and management.

The team will utilise its communication network to draw upon specialist assistance from a range of multidisciplinary services to meet residents' needs.

The limits to team authority

As manager, it is a basic requirement that you set limits to team, and therefore individual, authority. This needs to be done in a responsible and ethical manner.

The limits to team authority will be determined by:

- their dedicated role;
- their contractual role and grade;
- their experience;
- organisational rules/boundaries;
- skills and knowledge within the team;
- their training history;
- gaps in knowledge/skills base;
- what they need to learn to close the gap;
- the learning curve they must run to complete their collective development.

Clearly defined limits to team authority will similarly affect individual authority. The determinants of these limits include:

- their contractual role and grade;
- organisational rules and boundaries;
- what tasks they are actually paid to undertake;
- understanding of their own limitations in terms of skills and knowledge;
- knowledge of whom to seek advice from;
- understanding of the support systems in place.

Think it over

What limits would you set to team authority within your practice environment, and why?

Case study — Defining responsibilities and limits to authority

You are a manager of a 46-bed residential home. To meet the residents' wide range of needs, you employ four teams of care staff and one team of permanent night staff. There are 16 care staff, four senior carers, and administrative, domestic, chefs and laundry assistants on duty during the day and early evening. Two teams work in close contact on any one shift, on a back-to-back system. You are aware, given the varying experience, training and specialisms of the staff, that limits to both team and individual authority must be applied. You need to manage an effective teamwork approach, safe in the knowledge that they understand the limits of their roles and tasks, as well as their responsibilities.

- What limits would you apply to team authority, and why?
- What limits to individual authority would you apply, and why?
- What determining factors would you employ to apply these limits?
- How would you feed back to staff to ensure that they understood personal and team limits to authority when on duty.

You provide sufficient information on your allocation of work in a manner and at a level and pace appropriate to the individuals concerned

As manager, you must facilitate effective communication systems with your work team in order for your practice setting to function effectively. 'Sufficient information on allocated work' implies that team members must have access only to such information which enables them to work effectively. This information may comprise:

- areas of the original assessment pertinent to allocated work;
- the care plan, drawn up with the resident and carer, that now must be actioned;
- information on resident choice and preference in all aspects of care, together with carers' views;
- relevant medical information – for example, whether prescribed medication is to be self-administered or to be administered only by senior staff on duty.

What safeguards must be applied?

Under the Data Protection Act 1998, which came into operation on 1 March 2000 and which replaces all previous Data Protection Acts (of 1984, 1987 and 1990), the manager must uphold eight principles which apply to data on residents:

- Data must be kept secure.
- Data must be relevant and not excessive.
- Data must be processed only for time-limited purposes.
- Data must be processed only in appropriate accordance with people's rights.
- Data must be accurate.
- Data must be lawfully processed.
- Data must not be kept indefinitely.
- Data must not be transferred to other countries without protection.

It is your legal duty to ensure only information that is essential to the team's allocated work is shared and remains confidential within the team. You must make a judgement as to what information is both sufficient and necessary for team members to undertake their work. It may be necessary for reasons of resident confidentiality to withhold either sensitive information or information that has no bearing on the actual work undertaken (and therefore would offer no legitimate reasons to bring it into the public domain).

Once information is shared with team members, it becomes a management responsibility to ensure a confidential system for storage, ongoing recording, sharing, receiving and retrieving information from within the team's network system. Individuals not involved in the allocated work will have no rights to access.

Think it over

Consider the different ways in which information is processed in the work setting. What procedures currently exist to protect resident confidentiality, and what improvements could be made?

Information process	How is it currently protected?	What improvements could be made?

Storing of information in:

Filing cabinets
On CD or floppy disk
In case files
In portable expanding files

Receiving information:

By phone
By fax
By letter
Email
Handwritten messages
Tape-recorded messages
Verbally

Recording information:

Within case files
Message books
Assessment sheets
Review forms
On CD or floppy disk
Resident files

Retrieving information:

Open/close filing systems
Portable binders
CD/floppy disks

In order to be certain that you provide sufficient information regarding work allocation at an appropriate pace that your team members can understand, cover the following points:

- Give clear instructions to both the team and individuals concerned.
- Be very specific about the nature and content of the task(s) you wish to be undertaken.
- Identify specific people you wish to undertake the task.
- Explain to people what is required of them and what you wish them to do.
- Be very clear about the way in which you wish the task to be undertaken.
- Always test for comprehension by direct questioning (do this creatively).
- Reinforce the importance of the task by stressing its importance.
- Make it clear when you wish the task completed, and set realistic deadlines for its completion.
- Test the process you have outlined. As manager, you must ascertain whether the process is effective. If not, contingency plans need to be made.
- Supervise both the individual and team, focusing directly upon newly allocated work.
- Ensure that supervision is supportive and encourage team members to identify any weaknesses in their practice so that they can be resolved in a mutual, interdependent way (by either you or the team as a whole).
- Establish a system of proactive supervision, which should provide evidence regarding how the task is being completed and how the team member is progressing. Set formal review dates. Discuss results and potential problem areas encountered.
- Maintain a professional developmental position. Never regress by focusing upon personality traits. Simply stick to facts and give appropriate feedback.
- Offer unconditional praise for work that has been completed; qualitative results demand a simple 'thank you'. Reinforce the value to place on both the individual and collective efforts of your team. This will increase motivation and promote positive inter-group relations.

Case study — Provision of information

You are leading a weekly allocation meeting at which 12 care staff are present. A new resident has been self-referred and presents with multiple disabilities.

- How will you communicate sufficient details relating to the resident without infringing the limits of resident confidentiality?
- How will you instruct team members about resident management?
- What criteria will you use to identify a named key worker?
- How will you explain to all staff what is required of them to meet this resident's needs?
- How will you test for comprehension?
- How will you decide on monitoring arrangements and methods of recording, which must be kept confidential and in a secure environment?
- What range of instructions will you give all staff members to preserve confidentiality?
- How will you break these down so that staff both understand and remember?
- How will you instruct staff members on methods of information retrieval for review purposes without breaking the bounds of confidentiality?

You confirm team and individual understanding and commitment to work allocations at appropriate intervals

When you allocate new work or review previous work allocations, you must test both team and individual comprehension of what they are required to do, in order to action the care plan to meet residents' needs.

Forums for action

Individual supervision

You are expected to focus upon the outcomes of individual key worker intervention at planned and regular intervals. Does the team member fully understand the care plan, the resident's needs and preferences, and responded to these needs? Observation and active feedback from residents, carers and other team members are a prerequisite to this process.

Daily assessment sheets, monitoring and review will offer evidence of whether progress is being made, as will third-party feedback from the primary health care teams. Additionally, planning and the direction of existing and future work give an insight into a team member's commitment to meeting residents' needs.

Where difficulties arise, as manager and supervisor you are responsible for giving appropriate support, advice, guidance and practical assistance, perhaps through joint working with another member of the team. Regular supervision is the key to maintaining enthusiasm, reviewing progress and giving constructive feedback, which must be understandable. While it remains the key worker's role and responsibility to coordinate and show work undertaken, accountability for ensuring constructive outcomes remains the overriding responsibility of the manager.

Think it over

Identify the advantages and disadvantages of individual supervision as a means of confirming understanding and commitment to work allocation. Use the examples to direct your responses.

Advantages	*Disadvangtages*
(1) Focuses upon individual input and development	If not actioned regularly, the process shifts away from confirming understanding, commitment and development and dissolves into a problem-solving exercise
(2)	
(3)	
(4)	

Team supervision

For work allocation purposes, team supervision would be used only to work on a specified area of teamwork. Here the resources of the whole team can be drawn together and focused on a specific task. An agenda will direct collective discussion. The manager should be seen to lead, motivate and encourage contributions from everyone in attendance. Encourage open and honest debate, and develop individual ideas into a collectively owned strategy.

This is a particularly useful forum in which to deal with areas of work allocation which concern the whole team, for example changing patterns of work, increased joint working or restructuring teams. This type of meeting does require an experienced and strong-willed manager to retain focus and prevent anger or diffusion of responsibility from distracting from the specified task. However, when whole staff teams need to be brought together, this forum is unavoidable and if managed appropriately can restore confidence, mutual respect, interdependence, comprehension and commitment through ownership of collective decision making.

While it is more time- and cost-effective than individual supervision, there may be logistical difficulties in bringing the whole team together without inconveniencing the residents. In such circumstances the manager must arrange for external cover.

Consider the skills you would require to manage a whole team meeting to confirm their collective understanding of new work allocations. Use the examples as a guide to develop your responses for a meeting addressing team restructuring.

Skills required	*Desired outcomes*
(1) To question and encourage open debate	Clarify understanding
(2) To give information, listen and seek to build on individual ideas to arrive at agreed collective decisions	Sharing ideas and resolving problems collectively

(3)

(4)

Reviews

The reviewing process informs the manager whether the interlinked processes of referral, assessment, care planning and implementation have met the presenting needs of particular residents/carers. It should also confirm whether the provider input has met its stated aims. In being able to evidence this process, the manager will be able to ascertain both team and individual understanding of this specific work allocation.

The review itself will both measure and reveal standards of care and the team's standards of service delivery. Care plans should be reviewed monthly, as required by the National Minimum Standards. In this way, individual and team commitment to and understanding of residents' needs are compared against levels of resident satisfaction and that of their external carers. The review must also be centred on residents' autonomy/ independence, improved quality of life, mobility and self-care, as well as a sense of security. Given that the review in itself is outcome orientated, it reflects and shows individual and team commitment to this process.

Regularity of review remains the key to ensuring creative team and individual work practices and the systematic meeting of needs. By law, the National Minimum Standards of case review stipulate that residents receiving residential or registered nursery care are formally reviewed once a year. Regional variations may require this to be every six months. However, particularly in residential care, it should be undertaken every six weeks to be certain that work allocation continues to meet residents' presenting or changing needs.

How might you improve the review process in your establishment to confirm individual and team understanding, and their commitment to total resident care?

Invite contributions from individuals and the team

By inviting contributions from both individuals and the team, you can either informally or formally confirm understanding and commitment to your work allocation process. Simply inviting contributions may not always provide you with the necessary clarity of information or evidence you require, however, so how should you encourage your team to make effective contributions?

- You must ensure that whatever you request verbally is both clear and understandable.
- Clarify this by questioning.
- Invite ideas.
- Try to be persuasive.
- Be aware of the import of your own non-verbal communication (NVC).
- Be aware of the tone, rate and fluency of your voice, as well as its pitch.
- Remain assertive but not aggressive.
- Ensure there is a non-threatening atmosphere – encourage one that is conducive to open-ended discussion.

Increasing understanding and commitment

You may try to increase the understanding and commitment of your staff individually, in small groups or as a whole team.

Individually

This is probably the most effective way.

Advantages

- Seek to identify the staff member's opinions.
- Clarify them.
- Discuss them.
- Allay any fears.
- Identify comprehension or lack of it.
- Clarify personal commitment to allocated work.

Disadvantages

- Time inefficient.
- Inconvenient.
- Costly – if you unit cost your time.

For equal opportunities purposes, it may be necessary to hold similar meetings with all team members. Then collate all the information gathered, to determine overall team and individual understanding and commitment.

Small groups

Advantages

- Individuals may be prepared to share more or risk opinions in the company of peers.
- Group support reinforces the ability to convey feelings and thoughts.
- Small groups are likely to convey either commitment or not, given their inter-dependency, but might seek collective options to meet residents' needs.
- Time- and cost-effective with minimum inconvenience.

Disadvantages

- Individuals may try to diffuse responsibility for either understanding or commitment among each other.
- They may use their unity to deny confirmation.

Whole team meetings

Advantages

- All team members are present.
- The whole team is given the same information and asked the same questions.
- Strength can be drawn from the resources of the team.
- Weaker/less experienced members feel less threatened.
- Discussion is much wider.
- Objectives may be individual or wider.
- Making verbal and non-verbal responses may be easier in a collective environment. Eye contact is more flexible.
- The fear factor is minimised.
- Direct questioning is more likely to be responded to.
- Problems arising can be openly discussed.
- Ideas from individuals can be built upon collectively.
- Ideas can be tested out.
- Group decision making will give clarity and honesty to statements about what can be achieved or not achieved (with existing staff numbers, expertise, timescale and resources).
- Clarity of team understanding and commitment will be a visible outcome.

Disadvantages

- Silent members can hide behind the most vocal.
- Diffusion of responsibility among members unless the meeting is well managed.
- Disagreement or confusion may arise.
- Open rebellion in numbers is possible.
- Difficult to organise and equally difficult to manage when discussing such a sensitive subject, as team members can personalise the area.

For all three methods, the advantages outweigh the disadvantages. As manager it will be your decision to use one or all three in tandem, depending on your assessment of staff mood or commitment. In any event, your sole purpose must be to narrow the gap between required, as opposed to expected, understanding, as well as an unconditional commitment to the work allocation process, to meet total resident care and not simply the particular preferences of staff members.

Your final judgement may require role replacement and team restructuring. Only by strong management offering a resident first choice will you achieve, with what staff you have, standards of care which reflect a genuine understanding, qualitative care and resident satisfaction.

Try it out

What method(s) might you use to narrow the gap between required (for practice) and expected understanding, and to produce total commitment to allocated case-work, in which residents' needs come first?

Case study — Understanding and commitment

You are a manager of a 23-bed residential unit and a day service centre for 10 residents. Within the last six weeks you have become increasingly concerned about the apparent confusion, lack of understanding of resident care plans and misinterpretation of written information contained in care plans. There seems also to be a poor attitude to the implementation of care plans and to your work allocation.

- How will you go about reviewing each case allocation with the designated key worker?
- What methods might you employ to clarify understanding?
- How might you seek to minimise your increased time and inconvenience for task achievement purposes?

Where team resources are insufficient, you reach agreement with relevant people on the prioritisation of objectives or reallocation of resources

All teams depend on a structured yet creative budget to meet the diverse requirements of service delivery. As manager, you are responsible for calculating the budget as well for contingency planning in the event of a financial shortfall. The budget becomes the total expenditure allowed in any financial year to enable your team to deliver its services.

You must publicise your budgetary requirements and explain budget priorities to both residents and staff. Both groups can then make informed decisions about priorities in light of the demand for resources. However, when team resources become insufficient, you have to re-prioritise your budget to ensure appropriate cash flow to allow your team to function.

Think it over

Do you understand your budget and its implications? In the event of a shortfall, how could you provide the services you have already publicised, taking into account the cyclical nature of demand for residential accommodation?

Within the private, independent and charitable sectors, budgetary discipline is a matter of survival. It also represents the difference between profit and loss, where the latter could lead to financial bankruptcy. The word 'profit' should not be regarded as a dirty one. It should symbolise what monies can be made over and above the existing budgetary restrictions. Profit is a guarantee of a healthy cash flow, uninterrupted staff wages and the delivery of care which meets both statutory and your publicised standards.

Within a residential care or nursing home, budgets will be worked out to meet the necessary ratios of team members to residents. Each home must determine the appropriate staffing levels and skills to meet the assessed needs of its own particular residents, which will then be approved by the National Care Standards Commission (NCSC). Increasingly, residential homes are being required to accommodate older, more infirm residents who, in previous years, would have automatically been referred for nursing home care. This is a consequence of under-funding and the lack of prioritisation of nursing home care nationally. Clearly, if admission to a private residential home becomes the only option, it must be part of a highly managed care plan involving multidisciplinary input and regular review by all parties involved; ideally, it should only be seen as a temporary rather than permanent arrangement in the interests of best practice.

It is currently national practice that, unless residents are diagnosed as requiring high-dependency care, and unless a bed in a nursing home can be found, they will more than likely be referred to a residential care home, to free up a valuable NHS hospital bed. Additionally, residents will be offered a choice of homes only within the ceiling which social services can afford, which becomes a postal code lottery. Clearly, if their preferences or needs are different, they can choose from an inspected and accredited list, although they or the family would have to make up the financial disparity.

If at any time your resources become insufficient, then you must either re-prioritise your existing financial objectives/targets or seek to reallocate and make sufficient financial savings in order to sustain profitability. In such circumstances, you must:

- communicate this information to residents, carers and team members;
- ensure that any such communication is genuine and open to constructive criticism.

In the event of a shortfall of resident capacity, which has immediate cash flow implications and might force closure, then agreement with residents, carers and team members becomes a prerequisite for survival. What you must do is as follows:

- Accurate estimates and timescales will be required to satisfy your social care commissioner that you can continue to meet customer/resident needs to their assessed levels of care.
- Ensure that 24-hour care to all residents is provided.
- Reductions in staffing levels will require changes to the teams, to meet residents' needs at crucial times of the day.
- Carer concerns must be both listened to and worked at within a partnership, to allow any transition to occur with minimum stress.
- Direct your efforts to rationalise in close counsel with your nominated accountant and make savings only in areas that do not erode standards of care.
- Savings from staff costs must be agreed with team members in advance to ensure their retention. These savings may be through reductions in overtime allowances and lieu time given instead, incremental pay gains being put on hold or reducing the size of non-essential travel allowances.
- Always seek to reassure residents, carers and team members that once the necessary savings have been made, resident care levels will be restored and any restrictions previously imposed will be lifted.

How would you manage both financial restrictions and resident care needs in tandem, when faced with a downturn of demand for accommodation within your establishment? Jot down your thoughts.

Case study — Insufficient resources

You are a manager of a 46-bed residential home, offering residential and day care facilities to residents who present with a huge diversity of medical, physical, cultural and mobility needs. Your establishment has been caught up in a recruitment crisis and you are finding it increasingly difficult to provide adequate staffing levels to meet residents' need.

- How do you foster agreement with existing staff to stay?
- What methods might you employ to encourage retention?
- What alternative recruitment methods might you consider to get you through this crisis?
- How do you avoid compromising care standards with fewer staff?
- How do you reassure residents and their carers that this crisis is only temporary? What evidence can you use to satisfy their concerns?
- How do you plan, over the short, medium and long term, to restore staffing levels?
- How do you distill these difficulties into a proactive recruitment action plan?

You inform your team and its members of changes to work allocations in a way which minimises the impact on time, cost and inconvenience

Changes in work allocation are inevitable in a mixed economy of health and social care. As manager, you will be required to adapt to market trends, new legislation and different residents' needs. However, you will be expected to lead your team through these changes using eclectic leadership styles and to motivate members to develop even more creative ways of service delivery to your resident group.

Changes to joint work

Joint work with residents is an accepted means of decreasing stress, sharing skills and knowledge, giving mutual support, and training less experienced staff through effective monitoring.

How do you inform?

You can inform staff formally or informally but always from an agreed basis in weekly allocation meetings, supervision or in team meetings. Consultation and equal discussion are the keys to effective communication and collective resolution.

How does it minimise the impact on time, cost and inconvenience?

The above forums are time-limited and cost-effective. They will be planned and managed so as not to interfere with service delivery.

Think it over

How would you develop a culture of joint work in your care setting while minimising costs due to misinformation and poor time management?

Changes to mentoring roles

Mentoring is an increasingly common developmental practice within both health and social care. It assists with staff retention, prevents stagnation and provides more experienced staff with acknowledged status as well as recognised skills and knowledge to train, support, advise and guide new members to adjust to new roles and occupy them with confidence.

How to inform

This is a delegated role; therefore it must be negotiated and agreed mutually, ideally in formal supervision. Sometimes it may be necessary to train new members to occupy this role. As manager, you may delegate responsibility to a new mentor; however, you are still accountable for any work undertaken and the quality of that work. Proactive supervision of both mentors and team members is required to achieve the degrees of competency in the delivery of care required of all care professionals.

How does it minimise the impact on time, cost and inconvenience?

You must realise you cannot perform every task which is within the remit of your team, in tandem with your management role. Selective delegation releases responsibility but not accountability for key mentor roles/tasks. The mentor can be both time- and cost-effective if appropriately supervised. Any inconvenience which might arise would probably be the outcome of poor planning/preparation, inadequate mentor training to supervise newly delegated role(s) and insufficient formal supervision to review progress.

How can a mentoring role assist with changes in work allocation while minimising impact on time, cost and inconvenience? Examples are included to assist you complete this exercise.

Role of mentor	*Outcome for team member*
(1) Share information about how changes in work role can improve personal practice	Share ideas, clarify own understanding and focus upon role change
(2) Offer constructive support	Assist with managing own stress levels, while developing a sense of self-worth
(3) To confront the reality of change that changing work allocation can create	Learn to take personal responsibility and challenge personal assumptions about self with respect to what one can do or cannot do
(4) Assist with case management	Manage time and resources more effectively

(5)

(6)

(7)

(8)

Changes to priority setting

Effective work allocation demands the setting of realistic priorities, collectively agreed to operationalise the residents' care plans. However, the priority setting is never static and will change as residents' needs change. As needs decrease, priorities of, for example, high-dependency care, might be retracted in a measured and monitored way to increase resident autonomy and self-reliance.

How do you inform?

The key to effective communication with residents is open and sensitive discussion conveyed with empathy. This is best undertaken within the bounds of a secure key worker relationship.

How does it minimise the impact on time, cost and inconvenience?

Changing the essential work allocation on a **priority rotating scale** ensures the need for accurate assessment of need, as well as managed care planning and implementation. It makes for effective budgetary practice, as less time and resources have to be invested in one person. It should be seen as a positive outcome of an accurate assessment of need and a well constructed and managed care plan. Inconvenience is minimised as levels of care can be transferred to other residents with greater needs.

Think it over

How might you inform a resident that existing work allocations are no longer required? What skills would you employ to manage this transitionary process?

Changes to work role

Changing work allocations does not mean changing the actual work role of the team member. You should ensure that any change falls within the existing remit of the team members' job descriptions. If not, they must be legally rewritten to reflect the actual role and task the person is performing, together with hours on duty and whether special requirements such as split shifts and weekend working become the expected requirements of the post-holder.

How to inform

In practice, team members would be informed through open and genuine debate, in both team meetings and in individual or small group supervision. In this way the whole team can come to appreciate the facts and why changes in their work role are required. You must ensure an honest and not a manipulative dialogue. Active listening, negotiation and compromise are the key skills to ensure that individual team members can be actively supported through transitions. The down side to misinformation or imposition is team dysfunction, low morale, poor standards of resident care and higher staff turnover.

How does it minimise the impact on time, cost and inconvenience?

If you are able to sustain a culture of openness, honesty and accessible information regularly updated at team meetings, this will facilitate change. Sometimes change to work allocation overtakes existing circumstances. However, in a team environment where members are encouraged to make contributions and inputs to meet changing demands upon resident care and service delivery, such a change to the work role is less traumatic and therefore more manageable. Negative outcomes, such as time wasted in constant negotiation and costly recruitment processes, can be minimised or even avoided.

Changes brought about when demand outstrips supply

Changes in work allocation may arise as a consequence of increasing residents' needs – perhaps high mobility needs, barrier care, high degrees of physical disability combined with serious medical conditions which leave residents bed-bound. High demands can sap the strength of the most resourceful team. A residential care home is not a registered nursing home, nor an extension of a geriatric ward at a local NHS trust hospital. Therefore it is good practice to ensure that you create a balance of residents referred to you with a mixture of needs. This ensures that the resources of the team and individual members are both challenged and developed in different ways. Continuous high-dependency care should be considered only as a temporary measure to assist partner bodies such as trust hospitals or your local social services department, usually during the winter months.

How to inform

You must ensure that staff realise in advance, in successive meetings, that this current situation is only a temporary measure to alleviate local pressures. Their help and support is both required and valued, and any suggestions they can make to cope in a period when demand for beds outstrips supply would be appreciated. Listen, record and prioritise staff concerns and ideas. If budgetary allocations can fund the employment of temporary staff to ease workload, then give it serious consideration. Additionally, reinforce the message to staff that current admissions will not represent future trends. Such a constructive response should alleviate concerns about the ability to cope in a fraught atmosphere.

Think it over

How might you go about informing your staff they will be caring for high-dependency residents, albeit on a temporary basis, and that work allocations will place increasing demands on each team member?

How does it minimise the impact on time, cost and inconvenience?

Information is communicated in advance and team members are forewarned about an impending crisis threatening their own community and the part they can play to alleviate pressure on local services, as part of a concerted effort to reduce imbalances within trust hospitals and localised primary health care teams. Support rather than team dysfunction is a more likely outcome. Proactive collective planning is required about meeting increased demands, changing workload allocation, restructuring teams, changing individual roles and work patterns. If such measures and contributions can be encouraged voluntarily, the actual impact is likely to be minimised in terms of total cost, time spent in wasted management and inconvenience to both existing and referred residents.

Think it over

What contingency planning would you encourage from your team to deal with an impending localised health care crisis, demanding change to work allocation, team structure and patterns? Examples are given for directional purposes.

Planning	Desired outcomes for practice
Information giving and gathering	Proactive team members to inform and seek feedback as well as encourage contributions about how to cope. Look for practical examples from staff, residents and carers
Ownership/accountability	Seek team member advice and guidance. Build an action plan based on their collective contributions
Proactive changes to workload allocation	Prepare for change in advance by identifying team member roles, key worker strategies, joint work and an overall change in work patterns

▼

Set realistic priorities	Establish team strengths and weaknesses. Set priorities for work to be undertaken. Identify a reviewing structure to monitor and review priorities of residents at regular intervals
Prepare for change	Partly psychological, partly physical. Reassure existing residents and their carers that their needs will be unaffected. Prepare staff
Training needs	Identify additional training which may be required. Secure assistance from local social services and primary health care teams for training inputs, advise, guidance and support
Prepare residents and carers	Existing residents and carers to be given ongoing support and reassurance about the quality of their care, which is not to be affected

Case study — Changes to work allocation

You are the manager of an established 23-bed purpose-built residential home, which is all on ground level and can therefore allow resident mobility within motorised or manual wheelchairs at all levels of the establishment. Recently you have engaged in a new plan to increase occupancy levels to 28 beds. The new extension has forced budgetary constraints to a new limit. You find yourself in a situation, albeit temporary, in which full occupancy can be attained only by enforcing new work allocation levels. Care staff will now have to work with a minimum of five more residents within existing team structures. You are currently not in a position to afford to recruit additional staff, and contingency planning, as a result of a shortfall in funds, requires you to make savings to ensure continuity of existing care standards.

Therefore, new work allocation will include split shifts, reversal and changed worker roles, as well as additional weekend and bank holiday working. No choice can now be given to working unsociable hours.

As manager, these questions require discussion and team resolution:

- How will you inform your team(s) of the current situations and its implications for their roles?
- What forum will you use?
- What skills and methods will you employ to minimise the threat of team rebellion, unnecessary cost, time and inconvenience in fire-fighting to retain existing standards of care as well as your present staff team?
- How would you go about sharing information with residents and carers to reassure that their care will remain unaffected?

C13.2

Learning outcomes

- You give opportunities to your team members to help define their own objectives and work plans.
- You develop objectives and work plans which are consistent with team and organisational objectives and agree these with all personnel in your area of responsibility.
- The objectives, work plans and schedules are realistic and achievable within organisational constraints.
- The objectives and work plans take account of team members' abilities and development needs.
- You explain the objectives and work plans in sufficient detail and at a level and pace appropriate to your individual team members.
- You confirm team and individual understanding of, and commitment to, objectives and work plans at appropriate intervals.
- You provide advice and guidance on how to achieve objectives in sufficient detail and at times appropriate to the needs of team and individuals.
- You update the objectives and work plans regularly and take account of any individual, team and organisational changes.

You give opportunities to your team members to help define their own objectives and work plans

As manager, in order to give opportunities to team members, to help define their own objectives and work plans, you must initially agree the objectives of the overall team.

- Irrespective of your practice setting, you must define, clarify and agree the objectives of the team.
- Then you must prioritise the objectives of the team.
- Then breakdown the objectives into individual team member roles for overall task achievement.
- Individual roles enable specific objectives to be met.
- Set a realistic time scale for objectives to be achieved.
- You must monitor individual and team objectives in tandem.
- Accurate records must be kept of the objectives set and the achievements made, for both team and individuals.

Consider how you might help team members set their team and individual objectives. What processes might you use? What would you do if you could not agree on team and individual objectives?

The setting of objectives needs to be undertaken in partnership with residents and their carers, so that their views and specific needs feature in team members' individual objectives and work plan. The work plan becomes the vehicle by which the resident's original assessment and care plan can be implemented in an individualistic way. It must be written in an understandable and jargon-free format that residents can read and comprehend in their mother tongue. It must include individual key (team) worker ideas and how those ideas relate to implementation. It must include what the team contribution represents in the delivery of care. It must be achievable and measurable to allow for monitoring and review of progress. Finally, it must be time efficient to ensure achievement of objectives within an agreed time scale.

Forums for opportunities

Several different forums give the manager opportunities to help team members define their own objectives and work plans:

- formal supervision;
- informal supervision;
- team meetings;
- training support meetings.

Formal supervision

Whatever type of formal supervision is chosen, be it individual, pair, small group or tandem, it provides specific opportunities for you to focus upon identified team member objectives to be used within their work plans. It is your role within this forum to listen and give accurate feedback, and to assist the development of ideas so that specific objectives can take shape. However, ensure that the fundamental ideas emanate from the team member. You may be required to prompt or persuade team members to give more thought to their objective setting, but always be prepared to compromise in order that team members feel sufficiently empowered to take risks in their formulation of objectives, and how these can be transferred into achievable work plans.

Formal supervision enables the above to occur in an atmosphere of equality, which promotes open discussion. The forum is planned, regular, with a mutually set agenda and a prioritisation of items for discussion. Ground rules for behaviour, feedback and recording purposes are agreed in advance.

The process focuses upon the team members' needs or concerns. It gives good opportunities for team members to set their own objectives and work plans. Achievement is observed and monitored to ensure success as well as professional development.

Informal supervision

Informal supervision will have a non-structured format but it gives daily opportunities for team members to approach you, as manager, or their peers to assist in their own definition of both objectives and workflows. If effectively managed, informal supervision can run in tandem with formal supervision. The key to success must be sound inter-group relations, where team members actively and openly support and trust each other. In such a non-threatening environment, team members can use each other as sounding boards, take advice and equally take constructive criticism without offence or fear. It can move almost from an experimental platform to a practice one and then followed through with support on demand. Only in such a culture of support and trust can this type of unconditional informal supervision succeed in assisting team members define their own objectives and their work plans.

Team meetings

The team meeting can provide team members with the necessary help to define their own objectives and work plans if, again, a culture of mutual support exists. As manager, it must be your responsibility to ensure that a sensitive and responsive relationship between the more experienced and the less experienced members exists to allow without prejudice the exploration of ideas. In this way, members can be encouraged to discuss concerns, identify their limitations and take on board new ideas without feeling insecure or inferior.

A framework for differentiating team objectives and team member objectives must be put in place and agreed upon. More importantly, the relationship between the two must be understood by all. This should allow individuals to plan their own objectives and work plans within this existing framework, so that the team meetings can respond to individual concerns with practical measures, such as joint working or peer support.

Think it over

Do your team meetings provide an environment in which individual team members are given opportunities to define their own objectives and work plans? Explain how and why, or what improvements could be made to this important forum.

Training support meetings

This represents an ideal forum. These meetings enable the manager to assist team members collectively to draw, share and critically reflect on their learning in relation to practice. Ideally, this forum should have a voluntary membership.

The supportive framework must give team members the opportunity to share ideas and practise setting objectives individually, in pairs or as a group exercise. The same rationale can be applied for work plans as an outcome of realistic objective setting.

Training may be in-house or external; the important point is that you must give different opportunities to team members to draw from their learning experience, the knowledge, ideas or skills and to transfer them into whatever objectives they seek. For example, the objective might be to 'Increase resident mobilisation'. The work plan would include: risk assessments; techniques of mobilisation; no lifting in any form; to employ only EU mandatory techniques for movement and assistance; learn to use a hoist; increase resident's autonomy.

The use of this forum is an ideal way of fostering team member interdependence, which they can continue in the practice setting and equally share with the wider team. The principles of trust, support and information giving and receiving then become an assimilated and accepted part of team culture. You must encourage the provision of these different opportunities to give team members the chance to set their own objectives and work plans to improve team practices.

Case study — Team opportunities for setting objectives

You are a newly appointed manager of a high-dependency residential care home, accommodating 22 residents. You find that staff have historically been dependent on their managers to set defined objectives and work plans.

- How will you go about changing this culture?
- What methods will you employ?
- What new forums might you consider to give new opportunities to team members to clarify and define their own objectives and work plans?
- How will you prioritise this process to meet the presenting needs of residents, carers and the team?

You develop objectives and work plans which are consistent with team and organisational objectives and agree these with all personnel in your area of responsibility

As manager, it is your responsibility to ensure that your objectives and work plans are consistent with both team and organisational objectives, and that they are agreed with all personnel in your areas of responsibility. The key to doing so is in the formulation of the service plan.

- Ensure that both your team objectives and work plans are included in your service plan.
- Ensure that your service plan focuses on residents and details how care is to be delivered.
- Ensure that the team agrees its own objectives and work plans and informs you of how it intends to meet the objectives and action the plans.

The service plan could be formulated in a series of team meetings or by away days, if they are affordable. Ensure that the formulation includes appropriate role allocation, drawing upon the strengths and resources of the team. Tasks must be broken down to simplify how the service plan will operate in practice. The key to formulation is active involvement by all team members to ensure their personal objectives can be prioritised and disseminated into one working document. From this document, achievable and agreeable work plans can be drawn up to meet different resident needs.

The document could take the form of a brochure written by the team which is creatively and accurately illustrated. It might take the form;

- Who are we?
- Where are we situated?
- What do we do?
- How do we do it?
- Who with and who for?
- Our future developments as a practice setting.

Ensure that the objective setting for the service plan, together with teamwork plans which action it, are collectively agreed. This can encourage ownership to ensure success. Accountability and the involvement of team members to be at every level encourages motivation, morale and job satisfaction.

Who are we?

We are a community village consisting of assisted accommodation, residential and high-dependency care.

Where are we situated?

In glorious countryside (within the green belt) in the heart of the country, which is Meridan, the Centre of England.

What do we do?

We provide some 30 individually designed, purpose-built bungalows which cater for couples and individual residents. Each one is designed to cater for people with a range of disabilities. The bungalows are in a large circle, giving them a village outlook. In the centre is a 46-bed residential home which can provide personalised care to residents who find living independently difficult. All rooms are en suite and cater for couples and individuals. Your care needs are our priority, hence personalised work plans are drawn up with you to ensure all your needs, preferences and wishes are met.

How do we do it?

Care is provided in the form of assisted living for those disabled and non-disabled residents who wish to live independently. Additionally, we provide residential care to cater for residents who require more intensive assistance to enjoy a better quality of life. To ensure this high degree of personalised care, we employ 25 care staff, five of whom are RGN qualified. In addition, we have three highly qualified chefs, a team of catering, laundry and domestic staff to maintain high standards of cuisine, cleanliness and hygiene, in a safe and luxurious environment.

Who with and who for?

Both the accommodation and care we provide are targeted to meet the needs of the older person, irrespective of race, nationality, gender, disability or culture. Several of our staff are bilingual and their languages include French, Spanish, Polish, Punjabi, Gujarati and Hindu. Our care programme, as outlined here in this service plan, is multicultural. Inclusive care is our priority, preserved within a well managed village complex. Your accommodation is as individualised as your care, with specific work plans drawn up by yourselves and your key worker, and supported by the care

▼

team to facilitate a different quality of life on your terms. You are the resident and your personalised care and choice of accommodation are our priority.

Our future developments as a practice setting

In our published budget we have a three-year plan gradually to expand the village concept.

In Year 1, 10 extra bungalows are to be built, fully adapted to people with disabilities, to accommodate both couples and single residents.

In Year 2, an indoor swimming pool is to be built in a conservatory setting with views from the poolside to the surrounding gardens and countryside. A small hydro pool will also be built on the same site to assist with muscular development. Both facilities will have trained staff, hoists and disability aids to assist you to enjoy the water therapy.

In Year 3, having met Standards 2000 for our residential care, we intend to continue our refurbishment and building programme to ensure the existing environment is improved yet further, with a view to working towards Standards 2007.

This plan would have to be annually reviewed in the light of changing residents' needs and financial constraints.

Launching the service plan

The service plan, consistent with team and organisational objectives, policies, values and future developments, has to be launched. You must:

- publicise the plan using a variety of media, such as brochures, CDs, videos and audiotapes, to ensure resident/carer comprehension;
- obtain feedback to ensure that the language used accurately communicates the purpose of your plan;
- ensure that both the values of the organisation and the teams which subscribe to them are communicated to your resident base.

The service plan must reflect the organisation's aims, objectives and future developments, and inform actual and future residents, carers and other providers how your team can transfer these into actual practice. Staff can introduce their specific roles, their teams, their different practices, their training and ongoing developmental training to satisfy residents of commitment and accountability to the delivery of their care.

Feedback

Obtaining feedback from a range of different sources will ensure security that the service plan can meet its designated purpose.

Monitoring

Once launched, the service plan must be monitored. Role allocation to staff is vital to ensure their continued ownership as well as extracting resident/carer evidence of its purpose and whether it lives up to this.

Review

The service plan must be reviewed at agreed intervals with staff, residents, carers and the other provider bodies. Their feedback will inform you of any failings and limitations, and what modifications need to be put in place quickly to ensure that existing and future needs are met.

Case study — Formulating a service plan

As manager of a 22-bed purpose-built specialist residential home for people with a physical disability, you wish to raise the profile of your setting to encourage a wider resident base.

- How would you draw up a service plan which accurately communicates this?
- How would you ensure your objectives for this plan are consistent with team and organisational objectives?

The objectives, work plans and schedules are realistic and achievable within organisational constraints

Whatever objectives and work plans that may be scheduled over perhaps a three-year period as outlined in your service plan, they need to be underpinned by your budget. The budget, like your objective setting and work plans, is set in advance against actual and projected needs.

Your responsibilities are as follows:

- You ensure that your budget identifies the performance levels and resident capacity on a monthly and quarterly basis to ensure solvency.
- The budget must, in published form, detail income (required and expected) as well as expenditure in any financial year.

- It must set achievable targets for your service plan.
- It must clarify the original objective setting, work plans and their time scale to ensure that resident needs can be met.
- Modifications to resident care as needs increase have to be built into the budget, which is why ongoing monitoring and review are essential.
- Service plan review has to be in line with a budgetary review to ensure delivery.
- Budgetary ring fencing of funds to overcome constraints – such as staff turnover, training, absence, agency cover and ongoing maintenance – must be an intrinsic part of the cash flow.
- The service plan and its budget should produce specific and achievable targets for income generation within each quarter and financial year.

Controls upon unit costs, be they for staffing or equipment, are necessary to remain within budgetary expectations. A budgetary control system can identify where the areas within the service plan are failing, so that proactive problem resolution can be undertaken. Equally, capital under-spent through careful controls allows additional monies to be reinvested in target areas and produces the income generation required for profitability.

While effective budgetary management underpins delivery of your service plan, you must also be aware of other constraints on objective setting and realistic work planning with residents to agreed time scales. What are these constraints?

Think it over

What budgetary controls would you institute to ensure the feasibility of your service plan?

Lack of specialist staff

To employ and retain highly qualified nurses in the face of a national shortage has become a major problem. You must therefore budget over and above the minimum wage to attract suitably qualified staff. Then you must ensure appropriate training to develop, challenge and stretch the individual, to encourage both motivation and retention. The same argument may be stated for care staff, where the turnover is noticeably greater. A refusal by managers to pay more than the minimum wage offers little motivation to staff who aspire to a career within the care industry. Therefore, you must budget for pay levels appropriate to the role, with regular review via appraisal, so performance can be rewarded with both pay and advancement. In-house NVQ or SNVQ training programmes at levels 1–3 are becoming a popular; they reward staff and help in staff retention, as well as enhancing service delivery.

Resident under-capacity

Under-capacity will produce budgetary problems. In this event, you must re-evaluate original objectives at team, member and resident level, to ensure needs can still be met.

Resident over-capacity

Residential and day care over-capacity produces extra demands upon staff. Re-evaluation of team objectives, team structure and leadership, member roles, and the agreement of new working arrangements can prevent high levels of occupational stress and subsequent staff sickness.

Complex resident needs

If the residents referred are increasingly older, infirm, lacking in mobility or more frequently in the early stages of dementia, this can produce huge strains on realistic objective setting and work planning. If resident needs change on a daily basis, traditional methods of working need to be modified to allow a process plan to be achieved where objectives move with presenting needs rather than remaining static.

Changes in demand for services

While your service plan will outline your care provision, it cannot wholly account for unforeseen changes in demand for care. For example, increases in demand for respite care versus full-time care will have both budgetary implications and will require more proactive objective setting and work planning with set time scales. Identify the number of rooms which can be reasonably occupied and contract out to ensure they always remain fully occupied. Use your networking skills to identify the different needs within the mixed economy. Be proactive and ensure that your practice setting can contract out with local social services department, as well as with the voluntary, charitable, independent and private sectors.

Changes in legislation

Standards 2000 had huge implications for the way in which accommodation can be used for residential care purposes. Additionally, the Standards require appropriate training of staff to care for residents whose infirmity or disability is beyond the current levels of expertise. Therefore, phased developmental training of staff becomes necessary and has to be unit costed.

What constraints play a factor in maintaining realistic objective setting and work planning within your organisation?

Case study — Organisational constraints

You manage a busy 36-bed residential care home. Recently, you found that your existing budget control system is failing to spot demands on supervision. This in turn is reducing your cash flow. Additionally, constraints within your setting now make it difficult to maintain achievable objective setting and realistic work planning with residents.

- How do you reassess your situation?
- How do you reassure residents that realistic objective setting and work planning are achievable within set time scales, as made clear in your service plan and in their own care plans?

The objectives and work plans take account of team members' abilities and developmental needs

As manager, it is your responsibility to take into account and differentiate between individual team members' abilities as well as their developmental needs. Their current abilities – in terms of their knowledge, skills and accredited qualifications – will have been audited and supervised to ensure that they remain appropriate to their current roles. Developmental needs will be couched in terms of future rather than current ability, that is, the tasks they will have to be able to undertake for professional as well as organisational development.

Work planning must take into account both current abilities and developmental needs. Two case studies provide examples of how this might be done.

Case study — Derrick Shennowo

Derrick Shennowo, aged 63, has developed Alzheimer's disease. He has been cared for by two key workers, Gill and Colin, for three years. However, in the last three months his physical and mental condition has deteriorated severely. His behaviour and mood swings have become unpredictable and violent, so much so that he now presents a danger to himself, other residents and his two key workers. Both Gill and Colin have unconditionally cared and nursed Mr Shennowo throughout his stay in residential care. They have both become emotionally attached to him, although they realise his condition is terminal. Both accept that he now needs a more specialised environment. However, both Gill and Colin state they have a problem of letting go and feel a sense of betrayal and failure.

The new objective is to prepare Mr Shennowo for his move to a new environment. The work plan is therefore to phase Mr Shennowo's move to his new setting, with a view of securing a degree of familiarity as well as to enable his immediate carers to go through their own process of letting go. Additionally, it must facilitate individual counselling for Gill and Colin via special counsellors from the local branch of the Alzheimer's Disease Society.

The developmental needs plan for the staff will incorporate a course on dementia care and management for both Gill and Colin, the focus being the establishment of professional caring relationships without over-attachment. Additionally, they might increase their networking skills to seek additional advice from local/national support systems. The overall rationale is to assist their preparation for future work with other referred residents suffering from this condition.

- How could Gill and Colin have been better prepared to work with Mr Shennowo in the first instance?
- What different kinds of support could have been drawn upon to assist with Mr Shennowo's dementia management with a view to improve his quality of life?
- Does the developmental needs plan offer both Gill and Colin the opportunities to become more aware of the implications of dementia care as well as to be able to cope with their feelings in future work with residents suffering with this condition?
- Is familiarisation with a new environment a realistic option for a resident in the advanced stages of dementia?
- How might you improve and develop the work plan, given its twofold rationale, and still meet both sets of needs?

You explain the objectives and work plans in sufficient detail and at a level and pace appropriate to your individual team members

As manager, you are required to explain to individual team members the required objectives and work plans in sufficient detail, and at the required level and pace to ensure mutual understanding.

To begin with, you must provide the information team members require to understand the process of setting objectives with residents. This will enable team members to make accountable decisions. Explain how the objectives will be achieved through the work plan. Enable team members to share opinions and feelings, and establish an agreed understanding on how to proceed. Identify with team members limitations of either understanding or of application. Provide the information at both the level of experience and at a pace team members can comprehend. Close any 'gaps' by ensuring that sufficient detail is communicated in a manner that is clear, complete and correct. Then test for comprehension and give appropriate feedback to reinforce or correct team members' understanding.

Case study — Dorothy Gray

Dorothy Gray is aged 90 and comes to your unit every eight weeks for a week's respite care. She is extremely arthritic, wheelchair-bound and is given 24-hour care by her immediate family and support workers.

Allocated team members, who become key workers for Dorothy during her week's stay, require sufficient background knowledge of her case history to facilitate her respite care in line with the agreed work plan. Dorothy has given written agreement to the sharing of this information, as required by the Data Protection Act 1998. What kinds of information would team members require?

- Current medical history.
- Medication required.
- Levels of achievable mobilisation.
- Dorothy's expressed needs, wishes and preferences of each period of respite care (these may change).
- External carers' expressed wishes and opinions.
- Dietary needs.
- Social activities.
- Emotional needs.

▼

- Creative needs she may wish to explore.
- Activities outside the residential home (e.g. church, shopping, bingo) that she may require assistance in pursuing.
- Support within the existing family network which can be drawn upon to ensure that Dorothy's respite care does not distract her from the activities she normally pursues.

The objectives of Dorothy's respite care are to give her a break from her existing carers and daily routine, and equally to give her immediate family a much-needed rest. The work plan is negotiated in advance between Dorothy and her external carers before each period of respite care. Dorothy has requested Elaine to be her key worker (of two years' standing), thus allowing for continuity of care. Her usual room is on the ground floor. Breakfast is to be taken in bed at 8:30 am, with lunch and dinner in the main dining room. Her dietary requirements include a low carbohydrate diet, plenty of fresh fish and fruit daily. She enjoys a glass of white wine with her evening meal and a small measure of whisky at night. She needs assistance with bathing and ironing of clothes. She wishes to take her main meal with residents Alice and John, her friends. Social activities (church twice a week, bingo three times a week and a visit to the local shopping mall) are to be facilitated by a private taxi at Dorothy's expense and choosing. Dorothy would prefer Elaine to accompany her shopping and to bingo, as crowds sometimes cause her panic.

How is the detail of the work plan explained to team members? The information to be shared will have already been agreed both orally and in writing in accordance with the Data Protection Act 1998. Details may be shared orally or in writing. The former gives the opportunity for immediate feedback and cross-examination but may receive a quick response without time for reflection, and the lack of an accurate written record may lead to disputes later. A written record provides a means of making difficult material more comprehensible and less emotionally laden. The disadvantage is that it can take time to produce and does not readily allow for changing opinions or views. Nevertheless, a combination of both methods – oral in the first instance, supported by a written statement of Dorothy's current needs, wishes and preferences – assists with both understanding and comprehension.

Case study — Neil Stone

Neil Stone is 69 and a recent amputee; he is a single man who has stated that he has led a homosexual lifestyle for the past 49 years. He has expressed a wish for a male key worker for his period of respite care, estimated to be six weeks, while alternative assisted accommodation is found for him. He wishes to partake in all the residential home activities and feels that his fellow residents should be made aware of his sexual preference.

- How will you communicate Neil's wishes to team members without prejudicing Neil's preferences?
- What forms of communication will you employ?
- How will you communicate Neil's expressed sexual preferences to your existing resident group?

You confirm team and individual understanding of, and commitment to, objectives and work plans at appropriate intervals

As manager, it is your role to test (and, you hope, confirm) individual and team understanding of both designated objectives and work plans. In this way you may satisfy yourself that individuals and teams realise what their work is about and that staff know how they are performing. This type of evaluation should occur at regular intervals to ensure consistency of team practice and quality of care.

We have already explored a number of forums in which this can occur, most notably in individual supervision, team supervision, review and small group supervision. The problem is to find a mode of communication which suits the levels of understanding of all team members. One such approach is a team briefing, which is a proactive and planned form of organisational communication.

Team briefings

The team briefing can be structured around specific objectives and work plans which staff are implementing. Within this forum all individuals are encouraged to identify their own objectives, discuss their work plans, evaluate progress, make suggestions, share ideas and, if necessary, re-evaluate the nature of work undertaken to meet different residents' needs.

The size of the meeting will vary according to the size of your work team. For optimum learning and task achievement, it should be limited to eight team members. If your team is larger, then break down the team into two or more groups to keep the process manageable.

It is suggested that team briefings should be held for a minimum of one hour, once a week. The continuity of the briefing process enables team members to prepare for, contribute to and evaluate work preparation and implementation.

You are responsible for creating an atmosphere which is conducive to collective communication. Therefore it must be relaxed, informal and non-aggressive. Individual contributions must be valued. The briefing consists of two parts:

- objective setting;
- work planning, progress and evaluation.

Objective setting

You must:

- know and understand the objectives which individuals and teams wish to set, and why;
- clarify with individuals the relevance of each objective;
- ensure that individuals and the team understand what the objectives aim to achieve and how they are to be undertaken;
- identify individual and team roles and their satisfaction with both;
- test for accurate comprehension by asking questions which encourage both individuals and the team to asses the validity of identified objectives in relation to residents' expressed needs;
- focus on the limitations or potential weaknesses of the set objectives and engage in appropriate problem resolution;
- establish realistic time scales;
- agree the objectives and how they are translated into the work plan;
- evaluate the implementation of the objective;
- promote resident involvement;
- continually monitor how needs have been met or unmet;
- re-prioritise objectives as residents' needs change.

In short, you must encourage team members to discuss the objectives, to clarify them, to share opinions, offer new ideas, challenge, constructively criticise within established ground rules and demonstrate commitment both to the operationalisation of the objectives and to each other. Thus the whole process becomes mutually supportive and encourages a culture of interdependency.

Try it out

Set out your criteria for individual and team objective setting within a team briefing in your practice setting.

Work planning

Within the team briefing session, your work plans become the vehicle by which objectives are translated into practice. They also serve to confirm actual team and individual understanding and commitment to this reviewable process.

You must ensure that the objectives agreed are attainable within the work plan. Individual team members need to understand what has to be done and to realise their individual and collective role. Consult with residents and carers on how objectives and work plans will meet their needs and incorporate their wishes into the overall plan.

Then, several points need to be agreed with the key workers:

- a time scale;
- the regularity of monitoring and how it is to be undertaken with residents and the team;

- final evaluation of work plan with residents and cares;
- feedback to the team.

At the end of this process, the key workers should assess with team colleagues the accuracy of the original objectives and the success of the work plan in meeting residents' needs.

A pro forma for the team briefing session may facilitate individual and team understanding of objective setting, work planning and its review. It could take the following format:

> Resident's name.
> Objective(s) set.
> Work plan to meet resident's needs.
> Named key worker(s).
> Agreed time scale.
> Monitoring/review.
> Final evaluation.

An example will clarify its use:

- ***Resident's name***. Joan.
- ***Objective set***. To be enabled for the first time to pursue both religious and spiritual needs.
- ***Work plan to meet resident's needs***. To visit different churches of Joan's choosing. Joan is unsure whether to move from an Anglican persuasion to Roman Catholicism.
- ***Named key worker***. Val.
- ***Agreed time scale***. Two months.
- ***Monitoring/review***. Every two weeks.
- ***Final evaluation***. Joan, having visited her local Anglican Church after a gap of 30 years, has become a member of its congregation. She felt the leap to Roman Catholicism was too large.

Case study — Shabbir Ahmed

Shabbir Ahmed is a widower, aged 89. He lost his wife following a car accident 20 years previously. Although he is able to care for himself, he is bored living on his own and wishes to take up full-time residency in your residential home.

- Will you designate a named key worker?
- What types of objectives will you consider to set with Mr Ahmed to meet his needs?
- What should the work plan consist of, taking into consideration this resident's expressed needs?
- What kind of time scale will be required for a transitory visiting process and for Mr Ahmed to feel satisfied that residential care is for him?
- How will you monitor this process with your key worker and team?
- How will you evaluate Mr Ahmed's work plan and how will you ensure that understanding and commitment to meeting his needs are maintained throughout?

You provide advice and guidance on how to achieve objectives in sufficient detail and at times appropriate to the needs of team and individuals

At times it will be necessary to provide appropriate advice and guidance to enable both individuals and teams to achieve identified and agreed objectives. How should this advice and guidance be given? Broadly, it may be informal or formal. However, the giving of advice and guidance remains a two-way process. It will largely be dependent on the accessibility of the manager to individuals and teams. Team members will need to feel comfortable in coming forward and seeking advice.

Informal advice

Informal advice may be characterised by observed practice or chance communication with an individual, or discussion with the team. It remains fluid, therefore ongoing, as a routine of good practice. However, irrespective of the encounter being informal, you must:

- focus on the identified objectives;
- identify individual and/or team perspectives and opinions;
- look for shared solutions;
- keep comments simple;
- avoid generalising the situation;
- seek resolution;
- request individual and team feedback at agreed intervals.

Case study — Informal advice

A chance observation while on duty reveals that Joan's clothes are made up of odd items. She does not appear as neat as she used to. You speak with her key worker, Ann, and query Joan's presenting state of dress. Ann explains that she is finding it difficult to identify Joan's clothes. You instruct Ann to clarify with Joan what clothes she is missing and to draw up an inventory of missing clothing. Ann should then work with her team members to find them. Additionally, Ann should familiarise the laundry staff with Joan's wardrobe and to arrange a separate wash, and always checked the clothes with Joan on their return. The time scale for wardrobe collation and familiarisation with other workers is one week. This speed will seek to minimise any distress Joan is experiencing. As manager, you will personally check the entire inventory and wardrobe within seven days and confirm the same with Joan.

How might you approach giving informal advice and guidance in order to establish a culture of open communication in your practice setting?

Formal advice

By contrast, formal advice and guidance are given within a host of planned, regular venues – individual or pair supervision, small group supervision, team meetings, briefing sessions or even during formal staff appraisal. The essential difference is that the advice given will be focused upon agreed, planned objectives, where either the individual or team will have reflected upon, prepared and evidenced progression or not.

You must:

- encourage a relaxed but focused attitude;
- identify and prioritise which objectives will require more time;
- encourage the individual or team to discuss progress made;
- openly identify any problems encountered;
- ask open-ended questions to encourage discussion;
- listen actively to responses;
- wherever possible allow individuals or the team to their find own solutions;
- plan an agreed course of action – keep it simple and achievable;
- identify the evidence required to show achievement of the objectives;
- test for comprehension by asking the individual and/or team to identify what course of action they must take in order to achieve specified objectives;
- identify resources required to complete the objectives (e.g. additional personnel or finance);
- identify realistic time scales;
- agree a formal monitoring system and times for review (e.g. weekly, fortnightly, monthly);
- agree a formal review of progress, to include all evidence required to satisfy requirements;
- break evidence down to manageable proportions;
- avoid a paper culture – this in itself promotes dysfunction, as well as indifference from other team members;
- identify your quality indicators in order to measure resident/carer satisfaction with objective setting;
- ensure your guidance identifies the additional support systems for both individuals and teams to draw upon from yourself or third parties (i.e. a mentor) – be clear about availability and accessibility;
- set a time for a final evaluation to ensure that the supportive system you have outlined realises outcomes.

Note that the time scale will vary according to the simplicity or elaborate nature of the objectives set. It might be a week, a month or six weeks. Whatever the objective, you must ensure sufficient time for task achievement according to the competence and experience of the individual or team, and the support given.

Case study — Formal advice

You are engaged in fortnightly supervision with Marie, who is one of three senior carers in your employment. She is responsible for managing a team of six care assistants. The team is composed of three new starters, and she has become concerned about their overall ability to focus their work as a team on agreed objectives.

You remind Marie of her own Woodcock team development training. You ask her to reflect on the application of the nine-dimensional priority system, designed to address needs in a dysfunctional team. You test for comprehension and identify both the results and outcomes of her previous training. You agree with Marie to hold a formal team meeting. You require Marie to brief the team regarding the purpose of the meeting, namely team development. The team's role is to identify their immediate needs as a working team and to prioritise these needs. Marie is to help if this task appears insurmountable.

The team meeting will then address the team's prioritised needs. The outcome might provide sufficient evidence to develop some initial team building (bonding) exercises, as team needs dictate.

Think it over

One of your team members, Mary, is key working a new resident, John Williams, aged 72 years, who has recently become wheelchair-bound. Mary is required to agree with John realistic objectives to maintain high degrees of independence. Mary finds John opposes any suggestions made. She asks for your advice and guidance. How do you respond?

Consider Mary's objective – increased independence for John. What advice might you give to ensure that this objective can be realistically achieved within three months?

You update the objectives and work plans regularly and take account of any team and organisational changes

It is mandatory that you update your objectives and work plans as part of your reviewing strategy. Equally, your review will take into account individual, team and organisational changes, as the three are interrelated and may affect realistic objective setting and work planning. A team briefing session provides the ideal vehicle to action this collective process in a managed way.

When do you update?

This will depend on the objectives set, the nature of the work plan, agreed time scales and review dates. Regular reviews, although time-consuming, will identify changes in residents' needs and the realism of both the original objective(s) and work plan to address and meet those needs. Delay or failure can produce higher unit costs of care if the care delivered is not actually needed. A dependent resident is a disempowered resident if the care provided does not meet expressed needs.

Think it over

How often do you update both objectives and work plans to meet different resident needs within your practice setting?

Why consider the changes that team and organisational structures can impose?

Changes to team composition, for example, new starters and their lack of experience, may require a radical rethink of how you meet your original objectives with the skills available. Equally, team dysfunction may impair the quality of work plans and can reduce the quality of care residents receive and pay for. Changes within or external to the organisation may also inhibit the manner in which you set objectives. Such changes can be legislative, such as Standards 2000. Alternatively, organisational change, such as expansion or relocation, may produce, if not managed appropriately, negative effects and resident/carer dissatisfaction.

What questions need to be raised when updating both objectives and work plans?

- Are residents and carers satisfied with their care?
- Do they consider their original objectives and work plans to have met their purpose and expressed need?
- What degree of resident/carer involvement was there in meeting both the objectives and work plan?
- Were their views listened to?
- If so, what action was taken to incorporate these in both objective setting and subsequent work planning?
- What faults in the process do residents and carers identify?
- What changes would residents and carers like to see, to ensure that their objectives and work plans meet their expressed needs?

- What evidence do named key workers put forward to show progress with the work plan?
- How do key workers feel about their role, in partnership with residents, in setting both the objective and the work plan?
- What have key workers learned by engaging in objective setting and coordinating the work plan?
- Do key workers have recommendations for change?
- How might such recommendations be incorporated within the work plan?
- How does the work team feel about their overall involvement?
- Were they adequately consulted about the detail of the work plan and their role in it?
- What has the team learned from implementing the work plan?

Are residents satisfied with their care?

What questions does the organisation need to ask itself?

- Has it responded to the needs of residents and carers?
- What evidence can it present to support this?
- Has it listened to residents, carers, key workers and the team?
- Does it need to change?
- If so, in what ways?
- How will it make that change and communicate this to all parties concerned?
- How will it work in partnership with all parties in the future to ensure the success of both objective setting and work planning?
- What has the organisation learned from this process to ensure that a resident focus is maintained throughout and expressed needs are met?

Practice outcomes

Briefing reviews represent an outcome of efficient, ongoing monitoring. They can promote an open culture for identifying changes in residents' needs and responding to these proactively. In this way, resident-focused management is at the forefront of the delivery of care. Resident/carer involvement allows them to set objectives and work plans with their key workers, the staff team and the organisation. Partnership becomes the key to good practice. Responsibility and accountability become a shared and cooperative process.

Updating of objectives and work plans within such a culture becomes the norm of good practice. Resident needs do not remain static and monitoring change ensures that the briefing serves the resident and not organisational commerce.

Case study — Olive and Brian

Two residents, Olive and Brian, moved to your community village five years ago. They sought assisted accommodation. Both could care for themselves but required assistance with basic household tasks and occasionally help with cooking. The original objectives and work plan, drawn up in partnership with both Olive and Brian, were to assist in maintaining their personal autonomy by providing only the assistance they both asked for. This work plan, reviewed every three months, operated in a balanced way until recently. Following a fall while on a shopping trip, Olive fractured her hip. Her current state of health, in her own words, has become fragile. The couple have requested that they relocate to very assisted accommodation on the same site, which would facilitate additional care of Olive in a more managed way.

- Consider the types of questions you need to ask Olive and Brian before engaging in updating objectives and work plans.
- Consider the options the Olive and Brian have regarding their accommodation and explain these to both.
- How will you facilitate opportunities for the couple's key worker, Margaret, to engage in the process of objective setting and planning work to meet their changed needs?
- How will you communicate the couple's new needs to your staff team?
- How will you involve the staff team in the necessary updating of both objectives and work plans to meet the couple's needs?
- Question what role the organisation has with respect to Olive and Brian's transition.
- What kinds of support might the organisation offer both Olive and Brian, as well as all other parties involved, in the delivery of their care, and revising objectives and work plans that will meet newly presenting needs?

Learning outcomes

- You clearly explain the purpose of monitoring and assessment to all those involved.
- You give opportunities to teams and individuals to monitor and assess their own performance against objectives and work plans.
- You monitor the performance of teams and individuals at times most likely to maintain and improve effective performance.
- Your assessment of the performance of teams and individuals is based on sufficient, valid and reliable information.
- You carry out your assessments objectively, against clear, agreed criteria.
- Your assessments take due account of the personal circumstances of team members and the organisational constraints on their work.

You clearly explain the purpose of monitoring and assessment to all those involved

As manager, you must explain and obtain agreement from your staff about the nature of their assessment in the workplace, what it involves and how their performance will be monitored. The purpose of assessment must be firmly linked to individual and team performance and not to subjective personality traits. Performance should be measured in terms of achievement in meeting residents' needs through objective setting and work planning.

It must also be agreed how team members will be rewarded for their efforts, be it through performance-related pay, job rotation for enrichment and progression, further training or additional annual leave, or any other criteria you can agree upon within organisational financial and other constraints.

In order to achieve a purposeful and fair assessment, you must explain the methods you will employ, and obtain both individual and team agreement to these. You may draw upon a variety of methods but you will need to prioritise these.

The most readily achievable and realistic methods of staff assessment are:

- observed practice;
- individual appraisal to mutually agreed objectives;
- self-assessment via individual development plans;
- supervision;
- resident feedback on whether their needs have been met.

Your monitoring systems must be explained and mutually agreed for task achievement purposes. Monitoring can be both formal and informal, providing appropriate consultation is made with both the individual and the team. Monitoring involves observation and supervision of work, to set objectives within the context of the work plan. It could form part of an individual's appraisal, self-development plan and resident review. Monitoring should not represent a new process; rather, it incorporates all these activities within existing organisational work patterns, but is agreed by individuals and teams, and has achievable time scales.

Try it out

What methods do you employ to assess the performance of your staff? How could they be improved?

Case study — Meeting new standards

You are a newly appointed care manager of a 33-bed residential home.

- What consultation techniques would you use with your staff to inform them about assessment and monitoring, with a view to raising performance levels?
- What techniques would you employ to reach individual and collective agreement?
- How would you monitor the performance of your staff group, in line with the National Minimum Standards of care which you now must build upon?
- How might you involve residents and staff in the assessment and monitoring arrangements?

You give opportunities to teams and individuals to monitor and assess their own performance against objectives and work plans

It is imperative that you motivate both your team and individual members to assess and monitor their performance against agreed objectives and subsequent work planning. Why? Self-assessment identifies gaps in actual performance; regular monitoring minimises the risks of gaps widening and provides staff with the opportunity to close any gaps and maximise personal performance. The process demands ownership and accountability, both individually and mutually, if you are to meet changing residents' needs.

Self-assessment

Self-assessment of work performance can motivate the team member to focus upon objective setting and work planning, as well as their own learning style. Your role is:

- to assist team members to review their setting of objectives;
- to monitor and review results of process with residents;
- to monitor the implementation of work plans drawn up in partnership with residents;
- to identify and close any gaps between achievements and objectives.

This particular model insists that key workers assess their original objectives and their impact upon work plans drawn up with residents. The process is designed to identify potential gaps, weaknesses or limitations to the actual work plan. The involvement of residents and carers is paramount in order to determine satisfaction with work undertaken. Additionally, third-party feedback from other team members offers further evidence as to whether residents' needs are being met. Collective discussion is the key to managing this process.

A gap may be described as resident dissatisfaction with elements of their care, such as lack of assistance with mobility, dietary needs being unmet, or lack of choice in relation to social activities. Self-assessment enables the team member, in partnership with the resident or carer, to take steps to close any gaps.

Think it over

Do you employ self-assessment as a means of identifying potential weaknesses in objective setting and work planning? What are its advantages in terms of promoting a higher quality of resident care?

Monitoring

After gaps in objective setting and work planning have been identified and steps have been taken to resolve them, you must ensure that your team members monitor the results of their work. How can this be achieved? One such method is to develop a monitoring results plan:

- identify how to overcome gaps in objective setting and work plans;
- set a time scale;
- set a review date;
- review outcomes.

The plan allows for opportunities for dynamic monitoring which is outcome orientated. Monitoring should focus upon the evidence required to ensure that gaps in both objective setting and work planning are identified and overcome. A set time scale ensures residents' needs remain a priority. A review date requires action to be proactive. Finally, a review of outcomes will validate the process and ensure that the agreed steps taken have met residents' needs.

Case study — Selma

You have introduced a staff self-assessment and monitoring policy which all key workers are expected to undertake as part of their designated work with your residents. A new starter, Selma, has recently been appointed key worker status.

- How will you provide the opportunities for her to assess and monitor her own performance against set objectives and existing work plans?
- If gaps are identified, how will you advise Selma to proceed?
- How does Selma negotiate new objectives and work plans to meet the resident's expressed needs?
- How does Selma monitor her own performance against newly negotiated objectives and work plans, to close any identified gaps?
- What steps does Selma need to undertake to ensure that the resident's needs are met using a monitoring results plan?
- How might outcomes be reviewed to validate the overall process?

You monitor the performance of teams and individuals at times most likely to maintain and improve effective performance

As manager, to ensure continuous improvement in work performance, you are required to monitor the performance of teams and individuals at times most likely to maintain and improve their performance. This may be achieved through:

- observed practice;
- formal and informal supervision;
- appraisal.

Observed practice

Observing team members' practice provides a unique opportunity to satisfy you that they and the team are working to the required standards. Observations can be formal and planned, or informal where situations present themselves. However, agreement must always be made in advance as part of the overall assessment and monitoring process, with resident, individual or team.

Identify what it is that is being monitored, such as risk assessment, safe handling techniques, empowerment of residents, communication skills, personal care, health care, privacy and dignity, social care and activities, or even taking complaints and maintaining protection of residents. The majority of these situations fall within the remit of the Care Standards Act 2000.

Always explain in advance with team and individuals the criteria you wish to observe, obtain agreement and offer immediate constructive feedback after the observation. Observation may also be undertaken using audio-video technology, which offers a more accurate means of giving objective feedback; with permission, it can also be used for future training purposes. Effective monitoring must always allow for the sharing of good practice if it is to remain developmental and performance led.

Think it over

Do you employ observed practice as part of your performance-led monitoring process? If so, explain why it remains effective.

Formal and informal supervision

Supervision of actual performance, be it for individuals or teams, either formal or informal, must be two-way, focused, reflective, developmental and mutually accountable process, actively aimed at improving knowledge, skills and occupational performance. Monitoring of this management tool at regular intervals, perhaps after each session, is one means by which you can be reassured that it serves to maintain and improve individual and collective performance.

Formal supervision is planned and regular. Agenda items are prepared in advance. Informal supervision is spontaneous. Either type of supervision will enable you to monitor the performance of individuals and teams.

What monitoring is involved in supervision?

- The standard of work completed.
- Depth and content of work.
- Tasks/objectives achieved.
- Residents' wishes and preferences.
- Assessment and work plan.
- The team member's abilities and limitations, and needs.
- Agreed tasks.

Be sure to discuss any difficulties.

You will need to ensure that the appropriate records are on file for statutory purposes, and that records or statements of supervision are made and are jointly signed with planned dates for the next meeting.

Outcome monitoring

The monitoring of outcomes must focus upon professional development: how the team and its members are performing in relation to organisational and their own objectives; how work plans are developing around residents' and carers' needs.

Outcomes must be measured in terms of the quality indicators set down in the Care Standards Act 2000. It will be necessary to show that National Minimum Standards are being achieved and to be able to set a benchmark for optimum performance and qualitative care in your practice setting.

Monitoring performance must therefore be seen as a process rather than an event. By continually monitoring desired outcomes at regular intervals, the supervisory process, both formal and informal, if managed effectively, will lead to improved personal practice.

Appraisal

An appraisal by the manager will seek to identify strengths and weaknesses and to resolve the latter with a view to ensuring that both individuals and teams perform to the best of their creative potential.

This statement might be supported by L. Mullins (1998):

> The process of management involves a continuous judgement on the behaviour and performance of staff. A formalised and systematic appraisal scheme will enable a regular assessment of individuals' performance, highlight potential and identify training and developmental needs. Most importantly, an effective appraisal scheme can improve the future performance of staff. The appraisal scheme can also form the basis of review of financial rewards and planned career progression.

This quote underpins the need for the manager to motivate individuals and simultaneously to monitor their performance.

Within the appraisal process, what are you monitoring?

In practice, you will be monitoring the performance targets which individuals and teams have chosen to improve, for example over the next quarter. You should set checkpoints at regular intervals, say fortnightly or monthly, to both review and measure the progress of how the target is being met. If targets have been mutually negotiated, kept realistic and are resident focused, then they are more likely to be achievable. Evidence of progress should be tangible, so that performance can be measured. At the end of a quarter, when the final review of the outcome of the set target area is undertaken, you must focus on achievement.

If the outcome has been met, the team member should be rewarded. This might take the form of performance-related pay or additional training; it should have been previously agreed.

Case study — A new appointment

You have recently been appointed manager of a small residential home specialising in dementia care. Although only in the post for two weeks, you have become increasingly concerned about a lack of consistency in performance levels of individuals in undertaking simple tasks. Effective monitoring of work performance to maintain standards and improve performance of individuals and teams now becomes your priority.

- How will you establish a system of observable practice to evidence performance levels and implement it in a non-threatening way?
- How will you change the monitoring of the existing supervisory process to focus on individual and team performance?
- How might you employ appraisal as a monitoring tool to improve actual and future performance of both individuals and teams?

Your assessment of the performance of teams and individuals is based on sufficient, valid and reliable information

As manager, any assessment you undertake, focusing upon the performance of either individuals or teams, must be based on sufficient, valid and reliable information. The assessment of performance should be seen as a dynamic developmental process rather than an event.

You must ensure that individuals and teams understand what appraisal means to their actual practice. The information given must be sufficient to enable them transfer to their practice mutually agreed targets that are measurable; the meeting of targets should be rewarded.

Appraisal performed using the five-stage method

Within this five-stage approach, information targets and progress can be seen, valued and measured. The process is systematic, with each stage being worked through before moving on to the next. The process is shown in Figure 19 as a series of steps to climb.

- First, you discuss with either individuals or teams their job descriptions and key areas of accountability. In other words, the areas of work for which they are paid. You also discuss with the individual or team how they might be rewarded, be it through performance-related pay, additional leave or training. The process is thus introduced.
- Second, you empower either individuals or teams to establish performance targets for chosen areas, within specific time limits, for example a shared care scheme between a family unit and residential setting, or reviewing the demand for beds to achieve a balance between respite care and full-time occupancy. Care needs to be taken to prevent work overload. Therefore, keep the areas realistic, resident centred and achievable.
- Third, you must focus upon how to action the target; this requires careful negotiation together with mutually agreed methods of measuring progress.
- Fourth, you must set check points weekly, fortnightly or monthly in order to achieve proactive assessment of progress and evidence of targets being met or unmet. The targets must be negotiated and may require some amendment to secure the desired outcome.
- Fifth, at the end of the chosen period, you must meet with individuals or teams to formally evaluate the evidence of achievement and, if appropriate, to reward success (as previously negotiated).

Use the five-stage model of appraisal as a means of assessment to ensure that information given to individuals to improve their performance can be managed and validated.

Figure 19. The five-stage model of appraisal.

You carry out your assessments objectively, against clear, agreed criteria

In order to facilitate genuine assessments with individuals and teams, you must agree accurate, realistic and achievable performance targets. Furthermore, the criteria agreed must be measurable. The five-stage appraisal model provides a mutually agreeable assessment vehicle by which actual and future standards can be improved, and the expressed needs of residents, carers, the organisation and the individual and team can be met. Rewards should be given for achievement.

Example of the five-stage model in practice: staff appraisal

- *Job content.* Care manager and individuals meet to discuss current job description and the key outcome areas for which they are paid to undertake. The individuals are to choose one area which they feel they can improve.
- *Performance targets.* With a chosen area, the care manager encourages individuals to set a performance target that focuses upon a resident, as well as organisational and own career aspirations for actual improvement to current practice. Keep it simple, realistic and attainable.
- *Negotiation.* Let team members take control and own their chosen area. Listen to their views. Identify what method of merit will be awarded upon completion and success.

- *Monitoring*. Set a time limit of no more than three months in which the target area is to be achieved. Listen to the individual viewpoint. Identify review periods (e.g. weekly, fortnightly). Encourage individuals to identify what evidence they need to collate for each review session throughout the actual process. Fix dates, times and venue for each session in advance.
- *Evaluate the outcome*. At the end of the quarter, evaluate the whole process and the key improvements which the target area was set to achieve. This must be evidenced to include resident, organisational and individual need(s). If achieved, bestow merit award immediately.

Your assessments take due account of the personal circumstances of team members and the organisational constraints on their work

Any assessment you propose to undertake must strike a balance between the personal circumstances of team members and conversely the organisational constraints on their work. Undoubtedly, there is an interrelationship between the two. However, you must be able to differentiate and manage your assessments within the boundaries of team members' occupational roles and the policies of your establishment.

The Care Standards Act 2000 prescribes in Standard 30 (30.4):

> That all staff receive a minimum of three paid training days per year (including in-house training) and have an individual training and development assessment and profile.

This minimum requirement will ensure that team members meet the National Training Organisations (NTO) workforce training targets and that your practice setting will therefore continue to meet the changing needs of your residents. Your organisational policies for assessment must be geared to meet National Minimum Standards. Resources such as time and finance must be budgeted for to meet this requirement.

It therefore makes for good practice to have a policy for contractual supervision, which can identify specific training needs and skills and can be worked with developmentally. As required by NMS, there is a formal requirement under Standard 36 of the Care Standards Act 2000 that all care staff receive formal supervision every second month or the equivalent of six times a year. This can follow in-house or external training, or continuous assessment, as laid down in Standard 28.1 of the Act, which requires 50% of all trained members of staff to have achieved an NVQ2 or equivalent by 2005. Clearly, all training must be supervised and monitored; it should also be outcome orientated for achievement purposes and appropriately rewarded.

You must retain awareness of the different circumstances and sensitivities of team members. Not all team members will approach assessment in a proactive way. Some may perceive it as a threat to their autonomy or their practice, while others may display anxiety at the very thought that their work will be observed, questioned and evaluated and a judgement made upon it.

Given this background of National Minimum Standards and different staff needs, any form of assessment must be sensitively managed, to avoid confusion or dysfunction. Ideally, it should be approached from an organisational basis.

Assessment should facilitate:

- team member initiative and imagination, expressed through individual and team practice;
- the recognition of individual, team and organisational success;
- the motivation of individuals and teams through personal ownership of organisational goals, kept realistic and appropriately rewarded;
- the sharing of responsibility between team members and the organisation in a competitive marketplace.

Assessment must foster the idea that the needs of people at work matter. The assessment of individuals should involve:

- the idea that individual team members' views matter and can make a difference;
- constructive and equal support;
- fair and accurate feedback regarding their own performance;
- help in achieving the individual's own goals and in identifying training needs via their personal assessment profile;
- individual efforts being appropriately recognised and rewarded fairly.

If assessment can be promoted as a valuable individual and organisational vehicle for facilitating equal and fair support, for enabling individuals to achieve, while at the same time being seen to contribute to the organisation's success, it may be more palatable and acceptable to staff.

Organisational constraints must be managed according to National Minimum Standards. Individuals must be similarly supported to meet those Standards and their different needs addressed to ensure that they are not disadvantaged. In this way, team members' aspirations can be harmonised in line with organisational development and changing residents' needs. Therefore, it could be seen that fair but proactive assessment remains the key to this process succeeding.

How might you ensure that your assessments follow National Minimum Standards, while recognising the different needs of your team, but do not disadvantage their individual development?

Case study — Organisational assessment

As the registered manager, you are aware that many of your existing organisational policies regarding staffing, together with management and administration, will be required to change to comply with the Care Standards Act 2000.

- How will you ensure that your assessment structure complies with the National Minimum Standards?
- How will you take account of team members' circumstances and needs when considering assessment?
- How will you provide opportunities to sensitise each member to the National Minimum Standards required of their professional practice?
- What steps might you take to support team members within the practice setting?
- How will you de-stigmatise the role of assessment to meet the new Standards as well as team members' aspirations and fears?

C13.4 Learning outcomes

- You provide feedback to teams and individuals in a situation and in a form and manner most likely to maintain and improve their performance.
- The feedback you provide is clear, and is based on your objective assessment of their performance against agreed objectives.
- Your feedback acknowledges your team members' achievements.
- Your feedback provides your team members with constructive suggestions and encouragement for improving future performance against their work and development objectives.
- The way in which you provide feedback shows respect for individuals and the need for confidentiality.
- You give opportunities to teams and individuals to respond to feedback, and to recommend how they could improve their performance in the future.

You provide feedback to teams and individuals in a situation and in a form and manner most likely to maintain and improve their performance

As manager, you must provide feedback to both individuals and teams as part of a continuous process of informing them of the outcome of specific and agreed work plans and events. It is important first to establish ground rules regarding the giving and receiving of feedback.

Your feedback must be:

- accuracy
- honest
- fair
- set in context
- backed up with evidence.

The ground rules regarding feedback

- *Confidentiality*. Information shared remains within the remit of the individual or team and is not disclosed to others; it is always given in a private environment.
- *Performance focused*. Feedback focuses upon individual and/or team performance only and not on subjective personality traits.
- *Outcomes*. Feedback addresses achievement and seeks to evidence this for developmental performance purposes only.
- *Constructive*. It will be a constructive process, sensitive to individual needs, irrespective of whether the feedback is positive or negative.
- *Prepared*. It will be thoughtfully prepared, given in writing and delivered orally in a calm, assertive and friendly manner.
- *Time scale*. Feedback should be delivered by joint agreement and at an agreed time after the event.
- *Joint process*. It must allow for two-way interaction to ensure the viewpoints of individuals and teams are heard and clarified, and address the agreed outcome area.
- *Plot solutions*. Differentiate between what has been achieved and what needs to be improved, and plot solutions together for task achievement.

Where will feedback be required?

Feedback should be given on:

- observed practice;
- appraisal interviews;
- supervisory practice – formal and informal;
- team briefings/meetings;
- joint work;
- work-based counselling.

The delivery of feedback

Feedback must be delivered in a supportive manner which enables both the individual and team to focus upon actual and future performance. The content must be kept simple, understandable, accurate and concise. Restrict the feedback to single events or outcomes, as this provides an opportunity for a detailed and in-depth discussion within realistic time limits. Ensure that the feedback is delivered on completion of an event or outcome. This maintains accuracy and focus. Ensure that your feedback values the individual or team, and convey the value of their contribution or performance. Offer praise for work well done; be warm and enthusiastic.

A positive approach is far more constructive than criticism. If the outcome or event does not meet required or agreed standards, assist the individual and/or team to understand why. Listen to their viewpoints, take on board their opinions and fears, and assist discussion about what was done, how it might be done differently and how it could be improved. Involve the individual or team in the process of plotting solutions and finding more effective ways of working.

Case study — Appraisal feedback

You have recently introduced an appraisal programme within your practice setting. You have phased this process in to ensure it remains manageable, and began with your senior staff to serve as effective role models to their respective care teams. Their final appraisal interview is today.

- What do you need to consider in order to provide effective feedback?
- What kinds of agreed ground rules might you employ during your feedback role?
- Will you agree these in advance?
- What manner will you adopt?

The feedback you provide is clear, and is based on your objective assessment of their performance against agreed objectives

It is essential that any feedback given is based on an objective assessment of either an individual's or a team's performance against agreed objectives. The objectives ideally should be mutually negotiated and agreed at the outset of your assessment. Therefore, irrespective of the type of assessment, you negotiate in advance the ground rules for the setting of objectives.

Ground rules for objectives

- *Content.* The objectives should be clear, concise, specific and accurate, which is evidenced through structured observation, written evidence and third-party feedback from residents and carers.
- *Preparation.* What evidence can the individual or team produce to support their objective setting and work planning to meet desired outcomes?
- *Presentation.* How was the event or task managed? What knowledge and skills were demonstrated? Was the verbal communication used appropriate to both the cultural and personal sensitivities of residents or others?
- *How were obstacles overcome?* Did the individual identify any barriers, and in what creative ways were they overcome?
- *Achievement.* Was the task or event achieved to the agreed criteria or objectives? Was this appropriately evidenced? How could resident satisfaction be quantified?
- *How to improve future performance.* How did the individuals/team evaluate their performance? Did they identify any limitations or any improvements that could be made? What are the implications for future training or skills-based learning? Look at potential training – internal (joint work), work-based assessment, NVQ levels 2 or 3, external college, or interactive (IT distance learning) – that could be undertaken to improve their future performance to meet new Standards as well as the changing needs of residents.

Try it out

Consider the types of objectives you would seek to agree and set in order to provide both clear and accurate feedback with a focus on work performance. Apply your agreed objectives in order to give accurate feedback on individual or team performance.

Your feedback acknowledges your team members' achievements

As manager, your feedback should acknowledge team members' achievements through constructive criticism, positive reinforcement and praise. Appropriate use of reinforcement plays a central role in encouraging team members to follow organisational guidelines and agreed objectives.

A simple practice illustration

At a team meeting you ask your team members for their suggestions about creating a programme of social activities for the festive season. One member, Paula, had prepared her input, which she shared with the team. Her ideas were well received by all. Other members were equally encouraged to build on Paula's ideas, thus enabling collective input and agreement. You thank Paula for her preparation; immediately her facial expression changes and she beams. The entire experience positively reinforces Paula's behaviour; in the future she is more likely to put forward ideas again.

Praise

Taking the trouble to recognise and congratulate team members on work well done reinforces self-esteem and serves to maintain and improve individual and collective motivation. Your praise should be focused and specific; it needs to be perceived as both accurate and authentic. It must always serve to encourage, and to allow recipients to feel good about themselves while at the same time to learn from the feedback.

Choosing your words carefully ensures the recipient understands how genuine you are and you mean what you say. Be specific, as in the following example:

> You really responded well to Mary's expressed needs. Your body language equated with your verbal expressions, demonstrating both empathy and unconditional personal regard.

The use of praise does need to be learned and practised. Managers often forget or even deprive individuals or teams of this valuable and simple reward.

Think it over

When was the last time you praised a member of your team? Try to remember the event.

Case study — Jane, Helen and Tom

A recent flu epidemic increased the incidence of reported staff sickness by some 30%. However, Jane, Helen and Tom volunteered without request to cover absent colleagues. Collectively they undertook split shifts and weekend work for some 10 days.

- How do you respond to their unconditional commitment?
- How do you reinforce such generous behaviour?
- How might you offer praise for all three serving as outstanding role models to the whole staff team?

Your feedback provides your team members with constructive suggestions and encouragement for future performance against their work and development objectives

In order that your feedback provides team members with constructive suggestions and encouragement for future performance against relevant work and development objectives, you must ensure that your feedback focuses on actual performance. In order to simplify this process, identify and use evidence of actual events, acts or behaviours which positively reinforces what members have done, which they can reflect on and learn from, and be encouraged to perform against.

Ideally, your feedback should creatively persuade members to focus on how performance can be changed, and thereby develop their personal and work-related objectives. Additionally, your feedback should encourage members:

- to generate their own ideas;
- to share those ideas openly;
- to test them against existing objectives and work plans to identify limitations and 'gaps' in their own performance;
- to close those gaps.
- to engage in continuous development, that is self-assessment, which is both current and developmental.

Feedback should assist in shaping existing and future performance. For your feedback to remain constructive and to encourage future work performance, it cannot remain static but must be dynamic. Then it is more likely to facilitate more creative kinds of continuous, outcome-related development.

One of your team members, David, demonstrates senior carer potential, provided he can be seen to develop continuously his performance.

- How might your feedback in both supervision and appraisal assist David to reflect and learn from his actual work experience?
- How might your feedback assist him to change and improve his practice?
- How might your feedback help him to evidence developmental change in his work practice?
- How might your feedback assist David to identify his limitations in work practices and encourage him to resolve these on a developmental basis?
- How might your feedback encourage him to engage in dynamic self-assessment to evidence his continuous development and improved practice?

The way in which you provide feedback shows respect for individuals and the need for confidentiality

Because feedback is a continuous process, the manner in which it is given must always demonstrate both acceptance and respect for the individual, combined with delivery in a confidential manner and environment. A culture of respect and confidentiality are fundamental principles of good practice. Therefore your feedback needs to demonstrate both unconditionally, in order that they become role modelled as the norm of best practice.

Respect

Whether feedback is given after observed practice or during supervision or appraisal, it is imperative that you convey:

- respect for individual efforts no matter how great or small;
- respect for individual needs and circumstances;
- respect for individual sensitivities;
- respect for individual choices – even if they are wrong, your feedback can point this out in a friendly and calm manner, which encourages mutual respect for each other's role;
- respect for individuals' decision making, so as to encourage future improvements through self-assessment and continuous development.

Respect for individuals is fundamental to the feedback process if it is to retain its meaning as a two-way giving and receiving exercise. Without the element of respect, constructive feedback loses its purpose.

Confidentiality

Feedback must preserve confidentiality. Establish ground rules for how feedback will be given and how confidentiality will be retained within an agreement or feedback contract.

- Feedback is given to individuals in a private environment.
- Feedback is shared only with the individuals concerned, unless otherwise agreed.
- Individual sensitivities regarding disclosure must be respected at all times.
- Feedback to more than one individual must remain within the dedicated environment.
- Sanctions for breaches of confidentiality must be imposed to ensure a culture of trust is realised.
- Feedback can be given verbally and non-verbally, but, regardless, the principles of the Data Protection Act 1990 concerning the receiving, giving and storage of information must be adhered to at all times.

Case study — Sylvia's supervision contract

You have introduced a new supervision policy within your care home. Supervisory contracts for all staff have now been introduced. A senior carer named Sylvia, whom you will be supervising on a one-to-one basis every 10 days, presents for her first session. As part of the supervisory contract, your feedback and the manner in which it is delivered must demonstrate both respect and confidentiality.

- How will you reassure Sylvia that respect for her person and performance will always be maintained?
- What examples might you give to show your commitment?
- What ground rules for preserving confidentiality will you agree and set?
- What role does Sylvia have in preserving the confidentiality of her supervisory process?
- How will you agree what information shared in supervision is confidential or not?
- What principles of best practice will you include in your contract to ensure that both respect and confidentiality within the feedback process are always maintained?

You give opportunities to teams and individuals to respond to feedback, and to recommend how they could improve their performance in the future

You must deliver your feedback in a private, professional and friendly manner. The atmosphere must be relaxed and conducive to open discussion.

Individuals and teams must be encouraged to discuss both the strengths and weaknesses of their performance. They must collectively understand the value and benefits of improvement. Ideally, look for joint solutions. Listen to the individual's or team's perspective and decide together how their performance may be improved. Set up an agreed action plan which focuses upon improving future performance. Keep it:

- simple;
- realistic;
- achievable;
- managed.

Feedback which is supportive, which does focus on what can be undertaken in a practical way and which engenders partnership is more likely to improve actual and future performance and achieve what become mutually desired outcomes.

Evidence collection

You must prove that you provide feedback to teams and individuals on their performance to the National Occupational Standard of competence.

You can show evidence of positive and negative feedback by referring to the first three sections of element C13.4.

You can show evidence of both spoken and written feedback by referring to the first two sections, including the case study material.

You can show evidence of three of the following: formal appraisal; that your feedback encourages team members to set and meet developmental objectives; that your feedback acknowledges team members' achievements; your feedback shows respect for individuals and the need for confidentiality.

Finally, for further additional evidence, you can also show how you maintain motivation, morale and effectiveness, by acknowledging team members' achievements and how you have sustained this through positive reinforcement and praise.

D4 Provide Information to Support Decision Making

This unit is about providing information so that sound decisions can be taken. It covers the obtaining of relevant information, its recording and storage, and its analysis. It also covers advising and informing other people.

The elements are:

- Obtain information for decision making.
- Record and store information.
- Analyse information to support decision making.
- Advise and inform others.

Learning outcomes

- You identify the information you need to make the required decisions.
- You use reliable and wide-ranging sources of information to meet current and future information requirements.
- Your methods of obtaining information are consistent with organisational values, policies and legal requirements.

You identify the information you need to make the required decisions

Information represents the foundation upon which all decisions are based, but you need to identify the right information in order to make the right decisions. Take a typical practice example: if the information you forward on about potential residents, via their original assessment and accompanying care plan, is inaccurate, and you have offered accommodation without undertaking a pre-assessment, then the outcome may be traumatic and costly for both the resident and your practice setting.

How do you identify the right information in order to make the right decision? The following criteria could act as a checklist with which to assess information:

✓ reliability;
✓ accuracy;
✓ relevance;
✓ precision;
✓ timeliness;
✓ thoroughness;

✓ sufficiency;
✓ cost-effectiveness (in particular, information which is obtained without delay or externally from research or contracting secondary suppliers tends to be expensive).

The format of your information

Some information will be quantitative, that is numerical, and some qualitative, or subjective. Staff costings, for example, will give you numerical information on hours worked, average hourly wage rates and weekly costs, which in turn will give you a weekly wage cost, an annual wage cost and total percentage of gross income. Such information is a prerequisite to effective budgetary management. Such information is considered in more detail in Unit B3, 'Manage the Use of Financial Resources' (see in particular the Appendix to that chapter).

Qualitative information is not so objective. In fact, it might be described as subjective, as it attempts to measure feelings and expressions of satisfaction, for example. How might this be recorded and used in care management practice? One way is to focus upon *outputs*. Consider, for example, how you might attempt to measure the satisfaction of residents and carers with the qualitative nature of their assessed and requested care. The information contained in their original assessment (on admission) and reassessments, supported by ongoing monitoring and review of their individual care plan, should have identified any weaknesses in service delivery, resident dissatisfaction, new needs or changed preferences.

Case study — A new referral

You receive a telephone referral from your local social services department, to accommodate a 92-year-old man. You are informed that he is currently blocking a bed in a local NHS trust hospital and now requires immediate discharge, as he has made a full recovery, is mobile and is able to care for himself. You are required to have accommodation available for him within four hours.

- How will you go about making a judgement on the accuracy, relevance, reliability and sufficiency of information given to support your decision making in this instance?
- How will you identify any contradictory or insufficient information given?
- What information for admissions does your internal system demand?
- Will you (or one of your authorised people) make an emergency pre-assessment in hospital of this man's current needs and wishes?

Use reliable and wide-ranging sources of information to meet current and future information requirements

Information is vital to everyday operational practice and planning. Your sources of information should be wide-ranging. These sources can be broadly categorised as internal and external. Internal information will provide you with the information of whether your care setting is meeting its designated objectives, while external information will give a broader picture of outside influences, such as changes in legislation, and will enable you to plan to meet changing statutory requirements as well as changing needs.

Internal information

Your own, internal information systems will generate a great deal of useful information. For example, your budgetary control system will produce records of expenditure, income generation and staffing costs. You will have other records from the assessment of residents' needs and preferences, and perhaps records of complaints about care. This information contributes to ongoing monitoring and review of individual residents' care plans. Personnel records should cover time-keeping, absenteeism, observed and appraised information on actual performance, training done and ongoing professional development. This information contributes to staff profiling, essential to work allocation and delegation.

Internal information also consists of the more mundane daily diary records, rotas, records of telephone, fax or email messages. However, the value of this kind of information should not be underestimated because it will influence decision making at all levels throughout the working day.

External information

External information (e.g. the Care Standards Act 2000) can have a profound influence on practice. Professional journals, such as *Community Care*, will provide information on a wide range of social work and policy issues. Additionally suppliers, such as wholesalers, will invoice your care setting for goods. This financial information represents evidence of expenditure required for budgetary formulation and costing cycles or forecasts, which will be basis for financial planning.

Think it over

How might you ensure that your sources of both internal and external information are reliable? Consider the areas you need to focus upon and jot down improvements you need to make.

Your methods of obtaining information are consistent with organisational values, policies and legal requirements

To ensure that your methods of obtaining information are consistent with your organisational values, policies and legal requirements (i.e. relevant statute), they must be the subject of regular review. Consider performing such a review in terms of the four methods of obtaining information identified below.

Verbal questions

Staff must be taught how to ask questions. This should cover the manner in which they ask questions as well as the content/wording of questions, so as to avoid direct and indirect discrimination.

Four types of spoken question are suitable because of their gentle persuasive but friendly nature:

- specific,
- probing,
- prompting,
- reflective.

You must always remember the principles of your business operation, which is the provision of qualitative care. To provide that care you need reliable information on the changing needs of residents and staff. Ensure your verbal questioning does not compromise the values and principles which your organisation and its policies have adopted.

Written questions

With written questions it becomes especially important to ensure that they are free of jargon, focused, simple and concise. Written questions lend themselves to a more formal (and therefore less friendly) way of obtaining information. However, written questions will be regulated by policy and rules regarding what type of questions may be asked, and by whom, their wording, and their timing and frequency.

Written questions must never infringe people's privacy or rights. Responses should, whenever possible, be voluntary. It cannot be voluntary, for example, with staff disciplinary action, where both spoken and written questioning become a contractual part of the terms of employment.

Reading

This method of obtaining information can form part of unit policy if it is assimilated throughout the staff group and is a required part of contractual practice.

General reading of innovatory practice within the care sector should be encouraged throughout the staff team. An effective manager will advise staff about *selective* reading, to prevent information overload, as well as about how to recognise bias in what they read. Effective use of reading can assist each member of staff to reassess their own practice as well as to challenge the value system of the unit, team and individual. Sustained reading can open windows of opportunity for all and assist developmental learning.

Listening and watching

The use of listening and watching must be regulated in order to prevent it being intrusive. Your value base and policy, as well as legal requirements, will have a bearing on how this means of gathering information, in particular, is used. You must ensure that there is initially a *need* to listen and watch. Ascertain why, where and by whom the listening and watching are to be done. Are there personnel trained in this dual skill? Question their receptiveness to what is seen and heard, differentiate between fact and interpretation, and ensure they recognise the barriers and how they are overcome. Clearly, this method does demand practice of the most sensitive kind and observed assessment of its employment is ideal. It remains an essential part of care practice, which must be taught to all in order that residents' and carers' needs are proactively met in all instances.

Try it out

Consider the four specific methods of obtaining information (i.e. verbal questions, written questions, reading and listening and watching). How might they be used consistently with your unit's value system, policies and legal requirements to demonstrate best practice?

Evidence collection D4.1 — Obtain information for decision making

You must prove that you obtain information for decision making to the National Occupational Standard of competence.

You must show evidence that you use at least three of the following types of sources of information: people within your organisation; internal information systems; published media; specially commissioned research; records and documents; recipients of the service.

You must show that you obtain both qualitative and quantitative information.

Additionally, you must show evidence that you use four of the following; spoken questioning; written questioning; reading; listening and watching; formal research conducted personally; formal research conducted by third parties.

Learning outcomes

- Your systems and procedures for recording and storing information are suitable for the purpose and make efficient use of resources.
- The way you record and store information complies with organisational policies and legal requirements.
- The information you record and store is available only to authorised people.
- You make recommendations for improvements that take account of organisational constraints.

Your systems and procedures for recording and storing information are suitable for the purpose and make efficient use of resources

It is likely that most settings will combine manual records with some degree of computerisation for their information systems. Computer-generated forms represent a combination of the two when they are completed by hand by your staff team. They are a very useful way of recording information. Examples include:

- daily resident assessment sheets;
- care plan monitoring forms;
- key worker sheets (see the Appendix for an example);
- fluid balance charts (see the Appendix for an example);
- accident report forms (see the Appendix for an example);
- handling assessment forms (see the Appendix for an example).

The advantages of such forms are that they require a minimum degree of literacy to complete, they are cost-effective and time-limited, and they are resident friendly, in that they enable residents to be involved in the decision making regarding the delivery of their care. Additionally, since many of these assessment forms are completed daily, they accommodate the recording of residents' opinions and feelings.

Their disadvantages are that manual records are duplicated, they demand updating, and their storage in a confidential and a secure environment may be a problem. Residents' files need to be placed in filing cabinets in alphabetical order, for ease of access. However, the volume of the paper generated places huge demands on office space. Problems regarding location, security and restricted access can be hard to resolve, especially in practice settings where offices are small and cramped.

Cramped conditions can cause problems when it comes to keeping information secure.

Information may start out in a manual format but much of it can be quickly transferred to disk format and held on a computer, and accessed only via an electronic password for security purposes. Your computer programme will enable you to receive external information from contractors, accountants, solicitors, doctors and so on, and allow you to email them directly. This will reduce costs and increase the timeliness and security of your information.

A combination of manual and computerised systems will enable you and your staff team to manage and monitor a flow of information. It will be necessary to ensure that the costs of recording and storing information do not exceed your budget. The operational procedures for the recording of information and access to it must be kept simple, and be specific to both manager and staff team, for everyday application in accordance with the principles of the Data Protection Act 1998.

Try it out

Identify with examples how you record and store quantitative and qualitative information within your practice setting. Additionally, specify particular problems you may encounter with your existing system and procedures.

You realise your manual information systems need changing – within your existing budget – in order for them to meet the requirements of the Data Protection Act 1998 in relation to the receiving, storage, recording and retrieval of information relating to your residents.

- What safeguards will you employ for the receipt, recording, storage and retrieval of resident information?
- What ideas do you have about the marriage between manual and computerised systems of information?
- Does the application of computers offer you better opportunities to record and store information securely, and what additional problems might this pose?
- How will you continue to record quantitative and qualitative information using a combination of manual and computerised systems for everyday practice?
- How will you redeploy space within the building in order to store and retrieve information securely?

The way you record and store information complies with organisational policies and legal requirements

As manager, you must ensure that your information systems comply with the Data Protection Act 1998. You should therefore develop an organisational policy that informs staff of how to record and store information as part of their contractual codes of practice, and that conforms to statute. Your organisational policy will be specific to yourself and your staff team. Your policy must be kept simple, realistic, achievable and affordable.

You are responsible and accountable for what you do and how your staff perform. A great part of your staff teamwork will be focused on recording manual information. Your own role (designated by yourself) may focus on the overall structure of the practice setting and its financial management. This role will demand a combination of internal and external information and the use of both manual and computerised records. While you can delegate to key relevant people, such as your senior care workers or nominated staff, you remain responsible for ensuring that both the recording and storage of information comply with organisational policy and the law.

Your organisational policy must be broken down into a series of points which inform staff:

- what information to record;
- how to record it;
- how to share information with their allocated residents;
- how to protect confidentiality.

The Caldicott principles

The six Caldicott principles originate from a 1997 government report by a committee chaired by Dame Fiona Caldicott. The report focused on patient identifiable information within the NHS and made a number of recommendations on how it should be processed. The recommendations, when turned into principles, can be employed in all work settings, including your residential unit. One of the proposals was for each organisation to have a 'guardian', that is, a designated person responsible for safeguarding the confidentiality of information. The Caldicott guardian could be yourself or a senior member of your staff.

Principle 1. Purpose of the information

The use or transfer of resident identifiable information within your organisation has to be justifiable. Examples could be the computer-generated forms discussed above, for which consideration would have to be given to when and how this information is used and by whom. Rules must be clearly defined.

Principle 2. Resident identifiable information should not be used unless necessary

Any resident identifiable information should not be used unless absolutely necessary and then only with strict controls.

Principle 3. Reduction of resident identifiable information

You must provide evidence to support the established use of resident information.

Each item of resident identifiable information has to be supported and evidenced for use established. Where there is no need to do so, do not expose your resident identity to a third party.

Principle 4. Accessibility

Staff working with a resident should be allowed access only to the identifiable information they actually require: the confidentiality of information on all other areas of a resident's personal life should be safeguarded.

Principle 5. Responsibilities

Your Caldicott guardian, using your organisational policy, must ensure that the rules on confidentiality are understood by all staff. Adherence to these rules must be both supervised and monitored.

Principle 6. Compliance with the law

Your Caldicott guardian must ensure that any use of resident identifiable information conforms to the law.

Try it out

Appoint a guardian and within your organisational policy set up a system where the Caldicott principles can become operational. Monitor your results, over the short, medium and long term, to ensure they can be tailored within the law to be both practical and beneficial for residents.

Confidentiality

When you have an organisational policy in place, your next priority must be confidentiality. In practical terms, manual records need to be kept in lockable filing cabinets. Each resident's file needs to be marked and appropriately secured so that only relevant people have access to the information, and then only to the specific information they can justifiably be shown to require. Filing cabinets can be electronically secured and only relevant staff need to know the access code, and your Caldicott guardian can legally ensure this procedure is followed.

Resident information held on disk or CD-ROM can be kept in a secure room and computer access passwords can be given only to relevant people.

Information procedures

There are several procedures which, if combined with a simple and practical organisational policy, will help your practice setting to record and store information legally and cost-effectively.

The banking method

The flow of confidential resident information within your practice setting can be controlled using the banking method. Information is 'banked' in one restricted area. This ensures that after information is received, only your relevant and authorised people are allowed access. Your Caldicott guardian would then be held accountable for your information bank to operate and comply with the law.

The banking method is an organisational policy device for restricting access to the flow of information. It can be adopted by other organisations to ensure that resident confidentiality is maintained when information has to be passed on (e.g. to primary health care trusts, your local NHS trust hospitals or social services department).

Proprietorship

With this method, information held manually or on computer has its own 'proprietor' who is registered to hold that information, access it, use it and justify its use at all times. This would be personally supervised by your Caldicott guardian.

Personal responsibility

Personal responsibility is a method your Caldicott guardian might consider to encourage a culture of organisational confidentiality. In this way, all members of staff are encouraged to think about resident confidentiality at all times to prevent the misuse, intentionally or through ignorance, of all resident identifiable information.

Case study — Record and store information legally

As manager of a 30-bed private residential home for older persons, you realise that your organisational policy for the recording and storage of resident identifiable information must be realistic, achievable and cost-efficient, so it complies with the law. How will you proceed?

- Will you action the Caldicott principles and appoint a Caldicott guardian?
- How will you transfer the Caldicott principles from policy into practice?
- How will you train your staff to record resident identifiable information in confidence?
- What methods of information storage might you consider to protect residents' confidentiality, as well as to comply with the law?
- How will you restrict access and use to that which is justifiable by law on all resident information held on manual or computerised systems?
- To encourage a culture of organisational confidentiality, what other methods for recording and storing resident information might you consider appropriate, and time- and cost-efficient?

The information you record and store is available only to authorised people

The information your record, be it from external or internal information systems, be it quantitative or qualitative, will be accessible via a combination of manual or computerised systems for your authorised people, subject to control. Your Caldicott guardian will ensure the application of the six Caldicott principles and the protection of resident identifiable information in accordance with the Data Protection Act 1998.

It is acknowledged that information relating to residents must be recorded and stored, but only in accordance with the Data Protection Act 1998. In practice, this means the personal information must be:

- accurate;
- relevant;
- not excessive;
- retained no longer than necessary;
- lawfully processed;
- stored securely and confidentially.

Similarly, any *transfer* of resident information to a third party, which must be done only if necessary, must follow a system of control (see above).

Your authorised people can be the 'proprietors' of all resident identifiable information. They will be required to justify its access and usage, to ensure that unnecessary information is retained no longer than necessary, and to reduce the volume of information in order that only essential information is retained. The proprietors become your role models for the protection, recording and storage of all resident identifiable information, in order that a culture of organisational responsibility is both inspired and complies with the law.

The 'proprietors' must be supervised by the Caldicott guardian to ensure that they use only information they require and that they apply your organisational policy of security to ensure that no other party has access to it. They will have responsibility to secure lockable or electronically secured filing cabinets together with access codes to computerised information. Your authorised people must therefore be dependable, thorough and honest.

Think it over

What criteria for appointing an authorised person to record and store resident identifiable information would you consider? Make a list to assist your decision making.

You make recommendations for improvement that take account of organisational constraints

The recommendations for improvement to your systems and procedures of managing resident identifiable information must take account of organisational constraints. The chief constraint will relate to the resources you have available. Your recommendations therefore must be compatible with your current resources and accurately budgeted in your business and financial plans. The Data Protection Act 1998 became law on 1 March 2000. It was expected of all managers to plan and accommodate the eight new principles in their budgets and objectives as from 1 April 2000.

Think it over

Consider and identify the constraints which your recommendations are likely to impose on your practice setting and write an action plan with a view to overcome and comply with the legal requirements of the Data Protection Act 1998.

You are likely to face the following specific organisational constraints and demands:

- additional costs;
- changes to job descriptions (new duties);
- time for the administration of your new system;
- replacement of equipment (i.e. lockable filing cabinets and new filing systems);
- new software to protect computerised resident information;
- training and supervision of both your Caldicott guardian and new information proprietors to the required standards.

To overcome these constraints and meet these demands you must exercise your management skills. Three will be pertinent:

- proactive planning;
- managing a transitory process;
- effective budgeting.

In order to establish a culture of confidentiality, you are not managing an event but a transitory process, where your relevant people will have to be sensitised, trained and supervised. Your budgetary skills will enable you to plan for the purchase of new equipment and software.

Changes to job descriptions will have to be negotiated. Depending on the size of your organisation, it may involve detailed discussion with third parties, such as relevant trade unions and solicitors. The cost and time spent on training are very much the manager's perogative. If you understand the legal requirements, and you know what system and procedures you wish to have in place, then you may decide to arrange in-house training for your relevant people (perhaps one hour per week, over 12 weeks), complete with weekly monitoring and supervision of progression. Alternatively, you may choose to bring in a specialist external trainer, although this will be expensive. You might contact your local college of further education, which would probably be able to assist at a minimum cost. Interactive distance learning via the Internet is another possibility. Remember, individual learning styles differ and people learn at different rates.

In-house training can aid discussion about the management of resources.

Organisational constraints will always remain, but they can be overcome in a cost-efficient and managed way. Moreover, constraints offer no protection if you fail to meet your legal obligations.

Case study — Working with organisational constraint

You recognise that to operationalise your recommendations for new systems and procedures, to protect all resident identifiable information and to comply with the Data Protection Act 1998, there will be certain organisational constraints to overcome. How do you proceed and simultaneously comply with the letter of the law?

- How will you prioritise the constraints you face?
- What benchmarks or rating system might you employ to assist you in this process?
- What methods will you employ and why?
- How will you work with both your organisational priorities and constraints but still comply with the law?
- How will you supervise this process?

D4.3

Learning outcomes

- You identify clear objectives for your analysis which are consistent with the decisions which you need to make.
- You use methods of analysis which are suitable to achieve the objectives.
- You identify relevant patterns and trends.
- You support your conclusions with reasoned argument and appropriate evidence.
- In presenting the results of your analysis you differentiate clearly between fact and opinion.

You identify clear objectives for your analysis which are consistent with the decisions which you need to make

The objectives for your analysis must be clear and consistent, as their outcome will be measured both quantitatively and qualitatively. Therefore, what objectives do you derive from your existing analysis, which inform decisions you will need to make?

Your first objective must be to establish a culture of confidentiality, which is planned and not ad hoc. It must be organisation-wide and actually contribute to day-to-day operations. If effective, it will lead to constructive changes in organisational policy on practice and the protection of all resident identifiable information.

Your second objective must support the former, and your analysis of the practical protection of confidentiality, which will be achieved with the help of your Caldicott guardian. This person will take responsibility for the management and flow of information, its access, and justify its use and confidential storage and transfer. In tandem with your guardian, who cannot solely manage this process, you appoint your proprietors from among your relevant people. These individuals will be registered, authorised and supervised by your Caldicott guardian to access resident identifiable information, only when required and justified.

Your Caldicott guardian is responsible for your access to and use of information.

Your third objective supports your overall culture of confidentiality, which is the upgrading of security of information held on manual and computerised records. Combined with this, you need to provide both safe accommodation for your records and ensure your equipment can hold information securely, yet be accessible to your relevant people (proprietors and guardian) at all times.

Your final objective must be to sensitise and train your staff to operate an information system which upholds confidentiality. Initial and ongoing training and supervision will be required to ensure understanding and compliance with the legal requirements of the Data Protection Act 1998.

Your identified objectives are therefore clear and consistent and meet their designated purpose to inform and guide the decision making you choose to engage in. Therefore, they are formal and planned, not informal and ad hoc. Any decisions made will be the natural outcome of this process. In this instance they focus upon:

- information security and ownership;
- updating, recording and storing resident identifiable information;
- identifying the training needs of staff;
- identifying current versus future needs in relation to obtaining, recording and storing information, which supports a dynamic culture of confidentiality owned by all staff.

Think it over

What objectives might you consider to inform decision making and yet still retain a culture of confidentiality in your practice setting?

Case study — Objective setting versus decision making

You recognise that to comply legally with the Data Protection Act 1998, you must identify and set clear and consistent objectives to work towards. These objectives, if effective, will inform your final decision making to action this process. How will you proceed?

- Why should you read the Data Protection Act 1998 and understand its principles?
- Will you analyse your current system for obtaining, recording and storage of information and why do this?
- Will you set realistic and consistent objectives which you can work towards, and why do this?
- How might you undertake this task?
- How will your objective setting inform your final decision making? Give examples.
- How can you be certain that your objective setting is formal and planned, and not informal and ad hoc?

You use methods of analysis which are suitable to achieve the objectives

Your methods of analysis to achieve your objectives must be kept simple, so that they can be readily understood by you and your relevant people.

The first step is to recognise that there is in fact a need for objectives to be set. Then a series of questions will guide you:

- What am I attempting to achieve?
- What information do I need?
- Whom should I consult?
- What solutions are available?

- What might be the advantages and disadvantages of proposed solutions?
- What would the likely outcomes be and who might be affected?
- What needs to be communicated and to whom?
- What action will then be necessary?
- How will the action be monitored and its effects reviewed?

Finally, there is a need to reflect critically on the entire process and its outcomes.

You are attempting to achieve not only compliance, but also a new set of objectives which seeks to improve the security of the recording, storage and transfer of resident identifiable information.

Always consult your relevant people, residents/carers, and significant third parties before you engage in any new objective setting. Consider their views, be prepared to sell your own ideas, but always be prepared to listen to third-party feedback, as it offers you an additional overview of possible solutions and so facilitates the successful implementation of your original objectives. Additionally, feedback allows you to remain proactive and make modifications where necessary.

Always consider the advantages and disadvantages of policy change. In this instance the advantage of your policy will be better security of resident identifiable information. However, there may be significant disadvantages for the rest of your staff team. Consider how they will feel. Alienation and discontent have to be sensitively managed if your new objectives are to succeed. The issue of alienation cannot be dismissed, as it will be an outcome of the process. Hence, consider alternatives where all staff play a vital role in your objective of establishing a culture of confidentiality.

Ensure your objectives are communicated to all, equally. You may consider a variety of different forums – team meetings, briefings, supervision and resident/carer meetings. All have a vital role for stimulating discussion, developing understanding and demonstrating that your objectives are about compliance with the law and not a personal whim.

By this stage your analysis will allow you to action your objectives. However, never be complacent – always monitor and review, and make alterations where necessary. A simple example might be improved training of your Caldicott guardian and proprietors.

Critical reflection is at the heart of effective objective setting. The ability to analyse your original objectives, purpose, your role and the process followed will allow you to take stock of the qualitative nature of the outcomes. Additionally, it will enable you to make proactive modifications to systems and procedures, as well as take into account individual feelings about input and involvement.

Analysis need not be a complicated process. It does need to be suitable to the achievement of your stated objectives.

Case study — Effective analysis

You wish to introduce a series of new objectives which will result in changes to day-to-day operations relating to the recording, storage and transfer of resident identifiable information. What role does analysis play in your objective setting?

- How might you ensure your analysis takes account of the qualitative nature of the objectives you seek?
- Will your analysis enable you to quantify your results?
- How will these results be communicated, and to whom?
- How can you ascertain that the analysis you have engaged in is suitable and achieves the objectives you seek?
- How can you be certain your analysis is formal, planned and structured, and does not appear informal or disintegrate into an ad hoc process which merely confuses all?

You identify relevant patterns and trends

It must be remembered that not all information is reliable and accurate. It will depend very much on how it was obtained, and on how it has been recorded, stored and transferred. Your skills in these separate processes will determine its reliability and accuracy. Therefore, your analysis is of import and should assist both your objective setting and decision making in order to accomplish your task of safeguarding the confidentiality of resident identifiable information. It is good practice to be aware of patterns or trends which might influence the actions you take.

In theory, there are two relevant methods of analysis transferable to the care service sector which might be used to identify different trends of organisational activity. The first method is entitled 'time series analysis', which, as its name denotes, focuses on how events change over time. The second method is sometimes referred to as the 'collation method' or the 'correlation method'; it focuses on how events alter as a result of the influence of other factors.

The time series analysis is suited to examining ongoing improvement in the security, recording, storage and transfer of resident identifiable information over a period of time. This might be compared with effective reviewing which, as a result of analysis, could be quantified for costing purposes or subject to qualitative analysis by measuring both staff and resident feeling or opinion. However, its application is more than just reviewing because its aim is to enable you to develop your vision of what you wish to see occurring in the future and to plan to realise it.

Conversely, the correlation method enables you to demonstrate a relationship between one event and another. When using this model you can identify the trend you will later rely on to support your conclusions. For instance, it would allow you to demonstrate the relationship between the use of manual information systems and the take-up of a computerised system. You could plot the trend to determine the reliance upon one or the other system. A positive correlation might be determined by an increase in the time- and cost-effectiveness of using computer systems, while a negative correlation could be demonstrated by an existing reliance on expensive manual and labour-intensive recording systems. Quantifying both determines the difference. Figure 20 gives an example. The trend supports an 80% take-up of computerised systems for the recording and storage of resident identifiable information between April 2000 and April 2005. So, in the space of five financial years, the use of computers for all resident identifiable information jumps from a mere 10% to a 90%. Not only is such an application safer, but it is also more efficient in terms of time, space and cost.

Recognising the trend in dependency and differentiating between fact and opinion in percentage terms, and quantifying both, also serves to demonstrate how the use of computerised information systems can outweigh manual reliance. While an annual trend can be calculated, it is also possible to analyse quarterly or even monthly cycles, to show an effect or outcome in more detail.

Using both methods of analysis – time series and correlation – it is more likely that you will be able to identify relevant patterns or trends in virtually every aspect of your day-to-day operations. This in turn might lead to changes in operational policy, as changing residents' needs dictate.

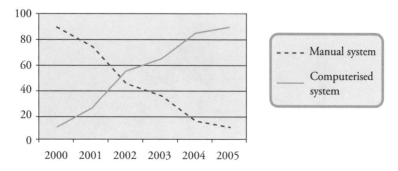

Figure 20. Adoption of the use of computerised versus manual recording systems, April 2000 to April 2005.

How might the use of either time series analysis or correlation analysis lead to changes in your organisational policy? Devise an action plan and implement it.

You support your conclusions with reasoned argument and appropriate evidence

Consider the analysis discussed above, which identified a clear trend towards the use of computerised equipment. The correlation analysis employed supported your original concerns relating to the secure recording, storage and use of resident identifiable information. The analysis was numerically quantifiable, but a qualitative dimension could have been added simply by asking staff and residents how they felt about the transfer of information and its confidential employment. Responses could be subject to the same correlation analysis. Allowing for changing opinion and a resistance to new technology, it might be suggested that the results would be similar or the same.

However, your conclusions, while objective, must not diminish the subjective feelings of staff or residents. The introduction of new technology will change an established culture within your practice setting. There may be opposition based on fear, insecurity or ignorance. These concerns must be worked with at an individual, empathetic level in supervision, team meetings or briefings, as well as resident/carer meetings. Only when you have established mutual agreement rather than imposition may you proceed with caution and support.

You need to weigh up the advantages and disadvantages of introducing new technology.

It is your responsibility to weigh up the advantages and disadvantages of introducing new technology into people's lives and to take into account its effects. You will be aware that day-to-day operational practice will change. The process of recording will speed up. Storage then becomes less of a problem given that all resident information can now be recorded on CD-ROM and the capacity and size allows for greater security.

The conclusions you draw must be based on reliable, quantifiable and qualitative information, reason, fact and subjective opinion. Conclusions should not represent an end to a process; rather, they mark a new beginning, which must be followed by support, monitoring and supervision.

Case study — Conclusions supported by reason and evidence

Changing residents' needs and new legislation have demanded the introduction of new technology into the practice setting. Your staff have been trained to use their new computer systems, and residents have now adjusted to their employment. On what basis do you draw your conclusions of its success, based on the evidence you have and the arguments that you have used?

- How will you re-examine your evidence, both quantitative and qualitative, and correlate the results?
- How will you obtain the views and feelings of staff and residents?
- Having obtained their views and feelings, how do you translate them into management practice or policy? What contingency plans have you made?
- Will your conclusions mark the end of your process or the beginning of a new one? Consider this issue based on the evidence you possess.

In presenting the results of your analysis you differentiate clearly between fact and opinion

In presenting the results of your analysis to either your relevant people or residents and carers, it remains vitally important that you differentiate between fact and opinion. Your presentation will be based on establishing a culture of confidentiality through the application of new technology. Your results will be informed by your previous exploration of methodology, namely time series analysis and correlation, and the patterns or trends which emerged from your study.

In this instance, you might demonstrate the take-up of the computerised equipment and subject to this to a quantitative and qualitative analysis. The results can be numerically broken down to support the facts of your case; subjective opinion and speculation cannot be given as evidence. However, your presentation must not dismiss group opinion but rather carry it with you in a supportive context. In this way you can engage with your staff or residents.

The presentation of the results of your analysis, although thoroughly factual, may be enhanced by giving particular attention to the employment of the following features:

- **Location.** Your presentation is likely to be in-house, so your relevant people will feel comfortable in their own environment. Equally they will probably feel more comfortable in your company than in that of a stranger.
- **Audio-visual charts.** You can support the results of your analysis with strong audio and visual messages. It increases the enjoyment factor and engages attention.
- **Flip charts.** Brief bullet points written with coloured pens may be used to support your results while you speak. Do not turn your back on your captive audience. If you decide to write, stand to one side to give flexible eye contact. It is advised if you use a flip chart, have your points pre-prepared so you can turn to the relevant page without difficulty.
- **Coloured paper.** If you seek to ensure that the results of your analysis become an interactive experience, then participant support is essential. Participants can be encouraged to write down their ideas. The qualitative nature of your presentations may be judged by participant involvement.
- **Posters.** Posters which support your presentation, bright and vibrant in nature, could be placed around the room in advance and this can serve to set the scene.
- **Handouts.** A handout is an effective tool with which to reinforce facts. They will support your argument in writing, and can be taken away after the presentation.

If your presentation is to be a success, ideally support the results of your analysis with factual information, and make it both visibly engaging and an interactive experience for your audience. In this way, facts almost speak for themselves, but opinions still matter and should be listened to with respect.

Think it over

When was the last time you attended a presentation? Can you recall what you learned and came away with? How was the material presented – in an engaging, creative, interactive way? Jot down your thoughts.

You must prove that you analyse information to support decision making to the National Occupational Standard of competence.

You must show evidence that you carry out both of the following types of analysis: formal and planned, and informal and ad hoc.

You must also show evidence that your analysis supports decisions concerning both of the following: day-to-day operations and changes in organisational policy which affect operations.

You must also show evidence that you use both quantitative and qualitative information.

D4.4

Learning outcomes

- You research the advice and information needs of your recipients, taking into account organisational constraints.
- You provide relevant advice and information that is accurate and appropriate to the needs of your recipients.
- The information you provide is accurate, current, relevant and sufficient.
- Your advice is consistent with organisational policy, procedures, constraints and legal requirements.
- You obtain feedback from recipients.

You research the advice and information needs of your recipients, taking into account organisational constraints

It is imperative that you conduct research in order that any advice and information you give are both appropriate and sufficient to meet the needs of the recipients. Your starting point for your research will be the residents' original assessment plans, any other reassessments, care plans, and monitoring and review forms. This will almost certainly identify requested or expressed needs for advice and information. Not all residents will request the same information or advice. However, there may be some common ground where you can discern a collective need for specific advice or information.

What kinds of information is needed? The most common fall into nine categories:

- finance;
- benefits and budgets;
- legal rights;
- unit guidelines;
- choice of menu;
- disability aids;
- accommodation;
- access to general practitioners;
- social activities (both internal and external).

The kinds of advice needed are widely divergent. You will need to give a mixture of formal, informal and 'random' advice.

Formal requests for advice by residents would include questions such as 'Can I smoke?', or 'Where can I smoke?'. Informal requests tend to focus on mealtimes, dining arrangements, choice of menu, seating arrangements. Examples would include 'Where can I sit?', 'Can I sit anywhere?', 'Can I sit in this person's chair?', or 'Can there be seating rotation arrangements?'. 'Random' requests for advice by residents might be exemplified by a request such as, 'Can my partner stay overnight and sleep in my bed?'

The organisational constraints likely to have an influence on both information and advice commonly fall into three categories, relating to the practice setting's structure, organisation, and flexibility. The first category relates to the practice settings, structure, organisation and flexibility. The second category tends to be financial, with a reliance on monies available, affordability, staff ratios, and so on. The third category might be considered ethical – the advice is likely to be on whether something is appropriate, whether it can be provided, or whether it can be justified.

Organisational constraints on formal requests for information, relating to all aspects of finance, legal rights and unit guidelines, arise through inadequate or poor management. Information on all these areas should be freely available in writing and other formats, for example in handout form, on tape, video, Braille, talking books, in different languages and through access to interpreters and signers.

A very real constraint is an inability to access public information systems or local professionals within local authority social service departments, law centres and charitable bodies. The Care Standards Act 2000 details in Standards 17 to Standard 17.3 how residents' legal rights should be protected, and residents' financial interests are detailed in Standards 35 to 35.6. Disability aids can become a constraint principally through lack of suitable space, cost and inappropriate training of staff. This is a management problem, which must be overcome for health and safety reasons, as required by Standard 22.

Access of general practitioners within the resident's own setting on a 24-hour basis does remain a constraint, unless localised arrangements can be negotiated with the new primary health care trusts. Problems resulting from the presence of locum doctors will remain due to pressures on the primary health care teams. Negotiation and diplomacy will help to resolve this constraint. You and the primary health care team must strive to reduce any failings in this essential personalised area of care.

Accommodation needs of residents with different and changing physical needs represents a significant constraint, particularly for registered homes which do not meet the National Minimum Standards laid down by the Care Standards Act 2000. Standards 19 to 26 detail minimum environmental standards. Since 1 April 2001, adjustments concerning individual and space requirements, identified in Standard 23, must be met in new extensions.

Constraints resulting from requests for advice at a formal, informal and random level will always pose immediate and particular personal problems unless managed sensitively and proactively. The example given of smoking is pertinent. Ideally, your unit brochure will identify guidelines to actual and potential residents and must disclose your smoking policy, not only for fundamental health and safety purposes, but also to meet the individual sensitivities of residents generally. It is now commonplace to impose smoke-free zones (no-smoking areas) in most public areas, such as dining areas and lounge facilities, as well as in all private bedrooms. You can identify a safe haven for smoking in a comfortable and relaxed atmosphere, such as a conservatory, which can be easily ventilated, but ensure controls are in place to accommodate non-smokers.

Informal requests for information, such as dining arrangements, choice of menu, dietary requirements and seating arrangements, can impose continuous organisational constraints given the changing dietary needs and preferences of residents. Sensitive management is required in what remains a significant and important part of individual and collective daily life. Ideally, your unit guidelines should allow for flexible rather than fixed dining arrangements. Residents should have the right to receive their meals in their own private bedrooms. However, staffing ratios can impose a significant constraint in this regard, as can health and safety regulations. Always bear in mind that some residents will require assistance with eating, and individual and collective sensitivities must be a consideration and managed with care. The Care Standards Act 2000 stresses diet as one of the most important factors in determining a resident's quality of life. Individual food preferences and cultural or religious preferences must always be observed. Standard 12 of the Care Standards Act (particularly 12.1 and 12.2) details routines of daily living which must be flexible enough to meet residents' expectations and preferences. This is also supported in detail by Standards 15.1 to 15.9, which gives appropriate advice.

Sensitive management of daily needs such as dietary requirements is required.

Random requests for advice, such as 'Can my partner stay overnight?', can impose legal and insurance constraints. Who is the partner? Might other residents be at risk? How do they feel? Standards 13.1 to 13.6 give formal guidelines on a resident's right to maintain contact with family and friends. You must observe a sensitive, legalistic and common-sense approach given the constraints you face, without contravening your residents' basic human rights or the sensitivities of others.

Case study — Information-giving and constraint reduction

Mary Gould is an 82-year-old resident, a widow for 10 years and a resident at your residential home for the last four years. Initially, she had pursued an active social life. However, more recently, following a fall and a hip replacement, her mobility has become more restricted. She now uses two sticks to get around, but has shown great determination to care for herself, to maximise her personal autonomy, of which she is very proud.

During a brief conversation she explains that she would love to attend the theatre to watch a visiting theatrical performance in a neighbouring town. She wishes to make this journey unattended and to finance the trip herself. What advice do you need to give to Mary, and what constraints need to be overcome for the trip to be achievable?

- Does Mary know where the theatre is, and can she safely get there?
- What health and safety checks do you need to make to ensure safe, accessible passage?
- Do you consider it necessary to explore with Mary her preferences of transport and research all options (taxi, bus, ring and ride volunteer drivers, and rail service)?

▼

- Do you consider it necessary to do a (telephone) risk-assessment of the theatre?
- Will you verify with Mary the total cost of the trip and her ability to afford it?
- What advice do you think is necessary?
- How might you give advice to Mary in such a way that she understands it?
- How might you verify Mary's understanding, and what methods would you employ to test comprehension?

You provide relevant advice and information that is accurate and appropriate to the needs of your recipients

It is important to provide advice and information in a form and manner, and at a place and time, appropriate to the needs of your recipients (who will primarily be your residents and staff).

What forums exist to accommodate these different needs?

For staff, examples might include:

- team meetings;
- supervisory sessions;
- appraisal meetings.

For residents, examples might include:

- care planning review meetings;
- presentation meetings.

Team meetings

Your regular team meetings – chaired, managed and set in a relaxed, warm and friendly environment – can provide a platform through its agenda to provide both information and advice. Information may sometimes be written, such as proposals for resident social activities, and reports on health and safety procedures. It should also be discussed during the meeting. Consider the example of a member of staff who has accessed through a professional journal inaccurate information regarding the date for the enforcement of the Data Protection Act 1998. She was led to believe it was in 1998. You can clarify this and satisfy the member of staff that it was enforced on 1 March 2001; hence the care home's preparation to ensure the security of all resident identifiable information in line with current statute.

Information given must be thought through. Conversely, information seeking is also a useful management tool. For example, a member of staff may seek advice about an operational procedure of 'no lifting'. Your advice might direct your team member to read the unit's policy document on handling and movement – that is, to seek information. You might also reaffirm the care home's policy on movement and handling and identify both safe and unsafe handling techniques. You could consider inviting colleagues at the same level to share their experiences and offer direct or indirect advice and formal information based on their personal practice, training and experience. In this way, as manager, you provide information and advice to a specific person who has made a request. This is performed using the spoken word and additionally it fulfills a specific need of one party.

Indirectly or directly advising and informing team members serves to enhance their knowledge base, and team members can participate in the information exchange process – which is essentially what a team meeting is all about.

Supervisory sessions

Supervisory sessions (one to one, pair, or small group) provide a forum for confidential information exchange. Individual team members will require specific information on areas of allocated work, together with advice on how to perform. They will require you to assess their practice, which is both observed and recorded (written), and will require feedback on your observation and perception of their progress.

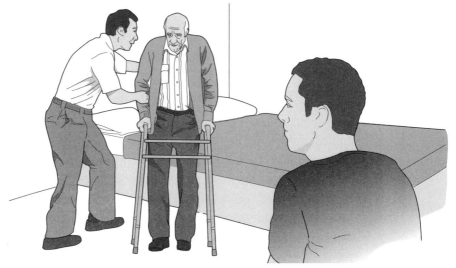

Team members will require feedback on their progress.

Your feedback has to be specific and the information shared is a judgement on how well a piece of work has been managed or where adjustments or modifications should be made. Your tone of voice, eye contact and body language must match your spoken words to avoid mixed messages and confusion; all necessary skills of non-verbal communication will be required and demonstrated in this setting. Team members will request specific advice on a variety of areas pertinent to their professional practice. Ultimately, they might seek your advice on how to progress, which provides you with opportunities to offer information, formal (probably written) or informal (verbal). You advise in detail what to do and how to evaluate and reflect on the piece of work being assessed. In accordance with the Data Protection Act 1998, all matters discussed and recorded, either manually or electronically, must be regarded as confidential and stored in a secure environment.

Appraisal meetings

In an appraisal meeting, you are judging performance based on evidence that has been jointly negotiated to meet team members' chosen targets. The evidence will be drawn from a number of sources, and may be written, empirical, tape/audio visual or from third-party observational feedback. Information analysis is performed in advance so you are prepared to ask questions, give information and seek information, to clarify and collate in order to make an informed decision.

The information you give may be legalistic or may focus upon principles of good practice. However, its purpose should be aimed at supporting your team members to realise their own potential as well as meeting your own organisational requirements. Your advice may be informal (in other words in your personal opinion), or formal, which directs the team member to a particular source to gather more information. If, for example, the appraised situation has a focus upon image presentation of the practice setting, then you may formally advise that team member to seek to employ visual aids to create a brochure which presents a strong visual representation of the joys of communal living within a caring environment.

Think it over

Identify a recent situation in which you were required to provide both information and advice to a resident. Jot down the specifics of what you said and why.

Care planning review meetings

Regularity of review is the key to meeting changing residents' needs. The care plan remains the vehicle by which the residents' needs are met. It never remains static. Your care plan determines and evidences your input, throughput and output, and represents the best endorsement of residents' assessed and expressed needs being met continuously. At a review meeting you will seek information from the resident, carers and team members as to whether their assessed and expressed needs are being met. If needs are apparently being met, you might use your initiative and advise on the reassessment of need; for example, mobility needs could be met with the use of external aids rather than continuous external physical care, thus maximising a resident's personal autonomy and reducing third-party dependency.

The information you provide must be precise, in accordance with legal requirements and principles of good practice. Accommodation of views and opinions, the giving of both formal and informal advice, together with information specific to improving the quality of a resident's life, become unified within this exchange. Nevertheless, agreement for any change must come first from the resident and carer or other representative, and equally from team members, so that a new process can be experimented with. Expect resident or representative requests for assistance or supervision when required and be prepared to inform, advise and reassure.

Presentation meetings for residents

Presentation meetings, either formal or informal, are designed to inform residents, their carers or representatives of new initiatives to improve their quality of life. You must always prepare your presentation in advance. Keep it brief, structured and informative, and introduce humour.

Consider an example. In accordance with the Care Standards Act 2000 you are introducing new individualised bathing appliances in the form of walk-in showers and baths with opening doors. The rationale is to ensure whatever a resident's disability, the choice of bathing can be catered for and managed either independently or with minimal assistance if requested.

The information you provide must be simplified and delivered at a pace your residents can comprehend. This is best done using a variety of media for reinforcement purposes, for example spoken delivery combined with visual material and a practical demonstration. In this way, your information exchange informs, guides and enables residents and carers to make decisions about use. A practical demonstration would reassure, inform and remove personal fears or prejudices. A question and answer session is a useful method of obtaining resident feedback. It is important that your advice sticks to the facts, in this instance for health and safety reasons. Be prepared to use your own initiative to answer unexpected questions.

Case study — Provision of information and advice

Mrs Angela Evans, aged 92 years, is a widow who has been resident for some 10 years. She requests specific advice regarding financing her care, which she is concerned about. She states that her personal finances are diminishing rapidly and she fears she may not be able to finance her care for much longer. How would you go about providing sensitive advice and information?

- Will you provide this advice and information in private and what measures will you undertake to protect confidentiality?
- Will you ask Mrs Evans whether she would prefer her carer or representative to accompany her for support? Why consider this?
- The information you provide must relate to the actual financial costs of her care. How do you relay this information in a sensitive and caring manner without causing unnecessary concern or distress?
- You determine the weekly cost of Mrs Evans' care. It amounts to £270 per week, of which the local authority subsidies £230, leaving £40. This balance is also made up by a special government subsidy to ensure that all people requiring residential care and experiencing financial hardship can have their residential care needs met. How might you explain to Mrs Evans that she has no need to worry about financing her care?
- How might you sensitively confirm that Mrs Evans understands the information you have given her?

The management of challenging behaviours

You are present at a team briefing session in response to a request by four members staff who are experiencing difficulty in providing direct care for an older resident whose behaviour is challenging and oppositional, and who is verbally aggressive and threatening. While no physical violence has been displayed, they fear the risks that this behaviour poses, to themselves, to other members of staff and to residents.

You have prepared in advance for this session, as you have a duty of care under the Health and Safety Act of 1974 to protect all residents and staff from any forms of aggression or abuse. Therefore, you have ensured that the information they need to manage this person's care is not only sufficient but also accurate, current and relevant. You have prepared in advance some written handouts, which explore some of the theories of aggression. Jargon has been dispensed with to ensure that the recipients can understand it. You have also identified a series of checklists drawn up from previous risk assessments on residents whose dementia management did involve working with aggressive behaviour.

In the first instance, you refer to the original assessment and care plan. There is no record of a medical or psychological condition which might contribute to the aggressive behaviour. Nor is there any statement from previous carers, social workers or primary health care workers to suggest such behaviour.

To put your information into context you begin by examining two theories of aggression, one entitled 'instinct theory' and the other 'social learning theory'. Instinct theory is primarily based on the early ideas of Freud, who suggested that aggression is an innate drive. According to this theory, aggression can be explained biologically and genetically without having to seek recourse to relevant social factors. By contrast, social learning theory perceives aggression not as instinctive but as behaviour which can be learned in any social environment. Additionally, this theory has direct practice implications for staff who work with aggressive residents, in that their aggression is likely to be perpetuated if they discover that they can obtain what they want or need by being aggressive.

The theoretical information can provide staff with the knowledge that aggression is known and a researched subject and they are not alone in managing it, which helps reduce fears of personal incompetence. The theoretical information is relevant because it helps put aggressive behaviours into a context in which they can be explained and rationalised. The assessment of contributory factors is required to provide information which focuses on the person.

In this instance, we might question whether this person is conveying negative feelings and behaviours about leaving his former home and entering residential care. From his assessment report, it was noted that he had been reluctant to move because he did not wish to leave his home. It was the persuasion of his immediate family that resulted in his request for accommodation. This person might therefore be experiencing some kind of bereavement transition of moving from one environment to another, and perhaps anger is being transferred towards his new home. This transference in some ways might help explain the negative, challenging and verbally aggressive behaviours. It would be important to assess whether this person had unmet needs.

It would also be important to point out that staff will hold either positive or negative attitudes and feelings towards residents. This could trigger negative responses from potentially aggressive residents. Equally, staff who are discontented are unlikely to handle situations such as this in a carefully managed way. Also, all staff will possess what are referred to as 'trigger points'. These are certain words, attitudes, actions or situation which they find particularly difficult to handle. Staff may also experience difficulties and problems in their personal lives. The negative emotions arising there can easily be transferred into the practice setting.

The information given will enable staff to focus on factors relating to this resident and the possible transference of anger; the resident will require sensitive understanding to manage within a caring environment. Additionally, the information given also allows staff to question their own feelings and attitudes, which may have inadvertently encouraged this aggressive behaviour.

Overall, the information is sufficient for nominated staff to perform a new risk assessment, and to manage the behaviour.

Think it over

Consider a situation when you have been required to provide information on managing potentially aggressive behaviours. What did you say? Jot down your thoughts.

Case study — Providing information to manage challenging behaviour

You are faced with a resident who has suddenly and for no apparent reason become exceptionally oppositional. His behaviours are alarming and distressing to fellow residents and staff. How do you ensure the information you provide is sufficient, accurate and relevant to meet this new situation?

- Will you exercise your 'duty of care' as registered manager under the Health and Safety Act 1974 and perform a risk assessment to ascertain current and potential risks to residents and staff?
- Will you research previous assessments, medical reports or third-party involvement of any kind to identify a trend or pattern to this behaviour?
- Observing the need for confidentiality, what relevant information will you share with your staff to manage this situation?
- What methods might you consider for imparting this information?

Your advice is consistent with organisational policy, procedures, constraints and legal requirements

In your team briefing, the advice that you provide to your staff members must be consistent with your organisational policy, its procedures, constraints and legal requirements which underpin its content.

In the first instance you would remind and require your staff to read the unit's policy and procedures for managing aggressive and challenging behaviour. This written document will inform staff how to react and work with presenting behaviours within set legal requirements. It will have been seen and authorised by appropriate social care commissioners, who will expect you to evidence any action undertaken to both local authority guidelines and legal statute, which is designed to protect everyone, including the most vulnerable. Clearly, older, infirm residents fall into this category. However, aggressive behaviours could lead, if supported with appropriate evidence, to a criminal conviction. Nonetheless, any violation of an individual's rights would be in contravention of the Human Rights Act 1998, which you are required to uphold at all times.

So how does your advice remain consistent with organisational policy, procedures, outside complaints and legal requirements? Your policy and procedure will serve to guide staff before, during and after an incident involving any form of aggressive behaviour. No one is paid enough to come to work to get hurt. It is advisable that your liability insurance stands at a recommended minimum amount of £10 million, and for this sum to be reviewed each financial year. It is your duty of care, under the Health and Safety Act 1974, to protect your staff from any possible harm. You must have liability insurance that is appropriately bonded to cover both staff and residents individually and collectively.

Within your policy document and procedures there are practice keys to be followed, which must be supported by your advice, under the contractual terms of employment. Any breach or contravention could result in disciplinary action and, if the evidence of any such action can be substantiated, criminal prosecution might follow.

Your policy and procedures are designed to minimise the risks and incidence of possible aggression and violence. Before an incident occurs, there are rules and guidelines to follow. They may seem basic and mundane but are fundamental to an effective operational policy.

The following points should be observed:

- *Establish a professional relationship with the resident* – most incidents involving difficult residents are much easier to deal with if there remains an established relationship based on mutual respect and trust.
- *Learn to recognise signals or triggers* – most people have their own way of displaying anger. Try to understand the trigger mechanisms, as these may indicate how best to respond to defuse tension and anger.
- *Do not display aggressive behaviour* – conveying aggressive behaviour is more likely to give an aggressive response. Do not allow a resident's

aggressive behaviour to result in an aggressive reaction from yourself. The outcome is more likely to escalate beyond the control of you both.

- *Always be diplomatic and patient* – listen actively to what residents have to say and ensure your body language reflects this. This can reduce the frustration a resident may experience.
- *Differentiate between aggression and assertion* – in most instances each individual has the right to be assertive and to protect basic civil rights. While assertive behaviour may be appropriate, aggressive behaviour never is.
- *Convey respect for another's viewpoint* – even if you fundamentally disagree with a resident's viewpoint, they have the right to hold them. The practice keys in effective resolution is to listen and not to interrupt, ensure you possess the courtesy to allow the person to complete what they have to say and then respond in a sensitive and empathetic manner.
- *Think proactively* – before engaging a resident who is known to be challenging and oppositional, think in advance of what you are going to say and act.
- *Voice your concerns to other team members* – be prepared to share particular concerns that you may have about a resident with your relevant team members, or senior staff on duty. This is not an act of inadequacy on your part – others may experience similar reservations.
- *Give yourself space* – if you consider that a situation is getting out of control and you consider yourself to be at risk, then it is your duty of care to leave. Delegate to others and explain why. This allows you more time to think about how you could take on similar incidents more effectively in the future. Being prepared to leave a situation without allowing a resident to be at risk is not an act of failure: it is simply about self-protection. However, always ensure that the situation can be managed by others with different experience and equally learn from the event. Acting on your own initiative and perception of the situation is paramount.

> ## What advice do you offer in relation to potential aggression?

- *Do not provoke.* Do not say or suggest with your body language anything that may provoke a situation or escalate events.
- *Tone and pitch of voice.* The tone and pitch of your voice can influence what occurs. Simply adjust both and lower your voice. By speaking calmly and respectfully you can reduce a negative atmosphere.

- *Remaining calm.* Whatever you feel inside, present a calm and confident exterior. Remember, you are in control and it is your responsibility to remain as calm as possible, to think rationally and to resolve the situation as far as you are able to do so.
- *Do not make ultimatums that you have no authority to enforce.* You must always follow written policy and procedures, as your actions will be judged against them. Legally you are not allowed to do so threaten something or someone, so do not make that fundamental mistake.
- *Diversion.* Think of ways that might divert a situation. Sometimes a simple statement, such as 'How about a nice cup of tea?', would do so. Do not sound patronising. By diverting attention in many cases the aggressive behaviour can be extinguished.
- *Do not allow yourself to become trapped or cornered.* Allow yourself and the resident opportunities to leave. Feelings of being trapped can trigger panic, which may result in unnecessary aggression. Under the duty of care, if you realise that a resident is a potential danger to others, then press a panic alarm or call on others for help, to ensure the situation is managed and dealt with appropriately.
- *What about the presence of others?* There may be other residents around who could help. Remember you have a duty of care to protect them. Nevertheless, peer pressure remains an effective tool of pacification.

What might be your advice to staff after an incident?

In the first instance, an incident form requires completion. It represents a procedural and legal document. It must cover:

- who was involved;
- what actually occurred;
- what provoked the incident;
- why it occurred;
- what realistically were your options at the time;
- what needs to be done now and why;
- what follow-up actions are required to protect residents and staff.

This form should be completed as soon as possible after the event when the staff member or resident has regained a sense of composure.

Record and identify potential aggressors. Without violating a resident's fundamental civil right or confidentiality, your recording system should enable you to identify instances or circumstances which might result in resident aggression. You have a duty of care to both residents and staff to prevent such situations recurring.

For both staff and residents, your policy must facilitate an effective counselling process. Immediately after an incident, it is important to be able to share feelings of hurt, anger or fear with an independent qualified counsellor. In this way, strong emotional feelings can be constructively, but more importantly empathetically, worked through. Counselling will result in the reliving or the psychological re-enactment of the event at an emotional and cognitive level. However, effective counselling should be just as much about healing as learning from the incident to minimise the risk of such situations recurring. It can also assist either staff or residents to understand why the situation occurred, which will help similar situations to be managed differently in future.

Your advice must also take into account both organisational and legal requirements. No Act of Parliament can prevent an aggressive situation from occurring, but your policies and procedures can minimise the risks of physical or psychological harm. It is your duty of care to have an effective and managed policy, and procedures in place that are regularly reviewed. However, constraints such as staff shortages and the delays of filling vacancies can increase staff stress. Such situations can result in observed lack of patience and tolerance, which can trigger challenging or aggressive resident behaviours. Similarly, inadequate budgeting, resulting in poor staff ratios or lack of specialist equipment, can result in adverse resident reactions. If residents' needs are not prioritised and met, then a negative consequence is almost an immediate and natural outcome. However, residents' needs require sensitive and caring management. Your practice setting should be about providing care and not control.

Making staff aware, through regular formal and informal advice, of your policies and procedures for managing aggressive or challenging behaviour is good practice. However, your advice must be measured to ensure understanding and it must be consistent with your policies, procedures, constraints and legal requirements.

Try it out

Determine your staff team's understanding of managing challenging behaviours. Give advice that is consistent to your current organisational policy, procedures, constraints and legal requirements. Choose formal or informal methods, but record your results.

Case study — Difficult behaviour

Charles Waller was recently referred to you; he is in the early stages of dementia. Your practice setting has a specific policy and procedures for working with dementia. Your staff have extensive experience of working with residents with this condition. Mr Waller has rapid mood swings, oppositional behaviour and occasionally is aggressive.

- Will you undertake a risk assessment with this resident and why?
- What areas and circumstances would your risk assessment cover?
- What advice will you provide your staff as an outcome of this risk assessment?
- Are your existing policies and procedures sufficient to protect and manage Mr Waller's care? Do they require reviewing, and if so how and why?
- What organisational constraints exist which might compromise this resident's care?
- Do your existing policies and procedures comply with all legal requirements?
- Can they be improved to ensure protection, security and unconditional care for this resident while accommodated within your practice setting?

You obtain feedback from recipients

In order to use feedback from recipients to improve the way in which you provide advice and information, it remains essential that you understand the different processes involved in receiving feedback.

Think it over

Consider different examples of recipient feedback and identify your current ways of providing advice and information. Jot down your thoughts.

To receive feedback, you must provide a confidential environment. Providing maximum privacy and minimum interruption should enable you to share more information that is more specific, accurate and appropriate to the expressed needs. Feedback from the recipients must be objectively and fairly assessed.

Receiving feedback can be a positive or a negative experience. However, ensure that the process remains constructive, supportive and sensitive to individual needs. Use feedback to focus on performance, outcomes, time scales, joint processes and ways of plotting solutions. Also use it to improve the content and accuracy of any advice or information you give.

Recipient feedback must enable you both to plot solutions. In this way, your information or advice must differentiate between what has been achieved and what needs to be improved. In order that you can proactively improve the way you provide information and advice to both residents and staff, you must evaluate the manner, style and pace they actually prefer their feedback. Consider alternatives, for example an over-reliance upon factual information may be inappropriate and not always wanted or required. Consider introducing humour but check that it is appropriate. Remain vigilantly aware of resident and staff moods, needs, feelings and sensitivities. Careful attention to your use of non-verbal communication is essential in the process of providing any information or advice; clarify whether your body language actually equates with what is being said, to avoid mixed messages or unintentional offence.

In conclusion, regular evaluation of recipient feedback remains a useful tool in developing an overview of whether your advice or information, be it formal or informal, is effective.

Evidence collection D4.4 — Advise and inform others

You must show evidence that you provide both spoken and written advice and information. This section has examined written information relating to finance, legal rights and unit guidelines, written in handout form. Additionally, refer to staff team meetings, supervisory and appraisal meetings, which are recorded. Refer to the example of written handouts for staff to explain and explore the theories of aggression.

You must also show evidence that you can provide advice and information in response to a request and on your own initiative. Acting on your own initiative is paramount when managing a situation that is getting out of control.

You must also show evidence that you provide information and advice to at least two of the following types of recipients: team members, colleagues, managers and sponsors, people outside your organisation and clients or their representatives.

Appendix: Examples of computer-generated forms

Key worker sheet

Sheet No.:	
Period:	
Key worker:	
Resident:	
Have there been any problems since your last report?	Yes/No
If yes, please comment:	
Are there any changes in medication?	Yes/No
If yes, please comment:	
Any changes in health conditions/family support?	
Please comment:	
Have the key worker duties been carried out as per schedule?	Yes/No
If no, please comment:	
Any recommendations?	
Signature:	
Date:	
Name (print):	
Authorised by (name):	

Example forms reproduced with kind permission of Appledore Lodge.

Fluid balance chart

Name:				
Date	Time	Description	Fluid intake in mls	Remarks

Accident report form

Accident reported by:	
On (date):	
Is the person who had the accident is a member of staff?	
Name and address of person:	
Occupation of person:	
Date and time of accident:	
Details of place where accident occurred:	
Details of the accident:	
Details of the action taken:	

Handling assessment form for residents who are not independent

On completion of this form, the resident will be colour-coded, in the box at the base of this form, indicating lifting instructions. More specific information is found in the Load Management Care Plan. The laminated sheet with the red, yellow and green circles will help you by giving instructions on how to colour code.

This form should be completed within 24 hours of the resident's admission and kept with the nursing care plans. There should be a re-evaluation when there is a change in the resident's condition. Main problems together with handling strategy and equipment to be used should be entered into the resident's care plan and evaluated regularly.

Name of resident:	
Room No.:	
Weight:	Average weight Obese Thin
Height:	Tall Short Medium height
Resident's sight:	Good Poor Unable
Resident's hearing:	Good Poor Unable

Resident's speech:	Good Poor Unable
Resident's disability/weakness/deformity (tick):	Stroke Alzheimer's Amputee Other (specify)
Handling constraints (tick):	Pain Stoma Skin lesions Poor skin Catheter Colostomy Other factors (specify)
History of falls	Yes/No If yes, specify frequency:
Equipment normally used (tick):	Wheelchair Walking stick Transfusion board Walking frame Turntable Hoist
Problems/capabilities (tick): day	Walking Standing Toileting Transfer to and from bed Movements in bed
Problems/capabilities (tick): night	Walking Standing Toileting Transfer to and from bed Movements in bed
Walking (tick):	Independent With frame/stick Assisted by 1 Assisted by 2 Unable
This resident is colour-rated (tick):	Red – do not lift Yellow – consult care plan/procedure Green – safe considering lifting procedures
Describe walking:	
Describe bathing:	
Describe transfer to toilet:	
Describe transfer to bed:	
Describe movement in bed:	
Signed:	
Level:	
Date:	
Evaluation No.:	

C8 Select Personnel for Activities

The following elements focus upon the essential processes of
(a) how you identify personnel requirements within your practice
setting and (b) how you address selecting required personnel and
the information systems you will need to select, inform and
feedback at each stage in the selection process. The learning
outcomes will serve to focus your attention to the detail required
of each in context.

The elements are:
- Identify personnel requirements.
- Select required personnel.

Learning outcomes

- You clearly and accurately identify the organisational objectives and constraints affecting personnel requirements.
- You consult with relevant people on personnel requirements in a timely and confidential manner.
- Your estimates of personnel requirements are based on an accurate analysis of sufficient, up-to-date and reliable information.
- The specifications you develop are clear, accurate and comply with organisational and legal requirements.
- The specifications you develop identify fair and objective criteria for selection.
- The specifications you develop are agreed with relevant people prior to recruitment action.

You clearly and accurately identify the organisational objectives and constraints affecting personnel requirements

As manager, it is your role to identify both the organisational objectives and the constraints which affect your personnel requirements.

Each practice setting will seek to identify its overall organisational objectives in the short, medium and long term. The objectives themselves represent the implementation of the organisation strategy document, which will have already been published and validated by external agencies, including any partner body with which the organisation will contract. Short-term objectives are those that may be achieved in any one financial year. Medium- and longer-term objectives are usually representative of an organisational plan, and relate to a three- to five-year time scale.

Organisational objectives may be simplistic, for example, to ensure all staff are trained to NVQ/SNVQ level 2 within 12 months. A longer-term organisational objective could be to work in partnership with a special provider body to facilitate both residential and therapeutic day care activities. To meet this objective, as manager, you would have to engage in proactive consultation with all interested parties – staff, residents and carers, as well as the partner body. Information would have to be communicated accurately and sensitively to all those concerned and appropriate feedback obtained.

Write a brief developmental plan for a residential establishment shortly to provide respite facilities to a group of 10 residents for one day a week. What would you need to consider? What would you need to communicate and to whom?

Each person in your employment should become, in essence, a stakeholder in the business. Ownership of roles and responsibilities assists in collective objective setting which can contribute to your service plan, focussing on personnel requirements. The opinion of your staff can influence decision making, such as the need to employ specific staff or retrain others to undertake the same role. However, the final decision in respect of identifying those realistic objectives, and the constraints which both influence and impact on personnel requirements, rests with the manager.

It can be helpful to represent the organisational objectives and constraints in table form. One technique is the SWOT analysis, which lists strengths, weaknesses, opportunities, and threats.

The skill is in identifying what positive action can arise from each.

Case study — Adrian Potts

Adrian Potts is a widower, aged 86. He remains active and can care for himself. Currently he attends your day centre facility once a week to socialise and take part in the activities. However, he has made a request to increase his amount of contracted time in the day centre from one day to three days a week. Unfortunately, due to increased service demand, you cannot offer additional day care at this time, but may be able to do so whenever a vacancy occurs. Naturally, Mr Potts requests that you keep him advised of when the service may be provided.

- What might you need to consider in terms of organisational objectives?
- What are the strengths and weaknesses in your plan?
- What organisational constraints might you need to consider?
- How do you propose to overcome the constraints?
- Represent the organisational objectives and constraints in table form. Consider a SWOT analysis to help you.

You consult with relevant people on personnel requirements in a timely and confidential manner

First, you will need to define who your 'relevant people' are for personnel requirements, where they are and how they may best be consulted. Good management depends upon good communication and consultation with relevant people. It requires integrity, clarity and trust. If you seek the views of others in consultative exercises, you will be more likely to engender ownership of the outcome and a willingness to participate in problem solving. The timeliness of the consultation is important, since information which arrives too late is of little use. Consider acting as a role model for others in relation to timeliness and punctuality.

Having identified your relevant people and agreed their role, you need to list the attributes likely to be required of prospective personnel to deliver the service according to organisational goals. This will help to direct your consultations with your relevant people.

Try it out

Write down your organisational goals and, for each, consider the qualities you will need in your personnel team to meet each of them. Begin to assemble a description of the skills, personality and attributes that you will look for in an employee who will do the job effectively.

A checklist is a good starting point, and you may choose to adapt the following model to suit your own needs:

- physique and manner;
- experience and education;
- general intelligence;
- special abilities;
- hobbies;
- personal circumstances;
- disposition.

This list is based on Alec Rodgers' seven-point plan. It may help your relevant people suggest a 'person specification' for a recruitment exercise and their ideas may therefore ultimately form the basis of a vacancy advertisement. This marks the first stage in matching your personnel to your organisational goals.

It is important for you to consider the ways in which you may motivate your relevant people to share their views and support your organisational goals. Your relevant people will tend to enjoy consultation if it offers a reward, and they will also prioritise the time taken. Maslow, Mayo, Herzberg and McClelland all researched ways of motivating groups and individuals. What all these different theorists concur on is that people respond to a work setting in different ways to satisfy different needs. No one single motivation exists as a universal panacea. Over-use of a stimulus such as pay will cease to have value if individuals have no time to spend or enjoy it. You need to have a grasp of what motivates your relevant people.

Having looked at how best to consult your relevant people in a timely manner and how to motivate them, what is the role of confidentiality in the process, and why is it important? You will need to understand the Data Protection Act 1998 and apply its principles in your consultation exercise. Consider the following questions:

- How will information from individuals be stored and exchanged?
- Will each group member be allowed access to the views to the rest of the group?
- How will differences of opinion be handled?
- What if people change their minds?

Remember that relevant people, during the consultation, may share sensitive or controversial views about personnel requirements, and may discuss specific people and name them. You will need to consider what information is shared, the manner in which it is shared and what information from the consultation exercise is recorded. You will need to consider that this information sharing will produce records accessible to staff, residents, carers and partner bodies within the care service sector. Records should therefore be accurate, relevant and not excessive; they must be processed in line with people's rights and be held securely.

A possible starting point would be to draw up ground rules for consultation which encompass the principle of confidentiality. These may include agreements not to mention people by name and not to hold any discussions which may be overheard. The role of confidentiality in the consultative exercise will underpin all your exchanges. You need to be aware of weak points and agree an approach to tackle them.

Case study — Motivation and confidentiality

This is your first meeting to begin the task of consultation in respect of personnel requirements. One group member arrives late and a third is unable to attend the session. You are keen for their contributions as they are experienced carers and have stated a willingness to play a role in personnel selection. Moreover, one group member begins sharing information in respect of a person known to you.

- Consider the time and venue for the meeting: is it available to everyone?
- What is the optimum size of the consultation group?
- Does the group represent the views of residents and carers who will use the service?
- Have you agreed ground rules on confidentiality?
- Have you agreed ground rules for attendance, duration and number of sessions?
- How will absent members be involved?
- What are the motives for group attendance? (Remember your reading around motivation: everyone needs to derive some benefit from the exercise.)

Finally, you will need to record and store information in accordance with the Data Protection Act 1998. Residents may request access to this information at a later stage, should concerns over staff suitability arise. Generally, a common law of confidence applies, which states that information cannot be passed to a third party without the permission of the provider. When the Freedom of Information Bill becomes an Act, all information held by public establishments will be accessible to the public. Consider this throughout each phase of your planning and recording.

Your estimates of personnel requirements are based on an accurate analysis of sufficient, up-to-date and reliable information

You have now identified, after consultation with relevant people, the skill mix required to operate your practice setting according to organisational goals. The numbers of staff required will of course be governed by health and safety ratios of staff to residents. You will also need to identify whether your requirements are compatible with your employee budget, and explore ways of maximising your workforce to show value for money.

In estimating personnel requirements, information needs to be accurate, relevant and retrievable from its storage point. A good starting place may be to identify your employee budget and where it is held. Deduct the cost of each staff member and consider unforeseen events. Can you cover sickness? Can you allow staff to attend training courses and still provide cover? Remember the Care Standards Act 2000 stipulates in Standard 30.4 that all staff receive a minimum of three days' training per year.

Your forecasts of your personnel requirements must meet the National Occupational Standard of competence. For this you will need to account for unplanned eventualities, as your home will need to function in times of staffing difficulties. Do you have a fallback position which is acceptable to the wider organisation and residents? Does your forecast take into account your legal responsibilities to personnel and residents?

If you have a practice setting where you have a vacancy, it will be helpful to ask some basic questions before seeking to fill the position. The new job need not match that done by the previous post-holder. Proactive recruitment demands that you undertake a job analysis before attempting to fill a vacancy. As manager you must consider the following:

- What type of job do I need to advertise?
- Does it remain the same job as originally occupied?
- Does the establishment still need this job?
- Does it meet its stated purpose?
- Can it be changed?
- Is it a job which could usefully meet changing residents' needs? (Focus upon under-represented groups, such as people with a disability, or black people or a need for male key workers.)

Consider methods of undertaking your job analysis:

- interview with the person leaving the post and current employees;
- structured observation of performance;
- study of staff profiles.

Now that you have thought through what you require, you need to work with relevant people to develop the specifications for the vacant post. The job description and person specification should cover:

- the purpose of the job;
- the roles and responsibilities of the post-holder and the wider team;
- the skills and knowledge required;
- prerequisite qualifications;
- experience;
- details of your practice setting and your current needs.

Proactive recruitment must focus upon the need to identify whether a vacant position does need to be filled. On this point you should consult with authorised people before beginning the recruitment process. Always consider the nature of the post, given changing residents' needs. This may provide the opportunity to change the post from full time to part time, using the hours of work flexibly to cover evenings and weekend working.

Proactive recruitment demands the writing of two basic documents by the manager, in consultation with relevant people. These include the job description and person specification. Both documents refer to the current post only; they must be reviewed in line with legal and changing work practices. However, when changes to such documents arise, you must consult with individual staff occupying same or similar positions to avoid discrimination.

Proactive recruitment is therefore a managed process to ensure that positions are filled quickly to meet both the residents' and the organisation's needs. Once a decision to recruit has been taken, the position must be advertised. Ensure that the advertisement is consistent with the written job description and person specification.

The following examples are job descriptions for a care assistant (Figure 21), and manager (Figure 22), reproduced with the kind permission of Broad View Care, a registered charity which provides residential care and services for adults with learning disabilities. These are examples of good recruitment practice.

Figure 21. Sample job description for a Care Assistant.

OUTLINE JOB DESCRIPTION

TITLE: Care Assistant

RESPONSIBLE TO: Manager

Job Summary:

To work within a team of caring staff in identifying and endeavouring to meet the needs of each resident in a way that respects their dignity and promotes their independence.

Key Tasks:

1.   To provide skilled and appropriate care to individual residents. This will include:
      a)   To follow and contribute to agreed training programmes and care plans
      b)   To help individual residents to develop their level of personal and social skills
      c)   To participate in occupational and recreational activities and encourage residents to do so
2.   To assist residents who need help with dressing, bathing and toileting, where necessary.
3.   To assist residents with mobility problems and other physical disabilities including incontinence; help in use and care of aids and personal equipment.
4.   To work together with all other staff in maintaining standards in accordance with the Philosophy of Care of the Home
5.   To be responsible for undertaking a range of household tasks, eg: laundry, ironing, general tidiness etc.
6.   To identify and discuss care needs with residents and other staff.
7.   To accompany residents where required to facilities within the community, eg: local adult education centre, swimming baths, shops, club, pub etc.
8.   To identify personal training and development needs and participate in the Staff Personal Development Programme.
9.   To bring to the attention of the Manager any inadequacies which may be to the detriment of residents' safety and welfare.
10.   To be aware of the fire procedures and be familiar with the fire fighting equipment and fire exits.
11.   To cover the absence of colleagues during periods of annual leave and sickness.
12.   Any other tasks as may be delegated by the Manager or Deputy Manager.

NB: **This is an outline Job Description only and may be amended – from time to time – in discussion with the postholder.**

JD: Care Assistant
August 2001

(Reproduced with the kind permission of Broad View Care Limited)

Figure 22. Sample job description for a Care Manager.

OUTLINE JOB DESCRIPTION

TITLE: Manager

BASE: 87 Narberth Way, Coventry, CV2 2LH

RESPONSIBLE TO:
(1) **Director for Care, for care/quality matters**
(2) **Director for Management, for administrative/financial matters**

****

PRIMARY PURPOSE: To manage 87 Narberth Way, its staff team and other resources, in an efficient and cost effective manner, so as to create an environment in which each resident is able to lead as full and as happy a life as possible.

PRINCIPAL RESPONSIBILITIES

1. To manage 87 Narberth Way, within the terms of Coventry City Council's registration requirements, the philosophy of care for the home and within Broad View Care's practices and procedures.

2. The Residents

a) To be aware of the needs of each resident (physical, psychological, social, spiritual and sexual).

b) To assist each resident in respect of dressing, bathing, toileting, mobility, minor dressings, nursing and other personal skills.

c) To establish a working care plan for each resident, that takes account their identified needs, their wishes where expressed, their skills and aspirations. Realistic goals and objectives are to be agreed for – and where possible with – each resident.

d) To monitor on an ongoing basis care plans, update and amend as necessary.

e) To explore – and implement – opportunities for each resident to develop their social skills, e.g visits to local shops, pubs, etc.

f) To explore – and implement – opportunities for each resident to develop their personal/domestic skills, e.g assisting in general cleanliness of the home, keeping their bedroom tidy etc.

g) To liaise closely with the relatives of each resident encouraging them to visit the home and to involve themselves in their care.

h) To liaise closely with the local GP, Dentist and other professional staff in respect of each resident.

i) To liaise closely with the day care manager of each resident and promote further day activities.

3. Staff

a) To ensure that the home is adequately and appropriately staffed at all times.

b) To manage all subordinate staff at the home.

c) To be responsible for the recruitment of new staff in the home.

d) To arrange induction training for all new staff in the home.

e) To work with each member of staff – as part of the staff personal development programme – in setting key objectives; identifying training needs and providing appropriate training opportunities.

f) To liaise with Broad View Care's Training and Development Manager in the organisation and provision of training courses.

g) To undertake counselling of staff where necessary.

h) To be aware of Broad View Care's disciplinary procedure; seek advice from the directors in the event of possible need to implement the procedure.

i) To ensure that all staff are aware of fire procedures, health and safety and food hygiene regulations.

j) To maintain records and manager staff sickness and annual leave.

4. The Building

a) To ensure that high standards of cleanliness and tidiness at the home are maintained at all times and maintain homeliness.

b) To ensure that all fire fighting equipment in the home is regularly checked maintained and maintenance records are kept.

c) To undertake periodic health and safety checks within the home, drawing any deficiencies to the immediate attention of the Director for Care.

d) To ensure that the general fabric of the home is maintained at a high standard, keeping a record of repairs/maintenance needed/undertaken and drawing any problems/deficiencies to the immediate attention of the Director for Care.

5. Personal

a) To identify own training needs and agree key objectives with the Directors as part of staff personal development.

b) To work with the Directors and staff in projecting a positive image of the home within the community.

c) To propose ideas and initiatives to the Directors for continuing to improve the services of the home.

d) To keep up to date with professional practices within this field and, if appropriate, maintain registration and PREP.

6. Financial

a) To practise good financial management, within the agreed budget for the home.

b) To ensure that proper financial procedures and records are maintained in respect of residents monies and petty cash.

c) To explore and promote fund raising initiatives, liaising as necessary with Broad View Care's Fundraiser.

d) To action any recommendations/requirements identified in annual financial audits, undertaken by the Director for Management.

7. To attend all visits by the Inspection Officer of Coventry City Council; work with the Directors in actioning any recommendations resulting from the visits.

8. To deal with any complaints in respect of the home; discuss as necessary with the Director for Care.

9. Any other duties as may be delegated by the Directors.

NB: **This is an Outline Job Description only and may be amended from time to time in discussion and following agreement with the postholder.**

JD Manager NW
August 2001

(Reproduced with the kind permission of Broad View Care Limited)

You are finding it difficult to recruit someone to fill a vacancy. In order to prevent a delay in the appointment:

- Will you engage in a thorough job analysis?
- Identify whether the role should change.
- Whom will you consult about this?
- Will you consider the needs of under-represented groups e.g. people from ethnic minority groups and disabled people, to meet the changing needs of residents?

The specifications you develop are clear, accurate and comply with organisational and legal requirements

You must ensure that you make clear reference to the organisational and legal requirements for the recruitment process. Concise information on these requirements should be available to job applicants; it may be sent out to them or held in an accessible place for easy reference. Organisational requirements focus upon defined areas of responsibility such as:

Figure 23. Organisational requirements in the recruitment process.

With specific reference to legal requirements for recruitment, you will need to be aware of the provisions of a number of Acts:

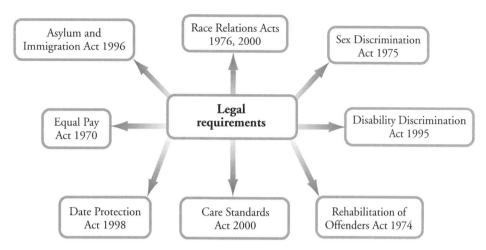

Figure 24. Legal requirements in the recruitment process.

Equal Pay Act 1970

The objective of this Act is to ensure that women receive the same pay and treatment as men, in the same or similar work by the same or affiliated employer in order for the claim to be considered valid. Pay is defined under the Act so as to include sick pay and redundancy payment. The work of women is to be given an equal value to that of men. Under the Act, women must also have:

- an equivalent work rate;
- the same right as men to join a pension scheme.
- the same fringe benefits as men, such as subsidised meals or additional holidays for length of service.

If people seek to claim for pay discrimination, they must ensure that they compare themselves to a man or woman in the same employment. The man or woman has to be employed in the same or similar work by the same employer, or affiliated employer, in order for the claim to be considered valid.

Sex Discrimination Act 1975

This Act makes discrimination, either direct or indirect, unlawful.

Race Relations Acts 1976/2000

The Acts make discrimination on the grounds of race, ethnicity, colour or national origin, be it direct or indirect, unlawful. Like the Sex Discrimination Act 1975, the Race Relations Act 1976 refers to direct and indirect discrimination, and serves to protect rights of staff, be they full time or part time or on temporary contracts. Direct discrimination means treating any individual applying for a job more or less favourably than another, perhaps because of their race, gender or marital status. A prime example of discrimination would be if a black person applied for a job as a care assistant, and at interview was advised that he or she would not fit in with an all-white staff or resident group.

Indirect discrimination arises when the requirements for a job disadvantage a particular minority group. An example would be a British Sikh man applying for a job as a community enabler for people with disabilities. At interview he is told that he would have to remove his turban to comply with uniform requirements. Such a demand would be in conflict with his religious beliefs and cultural requirements, and as such deliberately, though indirectly, disadvantage his application. This would be illegal.

Rehabilitation of Offenders Act 1974

This Act enables a person who has previously offended and received a sentence of 30 months or less to be rehabilitated and their convictions termed as spent. The nature of the conviction and the age of the offender will determine the time before the conviction is considered spent. Offenders with a background of consistent crime against individuals are required to sign the Rehabilitation of Offenders Act declaration.

Vulnerable groups such as children, older people and those with disabilities are protected by the National Police Register, which monitors the movements and rehabilitation of ex-offenders. Nevertheless, you need to be aware that it is illegal to discriminate on the grounds of a spent conviction.

Disability Discrimination Act 1995

This Act applies to any organisation (with certain exceptions, such as the armed forces) which employs more than 20 people. It gives individuals classified as disabled the right not to be discriminated against without justifiable reason. Moreover, employers must make 'reasonable adjustments' to premises to enable a disabled person to occupy a role for which he or she is qualified.

You therefore need to be vigilant not to discriminate against a disabled person at any stage of recruitment. Disability must not disadvantage a person's application.

Asylum and Immigration Act 1996

This Act carries a criminal conviction for anyone who employs an individual who does not have permission to work in the United Kingdom on or after 27 January 1997.

Data Protection Act 1998

All information received from prospective candidates must be recognised and protected as confidential. Only information on successful candidates need be retained and stored confidentially. Information on unsuccessful candidates should be kept no longer than is necessary; any processing before its destruction must of course also comply with the provisions of the Act. Information must not be transferred to other areas of your organisation.

Try it out

Consider whether the legislation relating to recruitment is adhered to in your experience within your practice setting. Make specific notes about any possible omissions.

Care Standards Act 2000

National Minimum Standards for care, defined in the Care Standards Act 2000, identify core requirements for all care homes providing personal or nursing care to older people. You will be conversant with the standards relating to your practice setting. For older persons, for example, Standard 29 states that 'service users must be supported and protected by the unit's recruitment policy and practices'.

The specifications you develop identify fair and objective criteria for selection

Specifications cover the key purpose of the job, the rules and responsibilities of individuals and the team in which they work, the skills and knowledge required by individuals and the team, and other details specific to your practice setting. From these specifications the selection criteria will emerge, against which candidates will be assessed. In essence, a person specification represents an analysis of the main characteristics required for an advertised role to be performed to competently.

The recruitment and induction of staff are interrelated. Together they represent the manager's task of selecting and introducing new staff of a suitable calibre to occupy positions to deliver a service to residents. According to P. Plumbley:

> People are the life blood of any enterprise, they are its vital asset. On them depends everything else. Capital and ideas or inventions are sterile without people to activate them. But people are a very variable commodity with an infinite range of skills, aptitudes and personalities . . . . Recruitment and selection is not simply about filling jobs, it is about building a workforce that is suitable and adaptable to suit the changing needs of the enterprise.

A variety of formats exist for completing a person specification, for example the Eyre five-point plan and the Alec Rodgers' seven-point plan (see page 230). The latter is slightly more detailed than the former; it was written and accredited by the National Institute of Industrial Psychology in 1970. The Rodgers plan is outlined in Figure 25.

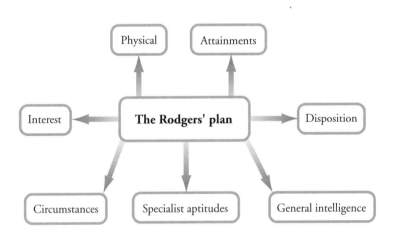

Figure 25. The Rodgers' plan.

These seven points will prompt you to prepare a detailed summary of the attributes required of a candidate to occupy any post. It is useful to tabulate 'Essential' and 'Desirable' attributes for each point, as in Table 3.

Table 3. Example of a person specification for a care assistant

Attribute	Essential	Desirable
1. Physical	Physically fit	None
2. Attainments	Minimum NVQ 2 in care	Ability to engage in advanced training (NVQ 3 and above)
3. General intelligence	Quick thinker under pressure	Alert
4. Special aptitudes	Excellent oral communication skills. Familiar with older people's needs. Excellent listening skills. Ability to record daily assessment sheets. Able to help residents read personal correspondence. Able to work in a team or individually with support. Ability to liaise with residents' families and other significant persons	Ability to learn new skills to improve resident care
5. Interests	To have a genuine interest in the care and support of older people in their daily lives. Ability to socialise with people of all ages, race, gender, or ethnic origin without distinction or prejudice	Orientated activities (directed activities which improve quality of life for older people)
6. Disposition	Sense of humour and friendly nature. Can work in a team, work under pressure and to time deadlines. Ability to resolve problems and to work with a varied work pattern. Demonstrate a commitment to developing antidiscriminatory practice and equal opportunities in personal work practices	People orientated
7. Circumstances	Able to undertake shift work (and split shifts as required) and to work weekends in rotation	Flexible to negotiated work needs and demands

While the seven-point plan provides a concise guide, you must ensure that your person specification rests upon fair and objective criteria. You must be aware that panel members define fairness and objectivity according to individual life experiences. Therefore, a system of weighting needs to be introduced.

Try it out

Your panel of interviewers will need to be motivated to undertake this exercise: its fun element should therefore be emphasised. It is a good exercise to check for cultural assumptions. Present a list of 'people types' and ask your relevant people to say what qualities they may ascribe to each. For example:

- a woman in casual dress;
- a 40–something man;
- a pregnant woman;
- a person wearing a suit.

Fairness and objectivity are vital in order to ensure equal opportunities in recruitment. Therefore, it is a key requirement that you and relevant people, some of whom will make up the interview panel, check against stereotyping.

Case study

You are a newly appointed care manager to a rehabilitation centre for people with acute and chronic physical disabilities. You find the staff's job descriptions are out of date and no longer match their current duties. Additionally, no person specifications exist. Vacancies exist for both care assistants and senior carers.

- Draft job descriptions for both posts.
- Draft person specifications for management appraisal and interviews.

After you have written what is required in the job description and the person specification, you will have to advertise the position available. How might you write a job advertisement to attract that special person? The following points cover the minimum information required in the advertisement.

- *Job title*. State the job title.
- *Job description*. Briefly specify the main duties involved.
- *The organisation's purpose*. Briefly describe what work the organisation undertakes.
- *Salary*. An indicative figure or rate should be given, as this is likely to be the most important factor in encouraging applicants.
- *Qualifications/experience*. If the post demands minimum levels of qualification and experience, this must be stated. Quite often salary will be dependent on both.
- *Location of post and organisation*. State where the organisation and post are sited.
- *How to apply*. Give the address and a telephone number of a named person for further details and an informal discussion. Also make it clear what the person needs to do in order to apply (e.g. fill in an application form, or simply send in a curriculum vitae?).
- *Special benefits*. These may include a company car, relocation expenses, private health insurance or assistance with child care arrangements.

The presentation of the advertisement will give applicants their first impressions of both the job and the organisation. Advertisements must not discriminate on the grounds of gender, race, disability or age. Remember that the Equal Opportunities Commission monitor employment advertisements at random.

Find two advertisements for a position in a professional journal or a local newspaper. For each of the eight points that should be included in a job advertisement, identify their strengths and weaknesses.

The specifications you develop are agreed with relevant people prior to recruitment action

The relevant people you consulted over personnel requirements will also be able to make a contribution to the drawing up of job specifications. They will have included team members, peers, senior managers, members of the selection teams and specialists in your field. Ultimately, you will need to recruit a selection panel from this group, and their involvement in and ownership of staff selection will be crucial to the survival of your organisation.

Advanced planning

Most interviews, be they one-to-one, two/three-to-one, or a panel, follow a particular process. Lack of planning/preparation may lead to a failure to select. There are several things you must attend to before the interview:

✓ determine the composition of the selection panel;
✓ set the time scales for participation;
✓ ascribe the roles of chairperson, lead interviewer(s) and observer;
✓ set questions relating to the person specification in advance, which will be asked to each candidate;
✓ decide on and prepare the interview room – allow for minimum disruption and maximum confidentiality.

Ensure that panel members have a knowledge of:

✓ organisational recruitment practices;
✓ equal opportunity procedures;
✓ ACAS advisory guidelines on recruitment;
✓ active listening skills;
✓ excellent communication skills;
✓ an ability to make considered judgements.

Ideally, your selection panel must have an appropriate mix of people in terms of age, race and gender, as well as representation from residents.

Think it over

Think about different ways of motivating your panel to undertake this task when they are likely to have busy schedules themselves.

Duties of the selection panel

The selection panel will have to do the following, in order:

- Write and agree person specification.
- Write and agree job description.
- Decide which questions on the person specification will be asked and how answers will be assessed.
- Agree on what information is to be sent out to candidates in advance.
- Draw up a short-list of candidates to be interviewed.
- Conduct the interviews.
- Reach a collective decision on the appointment.
- Consider references.
- Communicate within 24 hours to the successful candidate.
- Provide exit interviews to unsuccessful candidates (the manager should perform this upon request).

Try it out

Read your own job description and then 'match' it to your own person specification. Consider the contents of both and evaluate whether they were written accurately and in a manner which might attract suitable candidates to the advertised post.

Keys to good management practice

At the start of the recruitment process, you must:

- agree and draw up both the person specification and job description;
- agree how the criteria within the person specification will be assessed at interview;
- identify any additional information about the nature of the job or the establishment that you will need to send out to applicants to assist their preparation for interview.

You wish to recruit two new senior carers following a successful recruitment drive for care assistants. However, before any recruitment action takes place, you wish to agree with your relevant people the specifications for each position.

- How will you draw up and agree both the job description and the person specification?
- What time scales do you propose for these tasks?
- How will you consult and prepare with your relevant people and retain their commitment and motivation?
- What criteria do you need to consider and agree from the person specification, which will be used for assessment purposes at a future interview?
- How will you decide the composition of the interview panel? (You will need to consider age, gender, race and resident participation.)
- What other planning priorities do you need to be aware of?

Evidence collection C8.1 — Identify personnel requirements

You must prove that you identify personnel requirements to the national standard of competence.

You must show evidence that you identify requirements for at least four of the following types of personnel; internal, permanent, full-time, paid. This can be evidenced and appropriately demonstrated for all personnel, by referring to use of personnel specifications required for any person to occupy any post to the required standard.

You must show evidence that you involve at least two of the following types of authorised people: team members, members of the selection team. To demonstrate this you must refer to the specifications you develop, and these must be agreed with your authorised people prior to the recruitment action. Your authorised people are those you have consulted in respect of personnel requirements and are able to contribute to job specifications.

You must also show evidence that you develop all of the following types of specifications; key purpose of the posts, individual and team roles and responsibilities, required individual and competencies, as well as other details specific to the organisation. To demonstrate these you must refer to how you identify organisational objectives and constraints affecting personnel requirements. You must also refer to your estimates of personnel requirements, which are based on an accurate analysis of sufficient up to date and reliable information. Additionally, the specifications you develop are clear, accurate, and comply with organisational and legal requirements.

Learning outcomes

- You use appropriately skilled and experienced people to assess and select personnel.
- The information you obtain about each candidate is relevant to and sufficient for the selection process.
- You assess the information objectively against specified selection criteria.
- Your selection decisions are justifiable from the evidence gained.
- You only inform authorised people about selection decisions and the identified development needs of successful candidates.
- The information you provide to authorised people is clear and accurate.
- All candidates receive feedback and information appropriate to their needs at each stage of the selection process.
- Your records of the selection process are complete, accurate, clear and comply with organisational and legal requirements.
- You pass on your recommendations for the improvements to the selection process to the appropriate people in your organisation.

You use appropriately skilled and experienced people to assess and select personnel

After the closing date for applications, the interview panel should use the criteria in the person specification to draw up a short-list of applicants to be interviewed. A panel process is a much fairer means of assessing applicant suitability than leaving it to the manager alone. A panel also allows for appropriate race, gender, disability and resident participation in decision making. This may reduce the chances of discrimination. Increasingly more organisations, particularly from the charitable sector, seek resident involvement in the recruitment process. This represents a great step forward in recognising the role that residents play in organisational development.

The panel should ideally comprise the same people who drew up the job description and person specification, as they will be familiar with the criteria to be used. They will also be trained and experienced in interviewing. Additionally, a panel will represent a supportive vehicle for the less experienced interviewer and serve as a useful training venue.

Using the person specification, the panel should, collectively, read through the applications and make decisions as to who meets the criteria and will be interviewed. Applicants who only partly meet the criteria may be called for interview in the event of a low response. In any event, all applicants should be contacted by letter at least a week in advance of the interview, thanking them for their response and either inviting them for interview or politely stating why their application has been unsuccessful.

Case study — Select personnel

You are preparing to interview six applicants for four care assistant roles, to meet new resident demand as a result of a recent extension to your residential home, which has increased your resident base from 26 to 32.

- How will you ensure that your short-listing panel is suitably trained?
- How might residents become involved in the selection process?
- What preparations will you need to make?
- How will you organise and agree the different roles members of the panel will have during interviews?

The information you obtain about each candidate is relevant to and sufficient for the selection process

Your panel will best elicit information from candidates if they generally ask open-ended questions. Closed questioning is acceptable but it does require following up. For example, a question like 'Are you responsible for leading a team?' needs to be followed up to reveal related facts for confirmation. Remember that you can always rephrase a closed question as a more open one. For example, the earlier question could be rephrased as 'How did you lead your team and what leadership skills did you employ?'

As manager or panel chairperson, you will need to be aware of how panel members behave. Some types of behaviour should always be avoided, as they will fail to elicit the information you require to make a satisfactory selection and will call to account your interviewing styles. Examples of such behaviours are:

- *self-opinionated interviewers*, who simply give personal opinions and may even come across in a threatening or discriminatory manner;
- *compulsive interviewers*, who like to hear their own voice and take more time to convey their message than the candidate and so run the risk of overwhelming the candidate with the power of dialogue;
- *antagonistic interviewers*, who use an argumentative tone to make a point (the danger here is uncontrollable conflict);
- *directive interviewers*, who ask direct questions and give candidates little opportunity to say how they might meet residents' needs;
- *over-friendly interviewers*, whose questioning is too personal and subjective and who appear too friendly (the risk here is a lack of objectivity and possible hidden agendas being perceived by the candidate).

Don't let compulsive interviewers dominate the selection panel!

It is also important to be aware of the candidates' responses. Do not allow the interviewee:

- to wander off the subject;
- to interrupt questioning;
- to go over old ground;
- to take too long to reply;
- to engage in repetition.

What interviewing or questioning techniques might you employ? The percentage clock (Figure 26) offers an accurate measure of interviewing versus candidate input to obtain sufficient and satisfactory information to assist selection.

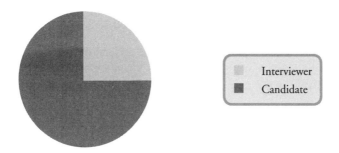

Figure 26. The percentage clock: interviewer takes up 25% of allocated time; candidate is given 75% of all allocated time to give a full account of skills, abilities and experiences.

Another constructive technique is the *fourfold method*:

- ***Open-ended questions.*** Avoid closed questions (which demand only a yes/no response) and give candidates every opportunity to discuss their skills, abilities and life experiences.
- ***Reflective questions.*** These enable candidates to reflect on content and give them the opportunity to offer an honest and in-depth response.
- ***Probing questions.*** These are primarily used to encourage candidates to give more detailed information.
- ***Candidate questions.*** Offer candidates the opportunity to ask questions in relation to their application.

Try it out

Using the fourfold method, make a list of questions and devise a mixture of each type, suitable for panel members to elicit the required information.

The way in which you end the interview is important. At the close of the interview, you must:

- request permission from candidates to take up references (if not already received);
- ask how much notice candidates require contractually to give their current employer, if the position was offered to them;
- state whether a medical examination will be required, subject to a general practitioner's report;

- inform candidates precisely when they will receive a response (the time span should be the same for every candidate);
- refer to the opportunity for exit interviews for unsuccessful candidates (specify the type of exit interview which will be provided for personal/professional development purposes).

After the interview you must ask all panel members to write up their notes and collate any scoring applied to specific questions. Then the panel can collectively make its decision, upon all evidence gathered, as to the appointment.

Case study — Obtaining information for your selection process

You are holding a series of interviews to appoint both care and domestic staff. However, you are aware of the obstacles which might prevent you obtaining sufficient information on each candidate to make a final selection.

- How will you eliminate the self-opinionated interviewer, the compulsive interviewer, the antagonistic interviewer, the directive interviewer and the over-friendly interviewer?
- What ground rules will you set to avoid such behaviour emerging at interview?
- How might you employ the fourfold method and use the percentage clock to elicit the information you require to make a selection?

You assess the information objectively against specified selection criteria

In order to assess information objectively, the questions and manner of each interview need to be the same. Therefore:

✓ check that questions used are relevant to the post;
✓ remove overt physical barriers, such as too many desks and chairs;
✓ ask the same questions in sequence to all interviewees;
✓ avoid being judgemental and making unnecessary assumptions;
✓ before asking challenging questions, ensure the interviewee is relaxed about the nature of the interview;
✓ ensure that your tone of voice and body posture are relaxed;
✓ do not field too many questions;
✓ do not send mixed messages;
✓ do not use a patronising tone of voice;
✓ do not interrupt interviewees or put words in their mouth;

✓ ensure that questions asked are relevant to either the job description or the person specification;

✓ make certain you understand the interviewee's answers;

✓ if not, seek clarification;

✓ give the interviewee the opportunity to ask questions;

✓ bring the interview to a close in a relaxed, professional manner.

Case study — Review selection criteria

It is imperative that you regularly review selection criteria in order that they continue to deliver the outcomes you desire.

- Will you check that questions used are relevant to the post being advertised?
- Do you use a set sequence questions with all interviewees?
- Is there an optimum number of questions to be asked?
- Are you aware of the import of your body language? What changes might you make to avoid giving mixed messages?
- Do you clarify answers given by the interviewee and what method could you use to aid understanding?

Your selection decisions are justifiable from the evidence gained

Once the interviews are over, a candidate needs to be selected for the appointment. Some interviewing panels use a scoring system or evidence matrix for fully answered questions. A scoring system identifies the quality and depth of answers to the standard that the candidate is required to give. Points for each answer are then awarded by each of the individual members of the panel asking respective questions. Equally, an evidence matrix can establish a rating to answers given on the basis of (a) outstanding, (b) excellent, (c) good, (d) satisfactory and (e) question not answered. Additionally, the use of observers gives some legitimacy to the process and can give additional feedback to interviewers sometimes preoccupied listening, making notes or perhaps unaware of the barriers to their own listening.

Once the appointment has been collectively agreed, successful candidates should be informed immediately, first orally, then in writing, requesting their acceptance. When acceptance has been given, it is best that a written contract, legally termed under Section 1 of the Employment Rights Act 1996, is provided.

In law, new employees should receive a statement of particulars within a minimum of two months of starting employment. However, a proactive care manager will ensure this statement is made at the start of employment, to avoid the potential for unnecessary disputes. The rationale is that, once the employee agrees to work for the new employer and the salary, terms and conditions are agreed and countersigned, the contract becomes legally binding.

An exit interview for unsuccessful candidates for developmental purposes is desirable for good care management practice and equally for practical purposes, as the unsuccessful candidates may still represent future employees.

As an outcome of the Data Protection Act 1998, any candidate may ask to see any written copies of information compiled on them by panel members at interview. Therefore, it becomes imperative that all panel members record only factual statements, which they can support. This must be part of their training and part of any evaluation of the selection process. Ensure consistency and eliminate the possibility of any discrimination in the recording of candidates' statements.

Try it out

Consider using alternative selection methods, such as a scoring system, or use of observers to ensure a justifiable decision at your next interview.

Case study — Tom's selection

You have interviewed four candidates for a vacancy for an experienced carer. One candidate, Tom, has emerged as the strongest. However, it is good practice to check that your decision is justifiable from the evidence gained.

- Would you use a scoring system to quantify answers given at interview?
- Would you employ an evidence matrix? For example, an essential qualification, NVQ2 in care, can be validated by certificate form at the interview.
- Consider using an impartial observer who might feed back on the overall process when panel members were asking questions, writing notes, but not actively listening throughout.
- How might a collective, unanimous decision be reached? Suggest a justifiable process.
- Once the decision has been made, what processes would you go through to communicate this to Tom, both verbally and non-verbally?
- How might you organise exit interviews for unsuccessful candidates?

You only inform authorised people about selection decisions and the identified development needs of successful candidates

You must inform authorised people (i.e. those on the selection panel) about decisions made at interview only after satisfactory references have been received and after you have verified your candidate's employment history, skills and abilities while in post, duties, special knowledge and disposition. Only then do you inform.

The development needs of successful candidates can be identified and managed within a planned induction programme. After looking at how to obtain a candidate's references, this section focuses on how the development needs of successful candidates can be ascertained and met in induction programmes, using mandatory TOPSS induction standards 1–5. It will also be necessary, under the Care Standards Act 2000, to ensure that induction is delivered and assessed within six weeks of a new employee starting work. Since 1 April 2002, inspectors from the National Standards Commission have had responsibility for verifying the suitability of induction programmes to ensure that they meet certain standards, and that managers take responsibility to assess the learning of their staff to the required standards nationally.

What does a manager need from a reference?

The reference must verify the name of the person, previous position, time spent in employment and experience. It should also cover specialist skills and knowledge, for example a nursing qualification, a first-aid qualification, a moving and handling qualification to RoSPA standards. The reference should mention the person's performance levels and ability to work in a team. Equally important is the attendance record, honesty and why the previous employer would recommend this person for this position.

Think it over

What other factual, yet confidential, information would you seek of a prospective staff member?

What must a manager not do?

It is important that you do not do any of the following:

- Rely on a verbal reference, as this will be difficult to verify and is subject to interpretation.
- Rely only on subjective opinions upon character, as this may be difficult to support factually.
- Make an offer of employment in advance and then request a reference.
- Influence an interview panel by suggesting in advance of the actual interview that the candidate's references provide the positive support you require. This would introduce bias and discrimination.

Case study — Reference request

Your interviewing panel is required to draw up a specific reference request form for an advertised position of senior carer. You inform the panel of the purpose of the reference. You emphasise the importance of confidentiality. As a panel, you require factual information about potential candidates to support their suitability for this position. You will only use criteria which can be checked against the person specification that is already written and ready to be sent out to both the successful candidate and the previous employer. Consider the following questions and develop them as your needs dictate.

- How long have you known this person, and in what capacity?
- Please describe their duties and responsibilities while in your employment.
- In your professional opinion, how well did they perform?
- Were they reliable?
- Were they punctual and have time-keeping skills?
- Did they have organisational skills?
- Were they honest?
- How well did they perform in team-based work?
- Why would you recommend this person for this position?

Staff induction

Having decided to appoint, you then inform your authorised people about your selection decisions, which you can evidence. However, the development needs of successful candidates are best identified through a structured and managed induction programme.

Staff induction is a term generally used to describe a process by which a member of staff (particularly a new one) is introduced to an organisational system. In theory, induction represents an extension of an already established recruitment and selection procedure. Therefore it should be structured with a view to transforming first impressions of an organisation or role into positive attitudes. Research within a variety of multinational companies has indicated that it can encourage higher retention rates as well as high performance levels.

Think it over

Jot down your thoughts and experiences, positive or negative, of what staff induction means to you.

To begin with, you have to focus on the subjective feelings of new staff entering or transferring to a new organisation. This can often be a bewildering experience, combining mixed feelings of wanting to satisfy employers, residents and colleagues, to be accepted and to succeed. It is not uncommon for someone to become exasperated when having to assimilate a new home, unfamiliar travel and different work routines all at once. A drastic change in lifestyle does require direct support from the manager.

Induction must focus on empowering new employees to reach their full potential in the shortest possible time. At the start of induction, new entrants should be greeted warmly. Even if there was a pre-interview observation visit to the practice setting, it will be necessary to re-familiarise new employees to their new surroundings. Introduce them to their colleagues and encourage them to write down their names, as they are likely to forget them.

Introduce new employees to their mentor. The mentor will be a trusted individual who will take responsibility for the new entrant without the constraints of a manager–employee relationship. Specifically in the case of induction, mentors will introduce entrants to all aspects of their roles and responsibilities, organisational administration, personnel criteria and practical matters. Irrespective of the work setting within the care service sector, the rationale is the same: to cushion the blow of beginning the new job, in order for understanding and learning to take place, and to enable entrants to perform their roles to organisational and residents' expectations and standards.

Induction programmes will vary from the mandatory six weeks to three months or even a year in some statutory agencies, and can be linked to the contract of employment.

No new employees can absorb everything that they need to know about the work setting in one go without the danger of information overload. It is therefore necessary to ensure that there is a gradual learning curve. Briefly, the mentor will attempt to expand on information the entrant has assimilated from the recruitment process. This may begin with a brief explanation of the organisation's structure and policy objectives, residents' needs, a detailed description of the employee's duties and responsibilities, and health and safety arrangements.

It is common practice within many larger organisations to issue to new staff a manual relating to health and safety matters, personal security, compulsory supervisory controls, appraisal, salary, disciplinary and grievance procedures, equal opportunities and legislative requirements, pension arrangements and policies on confidential practice, and so on. Manuals may also deal with equally important issues such as sick pay, overtime, staff rotation, flexible work, meal or break times, smoking policy, secure staff lockers, or even how to accrue time off. Even if these areas are detailed in writing, adequate time must be spent on each of them with the new employee.

Equally, time must be taken to meet staff, particularly those colleagues the entrant will be working with. Relationships will need to be built. It is also good practice to allow time for the entrant to be introduced to and to get to know the residents.

Try it out

Consider what functions you consider necessary to include in an induction programme in your practice setting. List them and give explanations for your choices.

Structure of the programme

A key feature of a well thought out induction programme is the regularity of supervision between mentor and entrant. The programme should also allow the line manager to support and measure progress, in a three-way relationship with the entrant and mentor. Other colleagues should provide additional guidance, advice and ongoing support.

While an entrant needs to be able to learn through experience, any risk to either the entrant or residents must be minimised. Ensure individual autonomy is supported by ongoing supervision.

A manager's induction checklist has been devised specifically for the care service sector. The checklist will ensure that a new employee benefits from the induction programme and that areas covered are evaluated. This checklist is given in the Appendix.

Potential problems with induction

The following is a list of potential problems to watch for within an induction programme:

- Allowing the new entrant to flounder and lose confidence because adequate supervision, both formal and informal, has not been put in place.
- Failure to match the entrant to a mentor with appropriate skills and qualities (this may leave a mentor deskilled by a lack of progress by the new entrant).
- The entrant not establishing the right kind of professional relationship with the mentor, which may result in conflict and allegations of unfair treatment unless identified early and resolved.
- Over-dependence of the entrant upon the mentor, which has the potential to cause friction with other work colleagues. Clear role negotiations and networking with peers may serve to reduce this.
- Stereotypes of previous entrants can undermine an entrant's confidence or can put an entrant under the undue stress of having to live up to an artificial image.
- Entrants being expected to take on extra work to satisfy their mentor's personal interest areas at the expense of their contractual duties. This has the potential to cause both resentment among work colleagues and conflict with line manager.
- Formal and informal supervision of entrants being seen as an intrusive or threatening experience. The mentor's supervisory experience will largely determine a positive two-way outcome.

Unless induction is managed, supervised and carefully coordinated, entrants can easily fail an induction process. This will result in either an extension of the programme or the entrant's dismissal.

The benefits of an induction programme

- It assists in improving overall standards and provides a benchmark for staff development at the start of a career.
- It develops a culture of supervised work. Within such a culture everyone benefits, including residents.
- It enhances a greater sense of responsibility among others.
- It should improve internal communication as well as networking systems for all staff, not only new entrants, which should lead to more innovative learning.
- It is likely to result in higher retention rates among new and current staff, which yields more efficiency, greater resident satisfaction and higher profits.

- It promotes stability and serves to harmonise a needs-led culture.
- It promotes a needs-led culture. Within this culture new entrants should be enabled to realise their abilities. Equally, residents benefit from consistent needs-led care.

Try it out

List the advantages of a well managed induction system as it might apply to your own organisation. Include areas of good practice you already use.

The information you provide to authorised people is clear and accurate

The recruitment process which you have in place must be both communicated to and understood by your authorised people. These individuals collectively provide the mechanisms by which you are able to recruit within the framework of your organisational requirements.

To be certain that authorised people understand what is required of them, map out their involvement in the recruitment process and be equally certain this information is *clear* and *accurate* and understood.

Think it over

How might you map out the involvement of your authorised people in the recruitment process, ensuring that any information provided is clear, accurate and understood? Jot down your thoughts.

Case study — Providing information to your selection panel

You wish to recruit additional staff and are aware that the recruitment process must be fully understood by your selection panel and that all information provided to them needs to clear and accurate, and meets legal and organisational requirements.

- Who plans the overall recruitment process?
- How might you agree on what posts do actually need immediate occupancy?
- How will you facilitate the writing of job descriptions and person specifications?
- Who will write the job advertisement and what media might you suggest for it?
- Who organises the sending out of application forms, the setting of closing dates and the provision of pre-placement visits by potential applicants?
- How might the roles be ascribed for these purposes?   ▼

- What criteria do you draw upon for short-listing?
- How might requests for references be drawn up and considered?
- How will you decide the composition of the interview panel to obtain a broad representation in terms of age, race, gender, disability and resident perspective?
- What roles will members of the interview panel have?
- What methods will you use to match your interview questions to the person specification?
- At interview, how do you quantify applicant's answers?
- What emphasis do you place on applicant references and why?
- How would you collectively arrive at a decision, which you can own and evidence?
- What systems will you put into place to feed back to applicants?
- Will you offer exit interviews and if so why?
- What emphasis will you place on contractual terms of employment and why?
- Where might an induction programme feature in the contractual terms of employment?
- How will induction be assessed?
- Might you include capability criteria to aid success?

All candidates receive feedback and information appropriate to their needs at each stage of the selection process

Candidates will require different degrees of feedback appropriate to their needs. These needs may relate to the candidate's language, degree of literacy or a disability (see the discussion of the Disability Discrimination Act 1995 on page 238).

Feedback is appropriate at three phases of the recruitment process, as shown in Table 4.

Table 4. The feedback process

Phase of recruitment process	Type of feedback to be given
After the placing of the job advertisement	Verbal information about the post and the organisation
During pre-placement visits	Verbal informal feedback during the course of the visit
After short-listing	Candidates not short-listed for interview should be sent a brief letter explaining why
After interview	Exit interviews for professional developmental purposes

Following the job advertisement, it is not unusual for candidates to request verbally more information about the nature of the post and the organisation itself, before they make a formal application. Your job advertisement may very well have an invitation for 'further enquiries'. This is where you brief your authorised people about what information is shared, to ensure they only share information associated with the job advertisement and the work of your organisation. Therefore, your briefing needs to be specific to the advertised post and its relationship to the organisation. You must remember that confidentiality should be your uppermost concern and it is your duty:

- to protect your residents.
- to protect your existing staff.
- to protect the integrity of the organisation.

The pre-placement visit provides an opportunity for you to meet the candidate informally, and to discuss in more depth the requirements of the person specification and the job description. It is important that your feedback to candidates is specific and very honest, and does not depart from the remit of the person specification and job description.

The pre-placement visit also enables candidates to develop informal impressions without commitment, as well as share aspects of themselves that they are unlikely to during a formal interview. The visit involves a two-way information exchange: candidates can ask questions, and you can develop your own impressions – being careful to avoid bias – of a candidate's motivation to proceed with the application.

A pre-placement visit allows candidates to develop informal impressions.

Candidates who are not short-listed for interview should be sent a brief letter explaining why they have not met the criteria of the person specification.

The next stage of formal feedback is after the interview. Successful candidates will be given a verbal offer of employment and feedback as to the aspects of their application that led to this offer; this must be followed up in writing.

Before employment can begin, candidates must be reminded, both verbally and in writing, that, by law, police checks must be undertaken. Any offer of employment must be conditional on the results of those checks. It is good practice to remind candidates that this process takes an average of at least six weeks.

It also remains good management practice to offer exit interviews to unsuccessful candidates. Ideally they should be a formal exercise, person to person, for professional development purposes. However, some candidates may prefer an informal exchange over the telephone. Exit interviews should be undertaken as soon as possible after the interview. Your feedback must be very specific to collective decisions made at interview – exit interviews are not about personalities. You may, however, suggest in what areas candidates may need more experience, qualifications or skills required for such a position and how and where this might be obtained. Your feedback should be positive, friendly and not leave the candidate demotivated, but rather optimistic.

Try it out

Develop a unit strategy for giving effective feedback to prospective candidates for any job you seek to advertise in the future. Your feedback must follow the entire selection process.

Case study — Jonathan's exit interview

You recently held an interview for a senior carer position. You received six completed applications. Four candidates were short-listed and interviewed. Jonathan was unsuccessful at interview. You have already spoken to him and informed him of the outcome. Additionally, you have agreed to offer him an exit interview for his own professional development purposes.

- How soon would you offer Jonathan an exit interview?
- Why is time scale so important to both you and the candidate?
- How might your feedback to prevent Jonathan feeling a personal sense of failure?
- How will you identify the areas of your person specification he did not meet and how might your feedback reflect this professionally?
- How will your feedback assist Jonathan to focus on areas of development he might undertake through assessable NVQ3 work-based training?
- How will you frame your feedback so that it presents as friendly, calm and positive?

Your records of the selection process are complete, accurate, clear and comply with organisational and legal requirements

A series of pro formas will help to ensure that your records are complete. The records you need to have in place are:

- appropriate job descriptions for the advertised post (see above);
- a person specification, preferably written in accordance with Rodgers' seven-point plan (see above);
- a short-list form;
- a interview form;
- an interview satisfaction form;
- a complaints questionnaire.

Examples of a short-list form, interview satisfaction form and a complaints questionnaire can be found on www.heinemann.co.uk/vocational under Health and Social Care.

You pass on your recommendations for improvements to the selection process to the appropriate people in your organisation

Recommendations for improvement are an outcome of a comprehensive evaluation of the entire selection process. Only then will you be in a position to make considered recommendations to appropriate people in your organisation. Where do you start?

Interview environment

- Does it afford minimum disruption and maximum confidentiality?
- Do seating arrangements remove physical barriers and facilitate conversation?
- Is the environment distracting?
- Can candidates access the environment without assistance?
- What barriers exist which can reasonably be adjusted to assist access to all, as required by the Disability Discriminations Act 1995?

- Does the composition of your selection panel give fair representation in terms of gender, race, age, disability and resident participation? If not, you might consider requesting assistance from other appropriate people in your organisation and training them, to ensure an antidiscriminatory approach to selection.
- Do your interviewers possess adequate knowledge, skills and training to perform the interviewing task?
- Have candidates complained about bullying, directive or over-friendly interviewing techniques?

Interviewing is not a static skill: it requires practice in each particular role, for example, observer, active listener, questioner, note-taker. Skills therefore require continual updating and interviewers may need some retraining. Similarly, a set panel composed of the same of people can produce stagnation, and so it is better to have a pool of people to draw upon.

Selection procedures

Do you need to revise any of your selection procedures? Examples might include job description, person specifications, short-list criteria, the interview form, satisfaction form and the complaints questionnaire.

Job description

The job description should list the duties and responsibilities required to perform the advertised, designated role. It must be accurate, as it will legally define the duties and responsibilities of the actual post. Is this description still relevant? Has it been regularly reviewed to ensure it meets the requirements of the post-holder? If not, the whole selection process is put in jeopardy. Therefore you regularly review all job descriptions within the practice setting.

Person specification

The person specification represents an analysis of the main characteristics required to perform the advertised job to the required standard. Here, examples have been modelled on Rodgers' seven-point plan. This specification provides the basis upon which all questions at interviews are asked. Special care must be taken, therefore, to ensure the relevance and accuracy of all the criteria. Was the selection panel pre-warned of any changes at the time of writing? Careful scrutiny of interview satisfaction and complaints questionnaire will provide evidence on these matters.

The short-listing process

The short-listing process is undertaken by the interviewing panel, by matching criteria from the person specification against completed application forms by candidates. The outcome of this process will determine whether a candidate is called to interview or not. Short-listing is a panel process and not a task to be undertaken by a single nominated person. Adequate time must be set aside and care taken to scrutinise each application form before final decisions are made.

The interview form

The interview form must be completed by panel members during the selection interview. All questions asked must relate to the criteria of the person specification and responses must be recorded factually. No hidden agendas must present at this or any other stage in the selection process. It is important that all panel members are trained in interviewing. However, different degrees of experience are likely to exist, so careful choice of roles and support for panel members are important to ensure fairness to candidates and appropriate development of your interviewing panel.

Selection interview

The selection interview must be a managed event, ideally rehearsed in the ascribed roles (chairperson, interviewers, observer). All selection interviews should be carefully evaluated using the candidate satisfaction forms and the complaints procedure. Interview satisfaction forms, as a rule of good practice, should be sent to all candidates as quickly as possible after interview. Enclose a stamped addressed envelope to ensure a speedy turnaround. These forms should provide vital evidence about how candidates felt about their interview.

Exit interview

Exit interviews should be made available to all unsuccessful candidates for professional development purposes. Identify the criteria which candidates did not meet and advise upon what knowledge, skills and experience they might usefully develop.

Complaints procedure

The complaints form/procedure is a necessary part of the overall selection process. It must allow all candidates to complain about their experience at interview and to say they felt discriminated against at any stage. A complaints form, with necessary instructions for completion, should be included in the application pack sent to all candidates.

Complaints may follow or precede an exit interview. In either case, they must be dealt with sensitively and professionally. The form enables the complainant to identify the reasons for complaint. Ideally, a note on the form should request its return as quickly as possible in order that it can be processed and dealt with.

On receipt of the form, read it carefully and compare the reasons for complaint with your selection criteria and recorded decisions made at interview. Be sure to examine all decisions carefully. Invite complainants for a further discussion, bearing in mind they should have already had an exit interview, and advise them that they can be accompanied by another person of their choice, if they wish. You should have a witness to record the proceedings. Set a time and date which are mutually agreeable. Meet and discuss the nature of the complaints. Listen and learn from the complaints.

If complaints are justifiable there may be grounds for a complainant to be re-interviewed. Equally, if the evidence you possess leads you to believe that the complaint cannot be upheld, then you must discuss why. If no agreement can be reached, be sure to advise candidates of their right to appeal. Record all information for an arbitration process, which is managed by ACAS, and cooperate with the process unconditionally.

An open and transparent selection process, well managed, will either remove or reduce the incidence of complaint. No process is completely perfect; however, it must be fair and in line with both equal opportunities codes of practice and relevant legislation. The process will be subject to external scrutiny for validation purposes.

Well qualified and experienced staff are difficult to recruit, so it makes good management practice and economic sense to have a well evaluated and constructive selection process.

Evidence collection C8.2 — Select personnel for activities

You must prove that you select required personnel to the national standard of competence.

You must show evidence that you select at least four of the following types of personnel: permanent, full-time, internal and paid. This can be demonstrated with appropriate job descriptions, provided with kind permission of Broad View Care Limited, a registered charity, and can be found on pages 234–5. Additionally, there is a person specification, written in accordance to the Alec Rodgers 7 point plan on page 241. A short list form, interview form, and interview satisfaction form can also be found in the Appendix.

You must show evidence that you obtain and assess at least four of the following types of information; biographical data, obtained and demonstrated within your selection decisions are justifiable from the evidence gained and supporting case study. References can be demonstrated substantially in Performance Criteria E, C8.2, with supporting exercises

▼

and a case study. Letters can be demonstrated, in particular, letters of appointment are discussed in Performance Criteria D as required and referenced under Section 1 of the Employment Rights Act 1996. Interview responses can be equally demonstrated in Performance Criteria D, your selection decisions are justifiable from the evidence gained post interview. This criteria also, in part, addresses an additional criteria (not required). Results of knowledge tests as it cross-references a mention of a score system or evidence matrix for fully answered questions which the selection panel would use to make decisions.

Think it over

Do you evaluate your selection process in order to make appropriate recommendations for improvement, which you can share and pass on to appropriate people in your organisation? Break down the separate parts of your selection process, and evaluate them with a view to recommending improvement.

Case study — Selection process overhaul

You have recently taken over a traditional, charity-funded residential home. You find little evidence of the use of selection criteria. You realise you have an impending inspection and wish to make improvements to this process. Where do you start?

- Will you review, in consultation with your staff, whether job descriptions match the staff's current duties? How will you go about this task?
- Will you train appropriate people within your organisation to participate in the selection process?
- What roles do you need to consider and what training might be available, both internal and external, to meet these needs?
- How will you prepare person specifications for current roles requiring appointment?
- Are interviewing forms a priority? If so, state why, and how you might construct one with your appropriate people.
- Would you consider drafting interview satisfaction criteria to measure the quality of your interviewing techniques and styles?
- How will you construct a complaints procedure which conforms to equal opportunities codes of practice within your selection process?

Appendix: A manager's induction checklist

This Appendix gives a simple checklist with which to ensure all new staff are given the information they need. To ensure that the induction programme operates to its full potential, you must clarify what new staff need to know. Induction involves investing time and resources in the inductee; the checklist will show that all the areas have been covered. A priority rating of, say, 1–3 (essential, important, desirable) might be applied to each section.

It becomes the manager's duty to have in place mechanisms to assess candidate learning and performance whilst undergoing their induction. Evidence of required learning will be the subject of external assessment by inspectors from the National Care Standards Commission, to ensure that the induction programme meets the new induction standards set out in the Care Standards Act 2000.

Induction checklist

Name of mentor:
Name of inductee:

Areas to be covered	Priority rating (1–3)	Date covered	Signatures	
			Inductee	Mentor
Introduction to staff				
Greet new staff member on first name terms. Introduce to mentor				
Introduce to staff on duty (develop worker relationships)				
Identify own role and responsibilities				
Go through job description				
Assimilate person specification				
Identify staff. List names and include specific areas of responsibility				
Key worker roles – explain				

Access to policies and procedures. Use of policies and procedures within the practice setting				
Dress code				
Identity card or badge				
Section complete				
Introduction to the building				
Provide map of building				
Access routes				
Toilet facilities				
Personal locker				
Fire exists				
CCTV camera operation				
Panic alarm buttons				
Telephone access points				
Main fuses, gas taps, stop cocks				
Section complete				
Fire procedures				
Main exit doors and their operation				
Procedures in the event of a fire				
Use of emergency lift				
Fire extinguishers				
Use of fire book and recording systems				
Fire alarm tests				
Emergency lighting				
Control panels and operation				
Fire officer visits and how to conduct and record				
Section complete				
				▼

Personnel				
Staff rotas/shift system				
Personal lockers				
Attendance sheets				
Staff rooms				
Breaks				
Holidays – both annual and bank holidays				
Lieu time and how claimed				
Overtime – rates and how to claim				
Policy on second jobs				
Smoking policy				
Equal opportunities policy				
Resident or user charter of rights				
Care values – communication and confidentiality				
Policy on receiving gifts				
Car mileage and travel claims				
Trade unions – representatives and how to join				
Employee services				
Occupational health				
Induction pack				
Section complete				
Personal development				
Inductee role and time limits placed on induction				
Supervision arrangements – with whom and how performed				
Mentoring arrangements				
Training and ongoing personal development				
Appraisal system and how it operates				
Disciplinary procedures				

▼

Grievance procedures				
Counselling system				
Evaluation of induction programme				
Section complete				
Service delivery				
The type of service and the particular needs of service user groups				
Care plans – how to record				
Care values and principles of good practice				
Filing systems				
Access to records. Always preserve confidentiality				
Safe working practices				
Policy on physical assistance/transference of people– safe handling				
Operation of manual aids				
Food control – safe food handling				
First aid				
Infection control				
Administration of drugs policy and named person(s)				
Legislative requirements to meet presenting needs of users and carers as well as staff responsibility to department or authority				
Arrangements for multi-agency work				
Daily task analysis				
Client care systems – the principles of care				
The effect of the service setting in relation to types of service user groups				
The effects of service setting on the service user				
				▼

The effect of service setting on the worker				
Section complete				
Sickness policy				
Sickness notification				
Self-certification forms				
Sickness monitoring procedures				
Long-term sickness				
Accident/assault procedure				
How to report and record an accident or assault				
Familiarise with accident form				
Familiarise with assault form				
Familiarise with procedure for investigation				
Familiarise with and read accident book				
Notification of relevant people				
Section complete				

D2 Facilitate Meetings

In order to facilitate meetings competently, you must be able both to lead the meeting and to make effective contributions. The outcome must be to promote participant involvement and the necessary sharing of information to make collective decisions and meet agreed objectives.

The elements are:

- Lead meetings.
- Make contributions to meetings.

Learning outcomes

- The type and purpose of different kinds of meeting.
- How to agree objectives.
- How to demonstrate appropriate leadership.
- How to encourage team members and others to participate in meetings.
- How to ensure meetings achieve their objectives.
- How to receive and provide appropriate feedback at meetings.
- The value of meetings.

The type and purpose of different kinds of meeting

Meetings vary according to type, purpose and formality. For example, the following two writers present their views of what a meeting is. According to Ann Dobson:

> A meeting involves two or more persons and can be anything from a friendly chat to a full blown, formal annual general meeting of shareholders from all over the country or world. Days that are full of meetings leave no time for action and meetings are meaningless unless they are followed by positive action. Meetings held at the appropriate time and conducted effectively can be very useful, but too many meetings can be counterproductive.

By contrast, Tom McMahon described meetings thus:

> For the communications orientated executive, a meeting isn't a box to be shaken, it isn't a set of checklists, it isn't a lot of hype. Instead it is a creative act, comparable to making a movie or making a stage play . . . your meeting must be tightly scripted to communicate its one key message with a maximum of emotional impact . . . the ability to drive home one message without boring an audience to death is what separates the amateurs from the professionals.

Both writers suggest that a meeting is designed to bring people together, which implies a sense of purpose to the proceedings.

As manager, you will attend different sorts of meeting. These could be broadly categorised into three groups according to the types of people involved in the meeting:

Strategic meetings – those involving partner bodies, such as the NHS trust hospitals, primary health care teams, social services departments, private companies and charitable/independent bodies (these meetings would be for contracting purposes);

Operational meetings – those involving senior managers and supervisory staff drawn from within the care service partnership structure;

Meetings with individuals – those involving front-line staff at all levels delivering care services, as well as residents and their immediate carers.

Alternatively, a more detailed categorisation could be made in terms of the purpose of the meeting:

Business meetings – those to discuss finance, budgetary controls, contingency planning/forecasting, policy making, procedural change, quality assurance, contract negotiation (tendering, commissioning), monitoring of service provision and strategic review of all services.

Resident/carer meetings – individual or collective as needs present.

Supervisory meetings – with senior staff responsible for the delivery of resident care packages.

Appraisal meetings – with key staff, to change or improve the nature of service provision within negotiated time scales.

Team meetings – with individual or external teams drawn from provider bodies within the mixed economy.

Training meetings – to identify team training needs or assist in the monitoring and evaluation of existing training plans.

Informal meetings – with all staff involved in the facilitation of care.

One-to-one meetings – with individual members of staff, focusing upon supervision, appraisal, training and support.

Irrespective of the type of meeting, and whether it is a complex or simple one, each meeting offers a forum for communication and the sharing of essential information for decision making purposes. The care service sector, as with any other business, depends upon the meeting structure, with all its variables.

Identify and list the types of meetings you are involved in (an example has been given)

TYPE OF MEETING	YOUR INVOLVEMENT
1 Resident Meeting	Minute-taker
2	
3	
4	

Why are meetings so important?

- A meeting is an invitation to individuals to participate in a process. The term 'invitation' embodies value and involvement. Residents, staff and partner bodies generally like to feel useful and valued.
- A meeting, if correctly managed, can disseminate essential information to a collective audience equally and without prejudice.
- A meeting may encourage ideas, the sharing of problems and the finding of solutions. Meetings may therefore be, for example, a manager's tool for strategic planning.
- A meeting can be a forum in which to resolve difficult problems or to take difficult decisions. A team meeting is frequently that given the shared ownership of ideals, objectives and common interests.

Think it over

Why do you think that meetings are so important in the everyday running of your practice setting? Jot down your thoughts.

How to agree objectives

Even before the meeting takes place, there are several points you need to attend to in order to ensure its success:

- ✓ Nominate someone to chair the meeting.
- ✓ Ensure there is an agenda – one to which all concerned may contribute.
- ✓ Distribute the defined agenda in advance – this allows all participants to prepare and also maps out the agreed programme of items to be discussed.
- ✓ Ensure that everyone knows why they are to attend the meeting – what their role will be.

✓ Set a time scale for the meeting in advance (one hour or two hours, perhaps, depending upon the importance or complexity of the issues to be discussed).

✓ Book a room which is accessible to and known by all those attending.

✓ Organise transport if required.

The agenda is the way in which to set objectives for the meeting. The agenda will give the meeting both *purpose* and *impetus.* When a meeting has a defined purpose, it is more likely to achieve its aims.

Preparing an agenda

The way to ensure that participants are clear about the *purpose* of a meeting is through a draft agenda which is circulated to all in advance. Agenda structures will vary according to the type and purpose of the meeting.

First, publicise the agenda. In an environment such as a residential, hospital or social work setting, place the meeting agenda in a visible area of the staff room. For an extended meeting involving multidisciplinary input from health, social services, education, for example, circulate the agenda to the participants.

You should invite participants to suggest items to be included in the agenda. It may be necessary to prioritise these, in terms of the order of matters to be discussed, given that there will be time restrictions. If you have an agreed agenda, permission will be required from participants to either delete or add items of importance.

Recirculate the revised agenda to participants, seeking their approval, thus making it final. Always circulate the final agenda well in advance, to allow time for participants to prepare their contributions. This can encourage a sense, import, ownership, value and purpose by all concerned in the meeting process.

Try it out

How are meeting agendas drawn up in your practice setting to meet their desired outcomes? Use the grid below to illustrate your response. You should prioritise agenda items in order of importance and timescale for discussion purposes to meet mutual desired outcomes.

AGENDA ITEM	HOW THEY ARE ORGANISED FOR DISCUSSION
1	For discussion
2	
3	
4	

How to demonstrate appropriate leadership

In order to lead a meeting effectively, the chair is required to possess a broad understanding of the different styles of leadership, as well as when to use them according to the type or nature of meeting in progress. Broadly speaking, leadership can be classified under three headings:

- authoritarian;
- democratic;
- laissez-faire.

Overt reliance on any one style would create resistance. Hence the chair must develop for the most part an eclectic style of leadership, drawing on the strengths of all three styles.

Authoritarian

Here the focus of power rests with one person.

Advantages

Potential troublemakers at a staff or policy making meeting are quickly dealt with to ensure the meeting achieves its stated objectives.

Disadvantages

Contributions by participants may be overlooked, ignored or marginalised, with the result that participants may feel demotivated, worthless and not acknowledged. The fundamental 'respect factor' is overlooked.

Use

You must use this style of leadership only to keep control and prevent the meeting being hijacked by a minority interest.

Think it over

When might it be necessary to adapt an authoritarian style in chairing a meeting?

Democratic

This style transfers power to the participants, rather than leaving it in the hands of one person.

Advantages

This style of leadership values the contributions and participation of others, which is reinforced by collective power.

What do you all think?

Disadvantages

Its principal weakness rests in resolving conflict, particularly in relation to contentious decision making, such as resident/carer complaints, team dysfunction or contractual failings by provider/partner bodies. In short, the presence of too many potential leaders may undermine the meeting.

Use

Use this style to generate ideas, to foster a group identity, and to encourage mutual support.

Think it over

Consider how you might employ a democratic style of leadership. Give examples of participant contributions in such a team meeting.

Laissez-faire

Here the chair sees herself or himself as part of the group.

Advantages

This style can encourage creative and spontaneous styles of leadership from all participants.

Disadvantages

Participants may become frustrated without adequate direction.

Use

You must use this style only in meetings where participants wish to pursue a specific area pertinent to a specific agenda area, and do not require interference from the chair.

Think it over

Consider the context of a meeting in which a laissez-faire approach is appropriate.

Case study — Lakeside Residential Home

The home is a private residence for 16 female residents. It is managed and owned by a Mrs Rachael Blake, who has 10 years' care management experience and a previous nursing background of some 12 years, mainly within NHS general hospitals. There are 12 staff, although four work part-time on a split shift system.

At Lakeside, staff meetings are held on the first Wednesday of every month, between 2 pm and 3 pm. All staff are expected to attend, and only sickness and booked holidays are considered acceptable reasons for absence. The monthly agenda is always written by Rachael, never circulated and produced only at the meeting. The roles of chair and minute-taker belong to Rachael. Agenda items are prioritised by Rachael and communicated to staff. No staff consultation or interference is tolerated. Open discussion of agenda items is allowed only at Rachael's prerogative. Each meeting follows the same format. Any disagreement with Rachael's viewpoint is frowned upon. When Rachael has finished discussing each item she regards the staff meeting as having met her stated objectives. The meeting is then closed. The only summary made is to reinforce those items she expects her staff to obey. The meeting is then adjourned. All staff are thanked for attending, and dismissed. At this point, Rachael leaves the room as the meeting is now over.

- What type of leadership style is being practised?
- What potential problems does this leadership style present, particularly in terms of staff participation at meetings?
- What alternatives are there?
- What modifications to both style and facilitation would you make?
- How would you improve the meeting process to encourage staff and resident/carer participation?
- How would you respond to resident and staff needs within the framework of such a meeting?
- What difficulties might you expect in introducing change, given the history of these meetings?

Choice of meeting arrangement to encourage appropriate team member involvement for task achievement purposes

You must choose the correct type of meeting to achieve its purpose. Consider the following examples:

- Financial or business meetings will require a formal meeting.
- Operational or multidisciplinary meetings with partner bodies may require initially a formal meeting and possibly even a public meeting with staff and residents.
- Discussion of concerns over practice issues between two or more managers or staff may initially require only an informal meeting.
- To encourage a team or the whole staff group to generate new ideas to respond to residents' needs may require a brainstorming meeting.
- Training for staff involving external trainers or speakers may require a conference meeting or venue.

The purpose of a meeting will influence its size. There are advantages and disadvantages to large and small meetings. These are shown in Table 5.

Table 5. Advantages and disadvantages of different sizes of meetings

Meetings	Advantages	Disadvantages
Large group meetings	More likely to share diverse opinions, reflecting participants' differing experience, expertise and background	Could create conflict because of the diversity of opinions. Individuals could avoid responsibility for essential decision making by hiding behind the views of dominant members or more eloquent speakers. Large group meetings require firm control from an experienced chair
Small group meetings	Can be controlled more easily than larger meetings. Everyone can be encouraged to contribute. It is also easier to influence the general opinion in constructive and sensible ways. Equally, a smaller meeting can be more productive if it prioritises and sticks to its agenda	A smaller gathering may offer a limited perspective on given issues. A great deal would depend on the criteria of the agenda and the expertise required from participants

▼

One-to-one meetings	They are easy to plan and arrange. Agenda setting becomes a shared exercise. Contributions from both parties can be discussed thoroughly and equally in an atmosphere conducive to the sharing of information. Participants can readily engage in constructive decision making. They encourages ownership and respect for individual expertise	They can become an oppressive exercise if democratic principles are ignored. Individuals are less likely to engage if they feel threatened or stressed. A lack of mutual respect can also contribute to an unproductive meeting

How to ensure meetings achieve their objectives

Preparing for the meeting

Preparation is the key to ensuring that the meeting achieves its stated purpose. The key points to remember are to ensure that the right people attend at the right time to reach the right decisions.

- Brief participants in advance of the purpose, date, time and venue.
- Ensure that participants are clear about their role and the need for their specific contributions.
- Background material addressing the subject matter to be discussed should be sent to participants in advance so that they can prepare.

Venue

The choice of location is vital to the success of any meeting. The environment must be appropriate to the needs of participants and the occasion itself. The venue chosen must be accessible (including to anyone with a disability); it should afford maximum privacy and minimum interruption.

Choosing a venue for a meeting

There are 10 rules to bear in mind when choosing a venue for a meeting:

- Assess an environment for its suitability in advance.
- Know the physical needs of your participants in advance.
- Ensure that the environment is comfortable but not distracting.
- Check the heating, lighting and ventilation are adequate.
- Effective air conditioning can be essential.
- Look for as much natural rather than artificial light as possible to maintain a dynamic atmosphere.
- Perform a risk assessment for health and safety purposes.
- Ensure there is access to clean toilet facilities.
- Ensure there are adequate catering facilities for the type and size of the meeting.
- Ensure there are arrangements for safe and accessible car parking.

What types of meeting environments do you use or have you experienced? Identify those environments which might be more conducive to generating positive outcomes.

Use the examples given below:

Type of meeting	Desired outcome
In-house team meeting	Break down whole team structure into key units of six, creating four management team meetings each week. Then circulate minutes between 24 staff for effective communication
Team training on safe handling techniques	Specialist training requires an external environment in order to avoid interruption or distraction

Seating arrangements

The seating of participants can have an enormous influence upon the success of a meeting. Consider the effect of the group process and how people interact in a formal or an informal way. The outcome can be seen in the defensive or tactical strategies participants adopt, which they may use in power games, leadership contests or even sabotage of the entire process.

There is one rule in securing ideal seating arrangements and that is to know your participants and be aware of the behaviour they can demonstrate. Thus prepare a seating plan in advance to give the meeting the optimum chance of achieving its desired goals. Additionally, managing meetings with a multicultural mix of participants does demand a sensitive awareness of cultural differences. For example, within Asian or Chinese communities, age carries great esteem, so the oldest person is given the most senior position. Other cultures, particularly European, place importance on hierarchy, expertise and title.

An example of a seating arrangement around a rectangle table is shown in Figure 27.

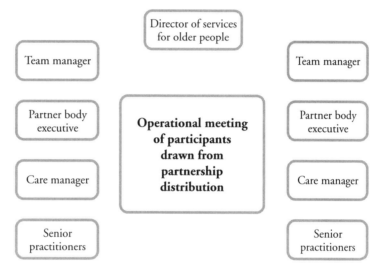

Figure 27. A typical hierarchical seating arrangement around a rectangle table.

A less threatening or informal seating position, which places discussion over status of the participants and generally promotes equality of contribution, is shown below. Its principal advantages are that it enables the chair to promote collaboration, relevant formal/informal discussion, gauge non-verbal communication and mood; it also facilitates flexible eye contact from all parties and engages all equally in the meeting.

An informal seating arrangement.

The chair's role in facilitating meetings

The chair is most often the one who has the authority to regulate the meeting, enforce ground rules, keep order, lead proceedings and coordinate process. Ideally the role is about coordination rather than control, although it is always essential to ensure that the meeting is achieving its stated objectives and keeping to the agenda. Within the care service sector the concept of an independent chair is now being encouraged, as this will promote neutrality rather than hierarchy and a focus upon partnership and open discussion. Equally, the idea of a rotating the chair among a staff group, for example, is gaining favour.

The chair must delegate the role of minute-taker or scribe, as a single person cannot perform both roles at once. The role of the minute-taker is described below.

The chair needs:

- to be an effective coordinator, communicator, negotiator and mediator to ensure the meeting follows its planned agenda;
- to be able to deal with any presenting problems;
- to be able to energise the group if it begins to stagnate and lose its way;
- to allow the group to pass through its own process in order to perform and decide its own course of action;
- to be able to summarise points made and agreed, to paraphrase and importantly to reflect back, as group needs dictate;
- to role model receptiveness when listening to opinions which the chair may not share;
- to have an eclectic approach with regard to leadership style;
- to be able to unite the group by eliminating any threats of aggression.

In relation to the last point, the chair must protect weaker, possibly vulnerable or less experienced members of staff, by not taking sides or abusing personalities or status, but by sticking to presenting facts for agenda purposes. Similarly, an ability to manage time efficiently is paramount if all participants are to be empowered to make full effective and considered contributions to the meeting process. The above skills, if demonstrated and role modelled appropriately, should assist in promote a sense of unity and purpose to the meeting itself and encourage contributions from participants.

Ground rules

The ground rules underpin both the meeting and effective participant involvement, and give the process a structure which can be explained in advance and demonstrated in practice. Helpful ground rules are as follows:

- The chair must open the meeting, introduce participants and include a brief summary of the purpose of the meeting and the negotiated agenda.
- Time limits must be agreed.
- Limits on behaviour (what is acceptable and unacceptable) must be agreed from the onset.
- The chair must then seek to involve all parties equally in both discussion and decision making. It is appropriate to allow participants to let off steam but negative outcomes must be avoided.
- The chair must not take sides, protect more vulnerable staff members, stay alert and, importantly, stick to the facts.
- The chair must encourage participants to express their views, and should then summarise and reflect back to ensure a maintenance focus.
- The chair must prevent irrelevant or rambling debate which distracts from the task.
- The voting procedures on decisions made must be beyond reproach – they must be ethical and correctly followed.
- The chair must check that the minutes are mutually agreed. This can be ascertained by both reading and orally paraphrasing all agreed actions. The importance of accurate records cannot be underestimated.
- A final ground rule which an experienced chair will exercise to manage a meeting is to reserve the right to cast the deciding vote, if necessary.

Taking minutes

Good management of the minutes will help a meeting to achieve its objectives. There are five golden rules. Minutes must be:

- short;
- understandable;
- accurate;
- agreed;
- circulated properly.

An example of good practice is given below:

Woodside Residential Lodge Staff Meeting

Minutes of the fortnightly staff meeting, held on Thursday April 11th 2002 at 2:30 pm–3.00pm.

Present (rotating chair policy)

Mrs Olive White	Centre manager
Ron Hughes	Care manager – Chair
Celia Jones	Senior care
Rachel Thomas	Support worker
Dean Richards	Support worker
Jayshree Khanti	Support worker
Tina Lea	Support worker

Apologies Angela and Katy

Items discussed	Action by
1. Unsafe Handling Techniques	RoSPA accredited trainer to be brought in next week (Weds 17th April, 11–12). Weekly programme focusing on assistance and management for six weeks. All staff to attend. Staff cover to be arranged by Ron.
2. Feedback from Inspectorate report by Ron. Generally very favourable. Minimum care standards met. Now need to focus on mid to maximum range.	Olive, Ron, Celia and Rachel to set up a working party to schedule how improved care standards can be achieved with residents and carers group.
3. Feedback by Dean on Therapeutic Activities Programme. Art and Craft very popular. Ergonomic activity developing phase – shopping and visits to local towns identified by residents are fully booked for the next two months.	More support needed. Celia and Tina to assist (volunteers)
4. Any other business	More staff cover on bank holidays. Olive and Ron to arrange agency input.

Next meeting to be held on Thursday 25th, same time.
Agenda items to Tina, new chair, by 22nd for prioritisation and organisation.

How to receive and provide appropriate feedback at meetings

The chair must foster an atmosphere in which all participants can readily share information. The atmosphere must therefore be entirely non-threatening. To give and encourage feedback in a professional manner is the key to effective communication within a meeting and it is the means by which decisions are reached.

The chair should encourage participants to share prepared agenda items and to pass on information – be it related to policy, procedure, staff morale or changing resident needs. Participants must feel that their work and opinions are valued; to feel confident enough to speak publicly, they must trust their peers and the chair, and have support if they feel overwhelmed, for example by information overload. The key for the chair is to use simple language, avoid jargon, be aware of non-verbal communication and engage in active listening to ensure that body posture matches verbal statements. The chair must convey warmth, support and appreciation, and to role model the receiving and giving of information to encourage participants.

However, giving feedback is not always easy and any concerns must be overcome if participants are to realise that it is a positive process and not a negative one. The chair must never become aggressive or angry, or focus on personal traits, and must always seek to maintain the confidence levels and self-esteem of the participants. You must absolutely clear about what they are stating, how best to empower them to express their viewpoint, in order to either provide one-way feedback or draw in the rest of the group for collective feedback, which can add greater depth to the debate.

There are some simple ground rules for effective feedback. You must:

- be able to be seen to receive feedback yourself, and to deal with it professionally and consistently, before trust is established in your role in providing it;
- actively encourage participation by all involved;
- encourage respect of both individual and group ideas;
- encourage collective responsibility for the content and manner of the discussion;
- ensure that participants understand that they own the meeting and are responsible for the outcomes achieved.

You are leading a small team meeting. The feedback from the team unanimously makes the point that they are unhappy with resident clothing care, including the labelling of residents' clothes, collective washing and loss of items. How would you receive this feedback constructively and reach a negotiated settlement which can be agreed by all?

Use your new skills and rules for holding a purposeful meeting in the following exercise. With members of your own peer or staff group, set up a series of three meetings. The topics for discussion are:

- Staff members to discuss home relocation and its implications for residents, carers and staff.
- Staff meeting to reduce the incidence of stress-related absences.
- Staff meeting to focus on identified residents' needs regarding: choice of menu; greater access to television viewing; religious or prayer sanctuary; extended choice of internal entertainment; cheaper hairdressing; greater choice of daily newspapers.

Elect a chair, a minute-taker, three participants and one observer for each meeting, which is to run for 20 minutes. Change roles and move on to the next meeting topic.

The value of meetings

We have discussed both the structure and management of meetings. It must be remembered that meetings can and should be about human issues, as they are about policy and strategy. In its simplest form, the meeting should help participants to understand the collective aim. In order to achieve that aim, the group, led by the chair, will pass through a number of unique processes in which they become aware of each other's roles and of how each can contribute to the whole inter-group process of task achievement.

One way of examining the work of groups in meetings is via its recorded minutes. These will inform you of the content and outcome of the discussion. What they will not tell you is the degree of satisfaction and involvement of members, in other words the process which the group went through to achieve its collective aim.

You must prove that you lead meetings to the National Occupational Standard of competence.

You must show evidence of leading meetings with two of the following purposes: information giving, consultation, decision making. For consultation you can demonstrate this by referring to preparing an agenda. Information giving can be demonstrated by referring to preparing a meeting and the four purposeful rules, which if followed ensure that the meeting achieves its stated purpose.

You must also show evidence of involving people from within your organisation, which can be demonstrated by referring to the advantages and disadvantages of leading large, small and one-to-one meetings, as well as the leader's role in facilitating meetings and the different processes of leadership involved.

D2.2

Learning outcomes

- How to prepare, consult and make effective contributions to meetings.
- How do your contributions to meetings seek to resolve presenting problems with simple solutions?
- How to acknowledge and discuss the viewpoints and contributions of others in a constructive manner.
- How to give clear information about decisions made at meetings.

How to prepare, consult and make effective contributions to meetings

Preparation is the key to making effective contributions at any meeting, whether one-to-one, small group or team meetings. As with leading meetings, you must ensure that much of the work is done in advance of the meeting, to free yourself of these responsibilities during the meeting itself. To give a brief summary of the discussion above, prepare for the meeting as follows:

✓ book a room which is accessible to and known by all those attending;
✓ give the meeting a set duration;
✓ nominate a chair;
✓ appoint a minute-taker;
✓ ensure there is a manageable agenda that has been contributed to and agreed by all concerned;

✓ prioritise the items on the agenda;

✓ distribute the final agenda in advance;

✓ ensure everyone attending knows why they are attending;

✓ organise transport, if required;

✓ book catering facilities, if required.

Having undertaken the above, you will be free to contribute to the meeting. Your contributions may be of several kinds:

- creative contributions;
- troubleshooting;
- decisive contributions;
- negotiation;
- mediation;
- representation.

Creative contributions

Ensures that you have new ideas to contribute to areas of discussion. By demonstrating this creative approach you can role model the style to encourage the same from other participants. Try to convey that their own creative ideas are not only valid but also of practical use. This will encourage a creative and uninhibited, atmosphere, with open discussion and a desire to put into practice the ideas that have been collectively generated.

Think it over

How would you introduce a new idea into the team discussion with a view to getting it agreed and implemented?

Troubleshooting

Your contributions can minimise disruption from the following kinds of participants:

The habitual late arriver. Arriving late for a meeting can disturb group process. Rather than embarrass the late arriver publicly, why not take him or her to one side and make it clear that this behaviour is unacceptable.

The invisible person – the person who contributes nothing to the meeting. Directly encourage contributions from such people, using phrases like 'Jim, what is your opinion?' and 'What do you think?' Convey a feeling that their inputs are of value and are needed.

The record player – the person who talks too much. Your contribution must be to steer the conversation away from them and actively encourage participation by others. This should encourage a record player to make more focused inputs to the discussion.

The brain box – the person who knows absolutely nothing about the subject you are discussing but who nonetheless talks incessantly. Your contribution must be to interrupt their flow and bring in others. Be decisive.

The terrorist. This is the person who makes aggressive gestures or rude remarks directly to the participants. Your contribution must be decisive – do not tolerate such behaviour. You will need to take this person aside and make it absolutely clear that such behaviour is unprofessional, unacceptable and could lead to disciplinary measures if continued. Once stated, retain the sanction.

Decisive contributions

Depending on the size of the meeting, you may get only one opportunity to make your response. Hence, your contributions must be informed, concise and attract the attention of all participants. In this way you can convey your essential points without having to make frequent interjections.

Negotiation

Within a meeting, negotiating is a key skill in securing a mutually acceptable solution. Your contribution when negotiating is to establish a result which you require but which also constitutes a favourable one for other parties involved. Successful negotiation will depend on your ability to be informed, to be alert and to compromise. In order to negotiate successfully, you should do the following:

✓ Prepare yourself in advance.
✓ Play the part.
✓ Be decisive in your participation.
✓ Know your aims.
✓ Avoid being distracted.

✓ Listen actively.
✓ Question appropriately – probe.
✓ Be flexible.
✓ Be willing to compromise.
✓ Agree the result.

Mediation

Within a meeting it is not uncommon for participants to disagree and not be able to move forward. Thus, the meeting becomes frozen. Mediation skills can break the deadlock. Your contribution must be to find common ground between factionalised parties and then to seek a mutually agreeable solution.

Mediation comprises the following steps:

1　Help participants to consider the problem from a different perspective.
2　Enable them to understand the other point of view.
3　Explain the issues factually.
4　Suggest alternatives.
5　Empower participants to think through mutually agreeable solutions.

Remember when mediating always to remain impartial.

Representation

You may be asked to represent the views of others who either cannot attend or who, for a variety of reasons, feel they cannot represent themselves well enough to get their points across (for example if English is their second language).

In order to represent their views accurately and impartially, you must first consult them to determine their views. If those views are given in writing, your role will be to familiarise yourself with them, ensure clarity of understanding, cross-check and be prepared to answer any questions arising from the written report. If you are in any doubt about your own competence to represent someone on this matter, delegate the role to a specialist third party.

If their views are related to you verbally, follow the same process, ensuring accuracy and understanding of content, and clarify what is required from your representation. Again, you may wish to bring in a knowledgeable third party.

Make only those representations you have been asked to make. *Do not*:

- interpret;
- use the representation for your own purposes;
- use it inappropriately.

You must:

- be impartial;
- convey accurately and precisely what has been requested of you;
- be respectful;
- field any questions;
- feed back on the results of representation, whether positive or negative.

You must always consider whether you are the most appropriate person to represent the views of a third party:

- Can you remain impartial without becoming overly involved?
- Are you sufficiently empathetic to both the views of those you are representing? (Receptiveness is different to conveying accurate empathy.)
- Are you, in this instance, sufficiently qualified to represent the views of another? (If not, you need to consider delegating this task to another person.)

Honest critical reflection will assist your decision making.

How would you represent the views of new starters at a weekly staff meeting, having been asked to reconsider mentoring arrangements which do not meet their practice requirements?

Making effective contributions to meetings

Whatever type of contributions you make, they should be:

- clear;
- understandable;
- concise;
- relevant to the agenda being discussed;
- original and creative;
- motivating;
- delivered in an informed and credible manner;
- practical (e.g. immediately applicable to residents' needs).

In addition, your contributions should inspire confidence and, where possible, surmount boundaries or potential deadlocks. Your propositions should also be agreeable to the participants attending, and if they are not initially accepted you should be prepared to try to persuade them of their value. Figure 28 provides a summary.

Figure 28. Observation of these points will enable you in most meetings to ensure that you make contributions in a concise and relevant manner and at a pace you can control.

How can you ensure that your contributions to meetings are relevant?

Playing the part

Professional appearance combined with informal comment can gain that additional respect. What you must remember is that not only are your verbal contributions important but also your appearance. It is a widely held view that people form impressions and make instant judgements based purely on appearance. So play the part.

Case study — Effective contributions

You wish to free yourself sufficiently to participate in a meeting to discuss training. There will be three care assistants and one senior care present. All four staff are engaging in the same pre-qualifying social work training, albeit with different providers and at different times. The purpose of the meeting is to identify progress, existing support and additional support required, and how to enhance their individual and collective learning. The group might like to ask members of their own support network to attend the meeting, as well as any valid external source e.g. college tutor or an external mentor.

- What preparations do you need to make to encourage those attending to participate effectively at this meeting?
- What roles will facilitate more effective contributions?
- How do you consult with others, as well as those staff members who have requested you represent their views at this meeting?
- How do you ensure that your own contributions are both clear and relevant to the meeting?

How do your contributions to meetings seek to resolve presenting problems with simple solutions?

No meeting is likely to be trouble free. Once a problem emerges, encourage participants to resolve it. This serves to encourage mutual ownership and accountability for decisions made and actions to be taken. Useful questions to ask are of the type:

- What are the alternatives?
- Do we have any other choices?
- What do you all prefer?

Also, by asking questions like these, you are inviting a collective response instead of imposing your own will.

You may ensure a professional approach is adopted to clarifying and resolving problems by observing a series of rules:

- Remain professional.
- Remain calm.
- Assess the nature of the presenting problem and seek a simple solution or energise the group to find one.
- Reduce tensions by diverting attention away from personalities (problems do not then become personal).
- Seek group support to identify common ground.
- Mediate to clarify statements made.
- Introduce humour into the proceedings.
- Always preserve participants' dignity.
- Stick to the facts.
- Do not get distracted.
- Allow the meeting to follow its natural progress so participants feel a sense of purpose to their role and each other.
- Encourage mutual/collective support.
- Foster inter-dependency.
- Help the group to move forward as necessary.

The remainder of this section looks at three different case scenarios which begin with a presenting problem, require a solution and have a determined outcome.

Potential problem: task not performed

You are contributing to a team meeting consisting of four care assistants and one senior carer. The meeting is a weekly event and lasts 45 minutes. Team members contribute to the agenda, share ideas and collectively seek to find constructive, agreeable solutions. At the previous week's meeting, Claire said she would evaluate security following a recent burglary. When asked for her evaluation she states, 'I could not find the time.'

Possible solution

Your contribution must be to remind Claire that was her agreed responsibility. Be sure that your body language and voice are calm. Ask Claire in a quiet but firm voice whether she requires any extra help from the team. Another member, Jane, intercedes and states she would be pleased to assist if necessary. Claire agrees and both clarify a working arrangement and decide that they can report back in writing to the next meeting. In turn Claire thanks Jane for her support.

Outcome

Unity within the team is preserved without scape-goating, and task achievement (i.e. home security) remains on track.

Potential problem: frozen meeting

You are at a weekly meeting chaired and run by the residents themselves. You reach a point when the issue being discussed is choice of menu. The majority of residents want to see more variety. Suddenly one resident backtracks and decides he does not want to see any change at all. In fact, he wants to see the menu remain as it is. His comments freeze the group.

Possible solution

Your contribution must be to keep calm and avoid disorder. Isolate the area, that is the menu, but do not present it as a problem. Insist that everyone has the right to voice their opinions but that they equally must respect the views and sensitivities of others. Remind the resident that the current choice of menu would remain but be a part of a much larger menu offering greater variety to all.

Outcome

A potential ambusher is pacified without feeling humiliated and the group benefits in that they can see that their collective views are addressed appropriately.

Potential problem: antagonism

You are contributing to a meeting chaired and run by carers whose dependants are residents within your home. One participant is unnecessarily negative and argumentative to every suggestion her fellow carers present. Hence the meeting becomes frozen.

Possible solution

Your contribution must be to remind the carer concerned of the actual purpose of the meeting. Stick to the facts of the discussion. Encourage participants to respond sensitively to each other and discuss issues in a calm manner. Introduce an element of humour to the proceedings in order for the group to re-energise and move forwards.

Outcome

Potential confrontation and disorder are avoided. The antagonist preserves her dignity and the group moves on without dissolving or fragmenting.

How to acknowledge and discuss the viewpoints and contributions of others in a constructive manner

It is good practice to acknowledge both the contributions and viewpoints of others in meetings, as this will foster constructive working relationships. Meetings should represent a collective rather than an individual process. However, for this to occur participants need to feel valued and to work together.

Value the individual

Recognise how each person has made a unique contribution to the meeting process. You may highlight particular inputs, such as preventing distraction, sharing new ideas with a prepared research paper, or supporting a fellow colleague. A generous effort needs to be publicly acknowledged so that collective praise can be made and seen to be made.

People who attend a meeting like to feel needed. After all, they have been asked to attend, and have prepared for the meeting and may have rearranged previous commitments in order to attend. Therefore it is reasonable to suggest that they believe their attendance can make an essential difference to both the process and outcome of the meeting. Acknowledgement that both individuals and the group are needed can lift the mood and resolve of everyone attending.

Reinforce a culture of individual and collective praise. Saying 'Thank you!' to both individual and group for efforts made encourages both the sense of being valued and needed. Equally encourage participants to thank each other for work done on their behalf. In doing so, individuals begin to trust, support and appreciate other members of the meeting. Praise is particularly useful in a staff team meeting.

Discuss the contributions and viewpoints of others

Discuss the viewpoints of all participants constructively. Never belittle or patronise. When someone has the courage to speak out and make a point alien to popular understanding or practice, explore it together and identify how it might work. The energising inputs that individuals can make will occur only within non-threatening, supportive environments, with people willing to experiment with the unfamiliar.

Encourage equality

Within the meeting, the participants must feel that their viewpoints are of equal value. Status is an unnecessary barrier in a collective gathering and only inhibits creative discussion. Equality is the key to ensure that individual viewpoints receive the credibility they deserve. (This will also reinforce feelings of being valued and needed.)

Encourage constructive feedback

Constructive critical feedback of opinions expressed can be helpful to tease out the advantages and disadvantages. Criticism without reason undermines the value of honest feedback and can be destructive in both small and large meetings.

Establish ground rules for professional behaviour

In order to foster a culture in which different viewpoints can be openly discussed without the threat of intimidation, then there must be agreed ground rules to govern behaviour. Keep them simple:

- Respect each other.
- Everyone has the right to speak.
- Content must be constructive not destructive.
- Do not discriminate in any way.
- Use language with sensitivity.
- Avoid interruptions.
- Support each other equally.

You are contributing to a monthly staff training meeting. How do you acknowledge the viewpoints and contributions of others in a constructive manner? Give examples within the following categories:

- participants encouraged to feel needed;
- encouraging a culture of praise;
- encourage equality;
- encourage positive feedback;
- establish ground rules.

Effective listening

Effective listening is not simply a predisposition to hear what participants say. Your contribution is to recognise and understand how participants receive information in open discussion.

Body language

An understanding of non-verbal communication can assist your acknowledgement of individual viewpoints.

Facial expression

Facial expressions and rate of speech must equate to avoid conveying mixed messages. Your contribution is to understand and equate the rate of speech with facial expression. Effective role modelling can assist all participants.

Eye contact

Making eye contact is usually interpreted as a signal to begin discussion. Your contribution must be to control the direction of your gaze in tandem with the rate and flow of conversation.

Direct eye contact is an example of non-verbal communication.

Head movement

Head movement can indicate a range of feelings. Your contribution must be to differentiate between the attitudes and feelings being displayed, be they sadness, agreement or even confrontation.

Gestures

It is worthwhile remembering that participants do not remain still when communicating. Your contribution is to interpret correctly certain behaviours, such as shuffling of feet or the drumming of fingers.

Body posture

A slight forward leaning of the trunk may indicate interest, enthusiasm and the point when a participant wants to express a viewpoint. Equally, a slouching posture may be either a relaxed position or an indication of boredom or of feeling ignored.

Proximity

The distance maintained between individuals may indicate the degree of closeness preferred and of feelings being shared. Your contribution is to discern from the signals conveyed how close is safe for both parties in a meeting, without damaging the overall relationship.

Case study — Non-verbal communication

You are contributing to a staff meeting about cover for staff sickness and holidays. Clearly, cover arrangements demand extra weekend and unsociable/split shift cover. You notice that several members have averted their eye gaze, have a bowed head, a changed facial expression, rigid body posture and changed their proximity to each other by moving closer.

- What do these non-verbal behaviours convey?
- How might your verbal contributions encourage constructive discussion?
- How might your non-verbal contributions encourage constructive discussion?

How to give clear information about decisions made at meetings

During a meeting, decisions made should be based on the collective views regarding the information presented. It is important to make provisions for the decisions to be followed through and monitored. Whatever decisions are arrived at, it is good practice to summarise all the information gathered which enabled the team to make its decision. To enable a group culture of critical analysis to emerge, it is important to allow participants to review their decisions, to ensure that potential further problems are:

- identified;
- discussed;
- resolved.

To ensure that everyone understands the importance of the decisions they have just made, test their comprehension by asking questions. Quite often, for example, staff members will reach a decision without understanding the implications for themselves or their residents. Develop a culture of accountability and ownership so that staff members learn the rules of collective decision making. To undertake this you will need to monitor how well individuals work with decisions made. This might be done through observed practice, third-party feedback from residents or carers, or in formal supervision.

Team dysfunction in relation to misunderstanding or misinformation can be avoided if all participants at a meeting – as well as those unable to attend it – have equal access to information and a record of the decisions made. However, this is not the end of the process: only by following through with careful monitoring of future work can you be certain that everyone has assimilated the information and understands the implications of the decisions.

Think it over

How can you test comprehension and develop a culture of accountability and ownership in the decision making at your meetings?

Formats for recording decisions

The minutes will be the main way in which to record the proceedings and decisions of the meeting. Decisions made will be recorded in the minutes, which will therefore offer a working guide to staff members present or absent. Absent members will require a detailed explanation of decisions reached and equally be allowed to give their viewpoint. However, there are other formats to convey information about essential decision making. These include the following:

- A detailed report explaining the background to the agenda item, the discussion of the information presented and the reasons why the decision was taken. This would then be circulated to all staff.
- A flow chart which diagrammatically explains the problem, solution and decision made.
- A video recording of an important staff meeting, which will visually and audibly record what was said, achieved and agreed.

The employment of alternative formats to convey accurate and concise information about decisions made and how they were made should ensure that all participants possess a comprehensive record.

Records should relate only to the facts of the meetings – there is no reason to include any degree of complication or jargon.

Evidence collection D2.2 — Make contributions to meetings

You must prove that you make contributions to meetings to the National Occupational Standard of competence.

You must show evidence in relation to meetings involving either people from within your organisation or people outside your organisation. Your evidence should relate to how you have prepared, consulted and made effective contributions to the meeting. Your contributions at a meeting must be concise and relevant.

You must also show evidence of representing individuals or groups. This can be amply demonstrated by how you acknowledge and discuss the viewpoints and contributions of others in a constructive manner.

RM2 Ensure Individuals and Groups are Supported Appropriately when Experiencing Significant Life Events and Transitions

This unit explores the organisational systems and structures that should be in place to support individuals and groups during times of significant life change. Many managers will recognise the action they need to take, or require their staff to take, to ensure appropriate support whenever a resident may be experiencing change. However, in many cases the action taken can be too ad hoc, when there should be a more systematic approach, underpinned by policies and guidelines. In line with the requirements for a high-quality service, an ad hoc approach to supporting clients during times of change is no longer acceptable. Therefore, policies and procedures should be implemented to ensure all levels of staff can work to consistently high standards in this regard. This unit will help you to establish or review and update such policies and procedures.

The elements are:

- Design and implement a service which addresses the needs of clients experiencing significant life events.
- Ensure the service responds effectively to individuals experiencing major life changes or losses.

You recognise the changes and life events that are likely to occur at different life stages, and the health and care needs associated with these

You will no doubt be able to recall a number of situations where you have had to deal with the effect of life changes on both your clients and your staff, not to mention yourself. While it is clear that change can often be positive, in this unit we are mainly dealing with difficult change and distressing life events for individuals. For example:

People leaving their own home to move to a residential setting.
This kind of event is likely to result in individuals going through the grieving process as they mourn the loss of their home and many personal items. There can also be a feeling of disconnection with memories and family events, especially for people who have lived for many years in the same location.

Residents leaving residential care to move to 'core and cluster' homes. Again, this kind of event is likely to result in a period of mourning for the life that once was. There could additionally be worries and anxieties about the ability to cope in a different, perhaps less sheltered environment.

Change of school or other institution. For many younger people, changing school or other learning provider can be a daunting prospect and support may be required to enable them to deal with the consequences, such as loss of friendship networks and, in the short term, loss of stability.

Clients experiencing the death of a partner or other loved one. Clearly, this significant life event is more likely to be experienced among an elderly group of clients than among a younger one although not exclusively so. This may be a time when additional help is required from other professionals, such as a bereavement counsellor.

People losing sensory or physical abilities. Most individuals will need support during the process of sensory loss; this could be in the form of learning new skills in order to minimise the effects of disability. Anger and anxiety as well as depression are likely to result from sensory loss, especially if clients are aware of the process and the consequences.

Change of carer after a long period of time. Clients can become attached to – or even dependent on – individual care providers. If this support is removed for any reason we can expect a an individual to undergo the grieving process in exactly the same way as an individual experiencing other forms of loss.

Change relating to an individual leaving the care system. Leaving the care system is another situation in which service users are likely to mourn a loss. This can even apply when an individual is pleased to be leaving. For example, after a long-term illness, going home can be a challenge and thoughts about emergency support needs are often uppermost in the person's mind.

Think it over

Think about the kinds of change you have experienced within your care setting. Does your experience match the examples listed or are there other examples of change that you would want to include? Make notes of the changes that regularly occur in your setting and especially among your service users. It is likely that these changes will form the basis of your evidence for this unit.

We know that human beings pass through several stages of life as they progress from 'cradle to grave'. These are:

- infant;
- young child;
- teenager;
- adult;
- older adult.

Each of these stages has the potential to bring about change of one kind or another. For example, some of the changes associated with adult life are shown in Figure 29.

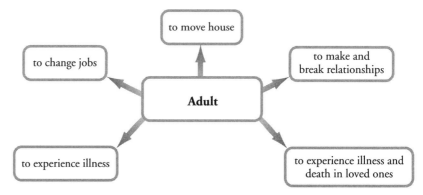

Figure 29. Changes associated with adult life.

Think it over

What changes have you experienced during your lifetime? Did you need support with any of them? How did you cope with the change?

While most people cope with such changes, each is still acknowledged as the creator of tremendous stress. Imagine, then, how much more difficult it must be for an older, frail person or someone with physical or learning disabilities to cope with the same kind of life changes.

Try it out

Complete the table to identify the support you might want if you were moving house.

Stresses and strains	Support required	Source of assistance
Finding a suitable place to live		
Planning the actual detail of the move		
Having to get rid of furniture and belongings that cannot be taken with you		
Leaving behind friends, family, memories		
Worry over whether the move is right		
Learning to meet new people and adopt new routines (e.g. travel to work)		

If one of your clients was in the same situation, would you need to make changes to the grid? That is, are their support needs different to yours?

Change for older people can be brought about through:

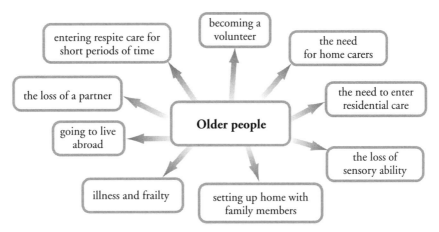

Figure 30. Changes associated with later adult life.

You recognise clients' care needs during times of significant life events

There is a duty to protect clients as well as to promote their autonomy. According to Braye and Preston-Shoot (1995), carers are also likely to have a strong desire to empower their service users as far as possible. This can be shown as a triangle, with the 'overriding need' at its pinnacle (Figure 31). This is not a static situation but is dynamic. It is your responsibility to ensure that carers give support that is appropriate to the individual at that particular time. For example, in some cases a client may need the emphasis placing on protection – perhaps they are no longer able to care for themselves safely in their own home. In this case 'protection' (in the form of a residential setting) may be the overriding need, rather than empowerment and autonomy.

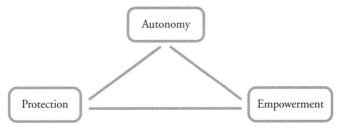

Figure 31. The triangle of duties owed by carers to residents. The triangle can be rotated so that the overriding need is placed at the pinnacle.

Whenever major change and upheaval occur in a resident's life, a set of needs will arise. According to Bradshaw (1972) there are four kinds of needs:

Felt needs. These are the needs that individuals identify for themselves. They are usually based on life experience. In some cases it may be that people do not actually know what they need because their experiences are limited.

Expressed needs. These can best be described as a request for action or service. It is a felt need that has been expressed, perhaps to a professional or to a family member.

Normative needs. The normative needs of an individual are decided by a health or care professional. These 'needs' are often seen as the same as those of the bulk of the population. The danger here is that professional viewpoints can clash with those of the person concerned.

Comparative needs. These are the needs that are identified by comparing one group of the population with another. So, once again, a professional perspective is used and this method of identifying need can actually lead to a form of rationing if one group needs a service more than another group. Funds are finite, and so there are always winners and losers.

Needs as perceived by the service user may be very different to those identified by the professional. You need only to think about the difficulties involved in care planning to see the potential for clashes of opinion in relation to care needs. Understanding the needs of another person can be very difficult. Empathy from staff is particularly helpful here.

An alternative to Bradshaw's classification of needs is the PIES classification. This can be easier to use when trying to identify the needs of a resident. PIES is an acronym for:

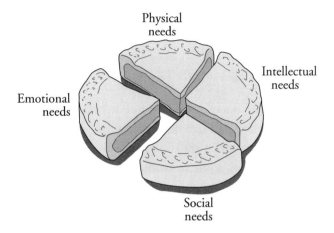

Physical needs

Intellectual needs

Emotional needs

Social needs

You may not agree with the choice of words used in the acronym – for example, you may prefer 'psychological' to 'intellectual' needs, or you may prefer to include other needs, such as spiritual and cultural needs. Nonetheless, these headings will at least give you the opportunity to explore needs on a holistic basis rather than encouraging one fixed idea about the origins of needs.

Think it over

How would you define the needs of your clients? What tools might you use to help you think through the different aspects of needs?

Case study — Identifying needs

Gregory is 24 years of age and has learning difficulties. He has spent the last six years of his life sharing a small group home with three other people. Ahmed is one of them and is his best friend. The social worker has just arrived to tell Gregory that he is to leave his home next week because it is being closed due to council cutbacks, but he does not need to worry because a place has been found for him at another centre, on the other side of town. Gregory is distressed because his friend Ahmed is going to be placed in a different care home and because he does not know how his treasured belongings will be moved safely.

Miriam has finally made the break from an abusive relationship, after 15 years. Her only regret is her decision to place her children in foster care until she has a safe and secure home to offer them. Everything has happened so fast that she feels she has no control over her situation at the moment and she is relying on her social worker more and more.

- What are the changes being experienced by Gregory and Miriam? (Think about physical, social and mental aspects in particular.)
- How can Bradshaw's classification of needs be applied to both cases?

It is relatively easy to identify the changes that are occurring in Gregory and Miriam's lives, for example, loss of home, loss of relationship and isolation. However, it is less easy to identify what might have been appreciated by both of them as a method of helping them to cope with change. What might you offer in terms of emotional support?

Recognising the implications of change

It is all well and good to understand aspects of theory relating to clients' needs, but unless staff can recognise when a service user is experiencing a significant life event or transition, see the implications and then take the appropriate action, some individuals will 'fall through the net'.

You should therefore ensure that there is a range of different mechanisms in place to support both staff and clients in the arena of recognising and meeting needs during times of difficulty and change. For example, every manager should have:

- an understanding of national and local policies relating to service user support;
- an in-house policy and procedure for coping with change;
- a training policy that includes dealing with change and providing emotional support for both staff and service user;
- procedures for working with appropriate external agencies.

It is important that you recognise the potential impact life changes can have on a whole range of people and situations. For example, admitting a new resident to a settled environment can have far-reaching effects on the other residents. If the new resident is a difficult person to deal with, there may be issues for staff allocated to the care of that person and of course the potential for difficulties with members of the family as well as other visitors to the setting.

You need to be aware how life changes can affect people.

However, remember that change is not always negative. There are some changes that are welcomed by most if not all of those involved.

Think it over

What changes might be welcomed in your care setting and why?

Case study — Coping with multiple sclerosis

Selina Wright has multiple sclerosis and needs to use a wheelchair. She lives in a high-rise flat in Birmingham and has three children. In most ways she can manage, but her flat has not been adapted for the chair and so she mostly stays in bed while her partner and children carry out all the household chores. She has just been informed that she has been allocated purpose-built accommodation in a bungalow in a central area close to all amenities.

- What effect is this change likely to have on Mrs Wright, her partner and her children?
- What effect is this change likely to have on Mrs Wright's care services?

You understand the legal and policy requirements underpinning the provision of services to clients who are experiencing significant life events

When we are discussing policy and legal requirements within the care field, we are moving into an area that is constantly shifting and changing. Keeping up to date is not easy but it is an essential element of a manager's role and responsibility. Therefore, you should have a good understanding of the legislative framework surrounding care practices in this country. Unit RM1 in this book will be useful reading in this regard.

In the main you need to:

- know and understand national and local relevant policies (both statutory and non-statutory);
- know, understand and recommend good practice guidelines;
- be able to apply your understanding to the care setting you manage.

Try it out

Test your current knowledge of policies and guidelines. Make a list of all the policies and guidelines you think are relevant to client change.

The five most important policies and guidelines to your role as a care manager are:

- the Care Standards Act 2000;
- the National Minimum Standards, for example those relating to care homes for older people;
- the White Paper *Modernising Social Services*;
- the National Service Framework for Older People;
- *Promoting Independence: Preventative Strategies and Support for Adults* (LAC (99) 14).

If you fail to meet the requirements of these national policies, action can be taken by the relevant inspectorate or regulator. Other policies and guidelines that you should follow and use in your decision making include:

- the Nursing and Midwifery Council's guidelines and codes of conduct;
- the Modernising Social Services Act 1998;
- the Human Rights Act 1998;
- the Disability Discrimination Act 2002;
- the NHS and Community Care Act 1990;
- *Home Life: A Code of Practice for Residential Care*, 1984;
- the Disability and Discrimination Act 1984;
- the Health and Safety at Work Act 1974.

Codes of conduct, policies and guidelines

Many professions have some sort of self-regulation in place. They develop codes of good practice or codes of conduct. Examples include:

- the General Medical Council's code of conduct for medical practitioners;
- the Nursing and Midwifery Council's code of conduct for nurses, midwives and health visitors;
- the Council for Professions Supplementary to Medicine's codes of conduct for dieticians, chiropodists, physiotherapy and so on;
- the Commission for Social Work's codes of conduct for social carers.

Professions which self-regulate can control to a great extent those people allowed to 'join their ranks'. They are able to monitor their work by having a defined expectation of the quality of service they should be providing. If individuals fail to meet these expectations, sanctions can be taken against them, usually, in the first instance, by the manager of their organisation.

Codes of conduct, policies and procedures are a useful source of information and are invaluable when you are planning or reviewing policy and organising staff development and training. Many policies deal with recognising cultural diversity and provide guidance for organisations on what is and what is not acceptable practice.

The full content of these codes of conduct, policies and guidelines goes way beyond the remit of this book. However, some aspects of these policies relate to providing support for service users and others. It is essential that you obtain and read copies of the codes of conduct and policies that relate to your service.

The Care Standards Act 2000 is a useful example of ways in which policies and guidelines can help managers plan for and then handle change for and with their service users in a constructive manner.

Care Standards Act 2000

This Act has a wide remit. In the main it deals with registration and inspection for all aspects of care. It brings into operation new regulating authorities and commissions. Of particular relevance here is section 23(1), which deals with National Minimum Standards for care homes for older people and, when they are completed, National Minimum Standards for other vulnerable groups of the population (e.g. children).

We can reasonably expect all National Minimum Standards to contain the same type of information; therefore we will use those relating to care homes for older people as a framework for guidance. These standards contain the sections shown in Table 6. Each of the sections provides guidance to a care manager on the standards expected for each issue when dealing with residents and their relatives and staff within the care setting. It is hard to imagine how any care manager can operate and function to a high level in the workplace without a good understanding of the content of these standards.

Table 6. The National Minimum Standards relating to care homes for older people

Section	Main content
Choice of home	Information, contract, needs assessment, meeting needs, trial visits
Health and personal care	Service user plan, health care, medication, privacy and dignity, dying and death
Daily life and social activities	Social contact and activities, community contact, autonomy and choice, meals and mealtimes
Complaints and protection	Complaints, rights, protection
Environment standards	Premises, shared facilities, lavatories and washing facilities, adaptations and equipment, individual accommodation, space requirements, furniture and fittings, services, heating and light, hygiene and control of infection
Staffing standards	Staff complement, qualifications, recruitment, staff training
Management and administration	Ethos, quality assurance, financial procedures, service users' money, staff supervision, record keeping, safe working practices

Obtain a copy of the Minimum Standards for older people and make notes of all the sections that are relevant to you. Identify major issues that require immediate attention and then identify those standards that can be achieved over a longer period. Think about your own support needs in meeting the requirements of the National Minimum Standards.

Aspects of the National Minimum Standards relate to supporting residents through change. For example, encouraging residents to be involved in the choice of residential care home or service provider if they are to stay in their own home will obviously be a source of support for those moving between care sectors.

The section on dying and death stipulates that managers must never regard death and dying as routine, and that staff training should be incorporated into all the policies relating to the care setting and, where appropriate, that specialist services should be introduced (e.g. Marie Curie or Macmillan nurses could be used to provide a joint service of care).

Standard 17 specifically requires that service users are enabled to exercise their legal rights, if necessary through the use of an advocacy service. This is a good example of supporting clients through change by involving external agencies.

You are able to design and implement a service that meets the needs of clients

Developing your own policies and procedures

Once you have a good understanding of the content of national policies and guidelines, you can begin to develop your own in-house version, based on the National Minimum Standards relating to your setting. The most appropriate place to start is by carrying out a review of your current policies and procedures. You should ask yourself the following questions:

✓ Are the organisational policies and procedures up to date, and do they contain the latest information?
✓ Are the different types and effects of resident change recognised and dealt with explicitly?

✓ Does the policy contain guidance on how clients should be supported?

✓ Is the guidance specific enough, for example in relation to when support should be offered, by whom and how?

✓ Is there a section on emergency procedures?

✓ Has cultural diversity been recognised and respected?

✓ Have the rights of people with a disability been accounted for?

✓ What part does choice play in the policy?

✓ How have service users been involved in the whole process?

✓ How have service users informed the development of these procedures?

✓ How often will the policy be reviewed?

✓ How will you monitor the success of action taken?

✓ How can you best inform and update staff?

✓ Who else needs access to the policy and for what purpose?

If you (and your organisation) are at the start of the process, and have no in-house policies or guidelines for supporting your service users, you will have to identify:

● your service users;
● aspects of change that may affect them;
● their support needs within the change scenario;
● how needs can be met by internal and external organisations.

Then begin to write you policy documents using the list above as a guide.

Evidence collection — Policies and guidelines

Using the National Minimum Standards for older people or other relevant policies and guidelines, develop or amend your own company policy to ensure appropriate guidelines are written for staff and others to cover supporting your clients during times of change.

Implementing systems and structures

Possibly one of the most important aspects of developing and implementing organisational systems and structures is consultation. This means that, at every stage of the process – writing the policy, implementing policy procedures and monitoring success (or otherwise) – staff, clients and others with an interest should be asked for their views and opinions.

When developing your policy you should ask yourself and others:

● What is the key purpose of the service (objectives)?
● How will you know that you have achieved that purpose (indicators of success)?
● How can you continuously improve the service you offer (evaluation)?

We already know from Bradshaw's work that there are different opinions on individuals' needs. We can see, then, that there will be different opinions expressed in answer to these questions. It is important that a shared understanding results from your activities. In this way policies and procedures are more likely to be 'owned' by the service user and staff.

Involving staff and residents in change

There are several accepted methods for obtaining the information you need. You could develop a questionnaire that goes to every client and member of staff, or you could run focus groups to discuss the issues. Each method will have advantages and disadvantages in terms of time, cost, client ability and, indeed, your own ability to understand and utilise these techniques.

Think it over

What would be the best way of finding out what your service users feel about the content of a new policy or way of working? What might be the implications for your organisation of using that method? You may need to think about 'time spent', about who could (or should) carry out the investigation and, of course, about cost. A further consideration will be how to store the information and then present it to others, perhaps as evidence of involving residents in decision making.

As the leader in your organisation, the way you choose to take a policy forward will affect whether it is accepted. Much policy implementation falls upon the shoulders of the manager. Many managers exercise power over their employees. This is perhaps best described as their having the capacity to alter the attitudes and behaviours of others. Within the health and social care setting, a manager's power is mainly obtained through social interactions. It is interesting to note that there are different kinds of power in operation:

- *coercive power* uses threats and sanctions;
- *reward power* uses positive reinforcement;
- *expert power* demands respect through a high knowledge base;
- *informational power* arises from the manager having access to information;
- *legitimate power* comes from holding a position of authority;
- *referent power* amounts to charisma.

Many contemporary managers use a range of powers, including 'connection' power – in other words, making good use of internal and external connections, a particularly important factor for those working in partnerships. When this is linked with expert and referent powers, most people will want to 'follow the leader'.

What kind of power base do you use? What is your preferred power base? Could you work differently? Should you work differently and if you did what difference would it make? Does your 'power base' involve staff in the change process or exclude them?

Case study — Involvement or exclusion?

Yusef is the manager of a day centre for people with physical disabilities. He has an autocratic management style because he firmly believes that his staff are mainly lazy and always striving to find ways of cutting their demanding workloads. He meets with the senior carers everyday and tells them exactly what must be achieved that day, by whom and in what way. His senior carers feel demotivated and have actually become low performers because subconsciously they know this is what is expected of them. They meet with their teams every day to pass on the commands and instructions. They then try to make sure that everything is carried out as prescribed. The workplace is filled with an air of apathy.

- What is happening at this day centre?
- How would the implementation of new policies and procedures be viewed by the staff?
- How might the situation be changed?
- What would you do differently, if anything, and why?
- How has the self-fulfilling prophecy been played out here?

Some suggestions for involving staff in change could include:

- Talk to the staff from inception to conclusion;
- Include progress reports at staff meetings;
- Ask for opinions and act upon appropriate advice;
- Acknowledge staff expertise and experience;
- Have a suggestion box;
- Ask staff to approach clients for ideas and involvement.

Some of these ideas can be used to involve clients in the change process. However, we need to recognise that some clients may choose not to participate which leads us into a discussion of the ethical issues involved.

Ethical considerations

At this point it may be useful to consider some of the ethical principles encountered in supporting and involving residents throughout the process of change. For example, in terms of your clients you could ask yourself 'Whose life is it anyway?' and 'What business is it of mine?' These are not easy questions to answer and different people are likely to give different answers.

You may find it helpful to consider four ethical principles or guidelines to help you think through your answers to such questions:

- beneficence (doing good);
- non-maleficence (doing no harm);
- justice (treating residents equally);
- respect for autonomy (respecting clients' rights and choice).

When examining support systems for service users (and staff), much of what you choose to do will depend upon the attitude you adopt. For example, if you feel that 'control' is important in the management of change (for reasons of beneficence), you may feel that you and your staff should make choices for service users, despite this being counter to the ethical principle of respect for autonomy.

Case study — Ethical guidance

George Ashcroft lives alone and the care agency that you manage provides for his daily care needs. One of your carers, Marcia, is becoming increasingly concerned about Mr Ashcroft. Due to his dementing illness, he is constantly asking for his son, Adam, who died several years ago in a motorbike accident. Marcia has found that if she tells Mr Ashcroft that Adam will come to see him tomorrow, he goes quiet for a while. She has asked you for advice on how to handle the situation. She feels that sooner or later Mr Ashcroft (or someone else) will realise that she is lying to him.

- How would you respond to Marcia?
- What justification would you apply to the answer you have given?
- How could you support Marcia further through training and development or other supportive systems?

Think it over

What other situations might you face as a manager that could lead you to consider ethical aspects? How would you respond to those situations and why?

Other ethical principles include the need to safeguard your staff and clients during change. This could be through the systems and structures that ensure confidentiality of information; for example, individuals going through major life events have enough to deal with without worrying about the confidentiality of the information relating to their situation. Many organisations guarantee confidentiality (subject to safety issues) within their mission statement. Is this something you should consider, or is it sufficient that the issue is included in your policies and guidelines?

You know of systems and methods for supporting clients and staff during times of change

Support systems can be either internal or external.

Internal support systems

Guidelines, policies and codes of conduct are clearly part of the internal support system that can be used by both you and your staff in dealing with clients experiencing change. We have already noted that the National Minimum Standards of care give advice and direction on handling death and bereavement as well as guidance on privacy and dignity (see Table 6 on page 315). Your internal support systems must be tailored to these standards.

Other internal support mechanisms include:

- developing supportive relationships;
- staff training;
- meetings and workshops.

Developing supportive relationships

Communication is a key issue in terms of developing supportive relationships with both staff and clients. All communication should be:

- timely;
- appropriate;
- relevant;
- at the right level.

Breakdowns in communication are often the cause of difficulties when a service provider aims to support clients during difficult times.

Case study — Breakdown in communication

Art Thomas recently left hospital after a hip replacement. He is 83 years old and very able apart from his current physical disability. His care plan was agreed when he left the hospital but unfortunately the occupational therapist could not attend the care planning meeting. On his return home, Mr Thomas tried to get out of bed by himself one morning, because his carer was late arriving. He knew the bed was too high but thought he could manage. He had to be readmitted to the same hospital ward with a fractured wrist and dislocated hip.

- What series of events led to this situation?
- How could communication have been used to prevent this kind of situation arising?
- What action would you have taken as the manager of the agency providing care for Mr Thomas?

Often it is not enough to simply provide a service user or member of staff with the required information: you must ensure the listener has understood the full implications of your message. The model developed by Shannon and Weaver in 1949 still holds good today (see Figure 32) . It explains how the communication process involves the use of appropriate methods for sending the message; for example, if the voice is to be used then the receiver (the ear) needs to be reached. The encoder in this case will be the spoken language. The intended message can be disrupted at any of the different stages shown in Figure 32.

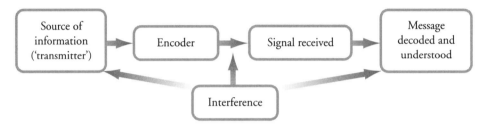

Figure 32. The Shannon and Weaver model of the communication process.

Try it out

What might cause interference with the communication process in your workplace or organisation? What could be the results of this in terms of service user support?

It is likely to be helpful if you adopt a philosophy of communication. For example:

- Make sure *all* your staff are informed about your organisational goals and plans.
- Tell *all* your staff about current activities.
- Inform staff of controversial and sensitive issues that affect the organisation (but remember to respect confidentiality).
- Encourage communication in every direction – up, down and across.
- Communicate quickly.
- Hold meetings that allow everyone to be open and honest.

Along with the importance of communication as a way of supporting residents, it is also useful to consider the work of Kitwood (1997), which looked at ways of demonstrating a 'positive person approach' to all aspects of care work. His research identified the importance of the following in developing supportive relationships:

- ***recognition*** – use of name and acknowledgement of the person as unique;
- ***collaboration*** – care carried out together;

- *negotiation* – recognising choice, empowerment;
- *play* – encouraging spontaneity;
- *relaxation* – the role of company and quiet time;
- *validation* – valuing emotions and feelings;
- *facilitation* – enabling action;
- *holding* – keeping people safe (psychologically).

Other methods of supporting clients can include:

- allocate a specific worker;
- introduce structured activity to promote positive social interaction;
- promote links with existing external contracts to maintain identity;
- gain insight into 'who they are' and what they like (their identity).

Needs vary, often according to the time of day, circumstance and situation. For example, people with physical disabilities may require more help at the end of a day, when they are physically tired from daily exertions, whereas people with Alzheimer's disease may have lucid times when the need for support is less. The type of change experienced can also affect the amount and type of support a client may require. Therefore, it is important that staff recognise the need to treat every individual and every situation as unique.

What comments might you wish to make in relation to this scenario?

How closely does your organisation's approach to developing supportive relationships fit with Kitwood's model? What would you need to change to ensure a closer match? How does this model sit with supporting staff?

Staff training

Possibly one of the most important mechanisms for providing support to clients and staff is through staff training and development. The intention should be to develop the skills and knowledge that your staff will require to support service users at difficult times in their lives.

When planning training for staff, you will need to consider:

- whether there is a relevant policy or guideline which underpins staff training, and if so how it can best be used as part of the training process;
- when training should take place (e.g. at induction or when the staff member has a good understanding of the job? Or should it be ongoing?);
- how the training fits into staff appraisal and developmental needs;
- who should deliver the training (in-house or an external provider?);
- what the content of the training should include;
- how the effectiveness of the training will be measured (otherwise how will you be able to tell that the staff development has worked?);
- what the training will cost, and how many members of staff need to be involved.

Case study — Physical intervention

Angela is a forensic nurse. She has found herself in a difficult situation. One of her patients has just been referred to the forensic unit from the youth justice service and is finding it very hard to settle down. Angela has been bitten twice by him and now he is following her around and making threats of further violence against her. She has had training on behaviour management and already gives clear messages about what is acceptable behaviour and what is not. She has now asked her manager for further support and a copy of the policy on the use of physical interventions.

- How might you support Angela and her client in this situation?
- What information would you expect to see in the policy on the use of physical intervention?
- What events could occur in your workplace that would require the use of a policy or procedures in the case of violence from a service user or between service users?
- Are guidelines available to you, your staff and others involved?

As part of their training, most carers will be expected to develop the skills and knowledge to identify that a client has a specific need. It should be accepted that along with change comes a range of support needs. Ways of meeting clients' needs in relation to change and significant life events should be covered in the training of your staff. The training should include:

- the provision of useful information for clients (tell carers so they can pass it on);
- the safe and appropriate provision of physical help;
- advice on what is acceptable support and what is not;
- emotional support systems (e.g. counselling and/or active listening skills);
- information on sources of external support (agencies and referral systems) and guidance on how and when to access them.

The training outlined above could be delivered internally, but in some cases specialised training may be required in relation to clients' needs or it may be more helpful to access the services of an external specialist service. For example:

- handling deep-seated grief and mourning for the loss of a physical ability, a home, person or situation;
- finding appropriate ways of dealing with the change or problem solving with service users.

Case study — Assessing needs

Steve and Maureen are going on holiday for the first time in three years. Maureen's mother, Mabel, has agreed to go into respite care for the three weeks that they are away. A great deal of attention has had to be given to the choice of care home. Mabel uses a wheelchair but is also frightened of closed-in lifts. She is a Christian and believes that she must attend church every Sunday (preferably twice). She enjoys her weekly game of dominoes at the over-60s club and frets if she does not see her friend Agnes regularly (because 'you never know at our age').

- Using PIES and other aspects of health and well-being, identify the needs Mabel is displaying in her choice of care home.
- How important is each need? How might your priorities differ from Mabel's?
- What information would you need to include in staff training to ensure that all your staff are in a position to support Mabel during her three weeks away from her familiar environment?

Meetings and workshops

One of your duties will be the organisation of appropriate meetings for all your care staff. These could be held for the entire organisation, individual teams, whole staff groups or one to one.

Meetings serve a range of purposes, including:

- day-to-day management of an organisation;
- information seeking and giving;
- updating policies and procedures;
- staff training.

The case study on physical intervention (page 324) is an ideal example of a situation which calls for a specific meeting to address a particular issue. It is important that you are clear about what you want to call a meeting for. It is no good holding a meeting for a meeting's sake! Know what you want to achieve and ensure that those people attending the meeting know what their role and responsibilities are in relation to it.

Other methods of supporting staff include the time taken to help new staff orientate into their job role.

Methods that could be used to support new staff include:

- key person to act as a mentor;
- time away from task to learn systems and procedures;
- regular supervision;
- being task-orientated in early stages.

External support systems

These are the systems and services that you can call upon to support staff and service users at difficult times. They should supplement rather than replace the internal services that you provide. External support services can include **advocacy**, **counselling** and **professional development**.

Advocacy

The views and opinions of service users are now central to all aspects of care delivery. Managers who fail to listen to the views of service users are likely to find themselves on the wrong side of an inspection report. Advocates are increasingly being used to help service users convey their views. Advocates are perhaps best described as people who speak (or plead) for others. You need to know what the role of an advocate is and how to make contact with an advocacy service, should a client require such assistance. The White Paper *Valuing People* has promised to make advocates available for people with learning difficulties and *Quality Protects* requires advocates to be available for children.

While the advocacy service is generally seen as a 'good thing', there are some examples of service users receiving worse treatment after an advocate has been brought in – as 'punishment' for involving outsiders! There is also the possibility of carers taking on a paternalistic or maternalistic role when advocating for the client and using their position of power to make decisions for the individual rather than encouraging autonomy and choice.

Case study — Support through a life event

Alf is leaving his own home to stay in the local hospice. His service provider is helping him to prepare for the move. Between them they have identified four stages involved in the move: planning; packing and preparing; making the move; getting to know the new environment. Bridget is helping Alf at each stage of the move because she has been his main carer for the last three years.

- What level of support would you expect Bridget to give Alf at each stage of the 'move process'?
- How could you support Bridget?
- What could an advocacy service bring to this situation that would assist both Alf and Bridget?

Counselling

Many care workers feel that they are able to counsel their clients whenever their skills are needed. However, in reality this is very rarely the case. People who offer a formal, professional counselling service have undergone rigorous training to ensure they are able to meet their clients' needs effectively.

It is important that managers and staff know when to contact the services of a professional on behalf of a service user rather than trying to deal with issues themselves. This is certainly a guideline that should be included in the policies and procedures for the workplace.

Professional development

One of the most important support mechanisms available to you as a manager is the professional development of you and your staff. In the main we have dealt with the development of your staff through the section on training, so this section will concentrate on your own development. During these times of constant change there is a real need for managers:

- to update their knowledge; and
- to increase their management skills.

Neither is easy to find time for when you are involved in the day-to-day running of a care establishment or agency. However, managers who are out of date and functioning at a low level of managerial ability are not an asset to an organisation. Indeed, we could argue that they are a liability! Therefore:

- read professional journals;
- talk to colleagues;
- attend training courses;
- find the time to attend *relevant* conferences;
- ask questions; and
- listen to clients and staff.

Remember that knowledge speaks and wisdom listens.

Evidence collection — Supporting individuals experiencing life events

With reference to your clients and their individual support needs during times of change, develop and implement a policy and associated procedures for staff to follow. Your policy should include the following headings as a minimum:

- rationale for the policy;
- client support needs;
- methods of supporting clients;
- staff roles and responsibilities;
- methods and purpose of referral to other agencies;
- external agencies used;
- emergency procedures;
- monitoring and evaluation methods.

Keys to good management practice

Supporting individuals through life events and change

- Develop and implement good practice policies and procedures.
- Know your clients and understand the changes that are likely to affect them.
- Recognise critical times of change.
- Be prepared for change.
- Ensure staff are fully conversant with handling change.
- Develop referral systems to outside agencies, making contact with external support networks.
- Keep yourself up to date with contractual requirements.
- Ensure that you have sufficient knowledge and skills to support both staff and service users.

F3 Manage Continuous Quality Improvement

This unit introduces you to the concept of 'quality' and the fact that we should all be striving towards 'continuous quality improvement' in all aspects of care provision. We explore the types of quality systems that are currently in use within health and social care and touch upon the historical context of their development, before examining the processes and techniques involved in continuous quality improvement.

We recognise that measuring quality is not only in the particular domain and interest of those people and agencies who have a purchasing/commissioning role within health and social care, but also in the domain of those who organise and provide care for others. It is entirely possible that, as the quality standards system becomes embedded in the way we work, any agencies or organisations that fail to measure up will see themselves out of business as their service is no longer purchased on behalf of clients. If nothing else, this should indicate to all managers that quality assurance is a key factor within health and social care and, what is more, it is here to stay!

The elements are:

- Develop and implement systems to monitor and evaluate organisational performance.
- Promote continuous quality improvements for products, services and processes.

You understand the background to continuous quality improvement in health and social care

The quality of service provision and of the outcomes obtained is a relatively new concept in the field of health and social care. When the welfare state was first formed, quality did not really figure – cure and health maintenance were key – but as care began to go wrong in terms of both cost and outcome, quality of provision began to raise its head.

Social care has to a certain extent explored the issue of quality for longer than health care. It was in the early 1960s that it was noted that many older adults lived in 'appalling' conditions in residential care. It was acknowledged that something 'had to be done' to improve the quality of their lives, and hence the first quality standards were introduced, in relation to living space, and so on. For health care, however, the concept really came alive only in the early 1980s, when the Conservative government tried to apply some of the more traditional, production-line aspects of quality to health and social care as a result of spiralling costs.

It is useful to note at this point that the traditional approach to quality developed through the production line. As products (say, light bulbs) were made, they would pass through several stages of development, but as they came off the production line a 'quality controller' would examine them and discard any that failed to make the grade. Although this system worked, it was expensive and time consuming (imagine all the time and money that had gone into making a light bulb only for it to be discarded at the end of the process). Therefore, a new approach appeared in the 1950s that concentrated more on each stage of production. This became known as quality assurance, a key factor of which was the involvement and to some extent the responsibility of the worker at each stage of the production process. Another key element of quality assurance is the participation of the customer or client, who also feeds back into the quality assurance cycle.

Quality assurance concentrates on ensuring that there is quality control at each stage of production.

As we have noted, quality became a more important agenda item for the government during the 1980s and early 1990s in both health and social care. There was a heavy emphasis on 'total quality management' (TQM). Directors of quality management began to appear in hospital trusts (they were often nurses), and in social care the Registered Homes Act 1984 brought in the system of external inspections and registration for care homes.

Practice has since moved much further on. Health and social care practitioners are now expected to be more involved in critical and reflective practice. This means constantly reviewing the service offered in terms of provision, resources, effectiveness and, of course, efficiency.

It can be argued, then, that quality assurance for an organisation depends upon the commitment, motivation and participation of every member of staff. We need to demonstrate professionalism and positive attitudes to quality at all times. These days it is not so much about the tools, techniques and procedures of quality assurance as about the staff who are applying them, although it is fully acknowledged here that we cannot do without the application of tools and measurements. However, it cannot be stated too strongly that the quality assurance process should be built around the people who are actually using (or receiving) the quality service.

Any managers who do not fully understand the issues related to quality and the impact it has upon a service are likely to find that their service is marginalised and under-utilised, especially when it comes to 'preferred provider' status (being on a list of suitable providers that are 'recommended' by purchasers).

Think it over

In groups, discuss the following issues, noting any points that you might want to take further action on.

- When did you last think about your service in terms of the provision you offer, the effectiveness of the service for clients and the efficiency of the service in terms of cost and value for money?
- How might you demonstrate a quality service to your funders, clients and staff?
- Who would you want to involve in the early stages of quality development in your workplace? Why?

You understand the purpose and setting of objectives

Standards are also known as 'objectives' and sometimes 'criteria'. Whatever term is used they are the 'indicators' of quality for that service. Thus, they are used (as a kind of proxy) for measuring quality. This means that unless an organisation has an aim and a set of objectives to work towards, there is very little chance of being able to measure 'quality' in any form that carries meaning and credibility. In this text we are generally going to use the term 'objectives'.

So what are these 'objectives' and who sets them?

Objectives are often used by the organisation as the 'stepping stones' towards improving service. It is these 'stepping stones' that are measured and monitored so that a manager can see how the overall organisation or sections of the organisation are working towards improvement. We can see, then, that care standards are used as measures of quality. If you meet a standard you are arguably closer to a quality service than the provider who fails.

Try it out

Obtain a copy of the Care Standards Act 2000. Note that there is a whole range of standards (objectives) to be met in social care. Examine those standards that relate directly to your organisation. Which ones do you already meet and which ones need further work to enable your organisation to meet the requirements?

The Care Standards Act 2000 has set quality standards for the care industry. These are broken down into a series of National Minimum Standards, for example the Minimum Standards for Older People, which also identify a range of criteria for the providers of care services. It is extremely unlikely that, at this point, any one provider of care services will meet all the criteria set. Nonetheless, you can use internally set objectives to act as 'stepping stones' towards meeting all of the national criteria. So how do you go about identifying the key features of an objective and then developing these for the organisation?

Think it over

Discuss with other managers how you might 'demonstrate' to an inspector that you meet the standard set in C8.1.

If you examine Standard C8.1 in the Care Standards Act, you will note that it says: 'The manager can demonstrate that he/she has undertaken periodic training to update their knowledge, skills and competence to manage the establishment'. This is a good example of a criterion or an objective that can be measured by others and then used to help define the quality of the manager in question.

The main points to note about setting objectives for your organisation to work towards is that they must be SMART:

(S)   specific;

(M)   measurable (be provable);

(A)   achievable;

(R)   reliable;

(T)   timely.

Think it over

Working with others, identify the reasons behind the SMART acronym. In other words, why should objectives be specific, measurable, achievable, reliable and timely?

Remember that objectives are used as a tool for measuring the performance of your organisation. Therefore, they must be written in a way that allows measurement. For example, an objective that is too wide-ranging or broad might read something like this: 'to meet the needs of the residents living in Happy Hours Residential Care Home'. Whenever you write an objective you need to ask yourself, 'How can I provide *evidence* of achieving this?'

If you can identify an example of 'concrete' evidence, the chances are that the objective will work. Compare the broad objective above with the management training standard (C8.1). The broad objective is much less likely to be of value to an inspector who has to make a judgement about the service in question.

The National Minimum Standards have been centrally set by a government body, but your mission statement (giving the aim of the service) and related objectives are likely to have been set by a local organisation, or an internal senior manager or business owner.

Evidence collection — Develop and implement systems to monitor and evaluate performance

Obtain a copy of your organisation's mission statement and, if they exist, the service objectives. Make notes on how you might provide evidence for the quality of your service by using this information. If you come across difficulties with any of the objectives (or if they do not exist) you may wish to discuss the situation with a senior manager or owner for action on policy development to be taken as part of your professional development.

Writing objectives

Writing objectives is not an easy task and yet without them the whole issue of measuring quality fails at the first hurdle. It is important for you, as a manager, to understand how to write and interpret objectives. Finding a starting point can be difficult, but it is not impossible. Perhaps you could start by asking yourself some fairly basic questions about your service. For example:

- Is your service accessible?
- Is it equitable to all?
- Is it relevant to the needs of your clients?
- Is it relevant to the needs of other consumers?
- Is it effective?
- Is it efficient?
- Does your service encourage or discourage participation from clients?

John has just taken up a new post as registered manager of Sunny Days Residential Care Home. He has been there six weeks and has observed that staff are demotivated, overworked through lack of numbers, and failing to respond to the clients and each other in an appropriate manner.

Ethel and Doris are two of the more interested and lively residents of Sunny Days. They tell him that every day is the same. There is no variety in their lives and neither of them can remember the last time they went out.

John feels that something needs to be done, and is thinking of writing an in-house strategy for improving the quality of life for both staff and clients. He has decided to call his strategy 'A Quality Service at Sunny Days'.

Working in a small group, use the basic questions about a service to write a series of objectives that John could use in his strategy. You will need to apply the SMART acronym to ensure your objectives are workable.

Once you have written your objectives, share them with another group to discuss ways of measuring their outcomes.

Evidence collection — Developing and implementing objectives

To begin the process of developing quality policies, arrange a staff meeting and subsequent one-to-one meetings to discuss the approach to quality in one specific area in your workplace. This could be a staff development policy (that would include induction and training and development), or a staff handbook or a health and safety policy.

Do not forget to keep notes and records of all your activities as evidence for your portfolio.

You identify a range of techniques and systems that can be applied to quality audit and monitoring in a health and social care organisation

Measurement is a vital part of continuous quality improvement: it allows for understanding of the way things work; it provides information upon which to base future business decisions; and it promotes best service and value.

There are several ways of measuring and monitoring quality in health and social care. These can be internal or external, but ideally should be a mix of the two. The two currently most used and advocated methods are:

- self-assessment; and
- external inspections.

Self-assessment

All organisations need to ask themselves about their performance from time to time. They need to know if they are meeting their clients' needs, if they are financially viable and most of all they need to know and recognise when they need to change in order to stay competitive and provide best value. Health and social care organisations are no different.

As we have already said, you need to know:

- what your clients want;
- how they feel about your service.

You also need to know how you feel about your organisation in terms of:

- performance;
- resource use; and
- improvements.

One of the ways you can address these questions is through self-assessment. You need to recognise that self-assessment is part of the continuous quality improvement process. You cannot continually improve your quality of service if you do not self-assess.

There are clear benefits to the organisation of self-assessment. For example, there is a 'systematic' examination of *everything* the organisation is involved in. A good self-assessment process will involve *everyone* in the process, as this will lead to healthy discussion about improvements and, of course, it will promote the overall culture of continuous quality improvement. It is also a useful way of preparing for external inspection and regulation. If you self-assess appropriately, you should (in theory) know exactly what the outcomes of an external inspection will be!

This is all well and good, but where do you start as the manager of an organisation? There are five clear steps to self-assessment, and having a good understanding of these is essential. Make sure your quality policies and quality criteria are in place first! Then:

- Compare your services with the quality criteria at this point in time.
- Identify your strengths and weaknesses against each criterion.
- Action plan to set targets for improvement.
- Monitor and assess the results of your action plan.
- Measure yourself again against the criteria and so back into the cycle (see Figure 33).

Ideally, a self-assessment would take place annually, but if you have major concerns about any aspect of the service it may be necessary to self-assess more regularly.

There is no one way of carrying out the self-assessments. You may choose to develop a few basic questions about a particular function of your organisation that allow you to answer with a quick yes or no, or you may prefer to examine the service in greater detail by using a scoring system. Whichever method you use, as long as improvements can be identified and dialogue is encouraged, you can be said to be self-assessing.

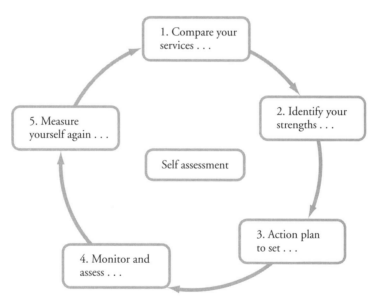

Figure 33. The self-assessment cycle.

Here is a page from John's list of standards for improving the quality of care and work for staff and clients at Sunny Days.

Quality criteria	Evidence from:	Score (1 = strong, 5 = weak)
We involve all our residents in care planning	Signatures on care plans Minutes of meetings Staff training records Survey of residents' views	5 – no clear evidence available
All our residents have a choice of menu at each meal	Questionnaire to residents Interview with catering staff	3 – choice not always available at breakfast, main meal of the day limited to two choices
Staff are well motivated and enthusiastic about their work	Interviews with staff Staff appraisal scheme Feedback from residents	4 – some staff demotivated

- What do you think of these?
- Could you make any improvements to the wording or the scoring?

Scoring the assessment

With an example such as John's scoring method from the self-assessment case study, it is possible to add up the overall score for the service and to work out the average (total score divided by number of questions). With the example given, the following average scores would show:

1 = strengths far outweigh weaknesses;

2 = strengths outweigh weaknesses;

3 = strengths and weaknesses are equal;

4 = weaknesses outweigh strengths;

5 = weaknesses far outweigh strengths.

However, we need to recognise that scoring is not the be all and end all of the audit. For some organisations, having a 'visual picture' of the service is sufficient in the early stages of a self-assessment cycle and they may want to wait until the second or third time around before they begin applying scores to their work. Once audit results are available, in whatever form, open discussion can take place among both staff and clients to identify the required action to bring about improvements. (Can you see how the self-assessment cycle is fitting in here?) This is discussed further in section F3.2.

Examples of self-assessment criteria

Policy and strategy

We have policies and plans to cover all aspects of our organisation's roles and responsibilities.

We constantly review and update our policies and plans.

We include feedback from our clients in all our planning processes.

Staff

We regularly update our staff training policies.

All staff participate in an annual appraisal process that includes constructive feedback.

Staff are actively encouraged to improve their qualifications.

Management

Managers are actively involved in consultations with staff and service users.

All managers regularly undertake professional development.

Managers actively encourage the promotion of effective communication.

Think it over

What evidence could you provide from your workplace to prove you are fulfilling the criteria?

Performance indicators

At this stage it is important to develop a set of quality performance indicators. In other words, what are you going to use as the 'performance indicator' for each of your quality objectives? It might help at this point to think of an indicator as a pointer or signpost that shows you are travelling in the right direction. It can tell you how far you have come and how far you still need to travel in order to reach your goal. Often, indicators relate to 'outcomes' and demonstrate a concrete, observable change. For example, implementing a 'no smoking policy' in a care home could be measured by the fact that no one smokes inside the building. Intermediate indicators give an indication of progress, for example, if you wanted all staff trained to NVQ level 2 in the next five years, the intermediate indicator would be the number trained each year.

Another example of evidence your organisation might use to 'indicate' to an external inspector that all clients are involved in care planning. You could (in theory) use the same sources of evidence as John in the self-assessment case study to demonstrate to an inspector that your service users take a full and active part in the care planning process, but only if the records are comprehensive and detail fully the discussions that have taken place. If you take short cuts with the information, for example not bothering to take minutes of meetings, you have lost a very valuable source of evidence relating to quality of provision.

The easiest (or at least simplest) approach to recording the information you require may be to use an audit questionnaire that relies on performance indicator questions with a yes/no answer. Such a questionnaire can be scored by a simple addition method. Table 7 gives an example. Once you are comfortable with this technique, you can progress to other methods of collecting evidence.

Table 7. An example of an audit questionnaire that relies on performance indicator questions with a yes/no answer, for the objective 'All residents are encouraged and enabled to make their own decisions about all aspects of their lives to the full extent of their abilities'

Indicator questions	Response (circle as appropriate)	
Is there evidence of service user participation in care planning?	YES	NO
Are care plans written in an accessible and easy-to-use format?	YES	NO
Is the service user invited to attend care planning meetings?	YES	NO

It is important to remember when devising this kind of questionnaire that if your indicator questions do not match the 'standard' set then you will not achieve reliable and valid evidence to indicate a quality service. In other words, make sure that the questions you ask during the audit are designed to measure the success or failure of the standard set and *not* something that is unrelated!

Think it over

Working with another person, add three more evidence indicator questions to Table 1 to give an inspector more evidence that the standard set is achieved in your place of work. You could think about the action you would take if clients failed to attend care planning meetings as a starting point.

Other important considerations when choosing performance indicators are:

- Who selected the performance indicator?
- What bias might this introduce?
- Is there any unwanted influence from other interested parties?

- Is the cost attached to collecting the data acceptable?
- Can everyone understand the indicator?
- Can the indicator be changed quickly and easily to respond to market changes?
- Can the indicators be accessed in good time by those who need to use them?

Evidence collection — Measuring quality

Decide now how you are going to measure the quality (think 'success') of a policy you are writing. Make notes of the intended process using the questions below to inform your planning.

- What performance indicators are required to measure the 'success' of the policy?
- Who needs to be involved in the feedback process?
- How are you going to measure (score) the assessment?
- Is staff training required to enable staff to participate effectively?
- If so, how will this be managed?
- What will you do with the results obtained?

Techniques for gathering evidence of quality

As you are probably aware, there is a wide range of techniques available for obtaining the evidence required to measure quality (we have already mentioned the audit questionnaire in the previous section). Key examples are:

- questionnaires;
- interviews;
- focus groups;
- secondary data.

Focus group

Secondary data

These are discussed under separate headings below. However, the techniques you decide to use should depend on how experienced you are at using them. Further considerations should also include:

- What is the purpose of the audit?
- Are the performance criteria available for measurement?
- What information is required and whom does it need to come from?
- What methods can best be used to collect the data?
- How will the results be reported back?

There are many views and opinions as to the best way to carry out a quality audit and each one has its own merits and disadvantages. If you have studied research methods, you will be aware of the debates about which approach is best. If your knowledge of research methods is limited, you may find it helpful at this point to dip into some of the texts available (See Bibliography).

However, if you are clear about the purpose of your assessment activities and the information required from them, then you are more than halfway there. You do need to remind yourself that contractors and managers are likely to require a scientific approach to assessment, which involves the collection of hard, quantitative data that focuses upon outputs and outcomes, such as the number of staff qualified to NVQ Level 2 and above. They are also likely to require a client-centred approach that includes information on people's feelings about and opinions of the service they are being offered. Thus, we can see that a mix of methods for the collection of data (i.e. your evidence) is most likely to be useful.

Questionnaires

As already discussed, these can be useful tools with which to measure outcomes. However, it is important that the questions are written in such a way that they actually measure what they are intended to measure. This is known as the *validity* of the research tool. Another consideration is *reliability*. In other words, will you obtain the same results no matter who asks the questions and collates the results? If the questionnaire is of doubtful reliability or validity, then the evidence collection will be flawed from the outset.

Other considerations include:

- How will the questionnaire be administered?
- Will everyone be able to take part or might some service users be excluded?
- What will be the cost in terms of finance, staff and time?
- Is there a better method of collecting evidence?

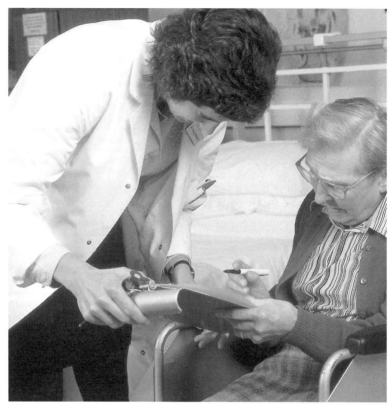

Will everyone be able to take part in the questionnaire?

Interviews

The interview is a very useful technique for obtaining information about feelings and attitudes as well as hard outcomes. Interviews are readily used by inspectors. All too often you will find that inspectors (and senior management) like to discuss systems and practices with all staff members and all clients to obtain a picture of what is happening in an organisation. However, the next stage of an interview is often the 'request' for hard evidence to prove that what is being said is actually happening in reality.

In an interview, the right questions have to be asked. Furthermore, it is usually beneficial to ask the same questions in a consistent manner across a series of interviews on the same subject with different people. It can be helpful, therefore, to draw up an 'interview schedule'. An interview schedule can take one of three forms:

- structured – each question is set and asked in exactly the same way to each person;
- unstructured – no questions are set, and only a general idea of the main areas to be discussed is outlined;
- semi-structured – the questions used fall between the above two extremes.

The main difficulty with interviews is in analysing the data captured. Many researchers advocate the identification of themes and patterns as a good way of turning the data into meaningful information. While this is certainly the case, you would need to plan the time it will take to do this into the overall assessment process.

The points to consider when deciding whether or not to use interviews for evidence collection are:

- the time it will take to carry out the interviews;
- the cost;
- the skills required;
- the service users' ability to participate.

Case study — Interviews for evidence collection

Sharon is visiting a small care home for people with learning disabilities. Her objective is to identify the methods used by staff to include residents in the decision making that affects their daily lives. At the home, she has a talk with Colin May (a resident) about the holiday he is planning and how he decided where to go. She follows this with a discussion with Eileen, Mr May's key worker, to find out how she enabled him to decide where he wanted to go on holiday. Once she had an image of the process that seemed to have taken place, she asked the manager for copies of Mr May's care plans, so that she could check when and how he had participated in the decision. Her next step was to meet with other staff to ask them how they enabled residents to take part in decisions about their everyday lives and how this was recorded.

- What are the advantages and disadvantages of Sharon's approach?
- How might the staff respond to her questions?
- Could she include anything else as evidence of resident 'participation'?

Try it out

Working with another person, devise a series of interview questions/performance indicators to use when checking that careful consideration is given to residents' rights in your organisation. The kinds of areas that you might want to explore for this task are:

- the ways in which staff address residents (observation is another method used for collecting evidence);
- the ways in which residents are/are not encouraged to participate in decision making;
- whether privacy is respected at all times.

Once you have listed sufficient questions, try them out in your workplace. Note the responses from staff. Check to see if the information relates to the quality in the way you expected. Compare your experiences and results with those of your partner. Make changes to the questions and try again.

Focus groups

A focus group is a useful way of exploring the views and opinions of a small group of people at one time. It is quicker and more cost-effective than interviewing people individually, and in some cases being a member of a group can encourage people to participate and express their own views more readily.

The recommended number of participants is between 6 and 12. Participants should belong to a single group of interest – for example, staff employed within the same organisation, service users who use the same care agency, or managers of residential care homes.

However, we need to recognise that the researcher will need to have certain skills in order to gather the desired information. These skills will include:

- an ability to put people at ease;
- an ability to facilitate discussion;
- an ability to listen and record information at the same time;
- an ability to analyse the information collected.

Try it out

Form a focus group in your place of work to explore a specific issue that you feel needs addressing. It could relate to a policy you are developing or it could be something entirely unrelated, such as menu planning, recreational activities for residents or a staff issue. Make a note of the questions and issues that you want to raise for discussion, find a suitable method for recording the information obtained and decide what you will do with the information once you have collected it.

On completion of this activity, write a short review of the process. This should include notes on how you felt when conducting the discussions and how successful you feel the method has been for giving you insight into the area discussed.

Secondary data

This is a particularly useful source of information for managers. Very often other people have carried out research into the very issues that affect your business. For example, you are likely to find that your local health trust or social services department has already carried out research to find out about the numbers and types of service user in your locality (potential residents or clients). Accessing this kind of information can save you a great deal of time and also provide you with a foundation on which to base your own quality improvement programmes.

Current trends in care provision can be identified from secondary sources. For example, the Health Service Plan 2001 identified an 'intermediate care' policy. This suggested that greater emphasis is going to be placed on community care in the future: rehabilitation centres will be used to give people a greater chance of full recovery and thus independence from illness. Clearly, this will have an impact upon your business planning. For example, should finance be devoted to the setting up of a rehabilitation centre as part of your service, or should you concentrate more on domiciliary care? It is information relating to trends such as this that should be guiding your decision making.

Think it over

Working with another person, use the Internet to find out the most recent census statistics. Access the demographic information on the numbers of older people in society today. What are the implications of your findings for you as the manager of a care setting?

Evidence collection — Techniques for monitoring quality

Select what you feel is the most appropriate tool to collect the evidence you require to measure the success of your organisational policy. Once you have developed your data collection tool, pilot it – in other words, try it out and see what kind of information it is giving you. Check to see if the information is:

- useful;
- relevant;
- accurate;
- easy to collect.

If you are happy with your results, use the data collection tool on a wider group of subjects.

F3.2

Learning outcomes

- You recognise current quality trends and requirements in health and social care practice.
- You understand ways of assessing and dealing with the implications of results obtained from quality monitoring.
- You recognise ways of including and motivating people in continuous quality improvement.
- You recognise your role in promoting continuous quality improvement.

You recognise current quality trends and requirements in health and social care practice

These days we are required to demonstrate our quality of service through the use of self-assessment, external inspection and 'best value'. These requirements are driven centrally by a government that is keen to see quality as the core feature of all care services and is willing to lead the process by setting the standards of required performance nationally for application locally.

In 1998, 'best value' was identified as the key element of a partnership between central and local government that has responsibility to provide quality services for all. However, in reality, the challenge is not just about offering a better service – it is about the greater challenge of continuous improvement, year upon year.

It should be clear then that 'continuous improvement' is the quality trend for health and social care and, as such, needs a base line or a starting point from which to begin the continuous improvement cycle. For many of us the challenge is to decide where to start.

Think it over

Working with others, discuss what you would like to see improved in your organisation, staff training, care planning, recruitment or induction processes? What difference would improvement make? How might you start the process of bringing about any necessary changes?

In the early 1990s, the Institute of Public Policy Research identified five different approaches to measuring quality that were being (or could be) used in health and social care. These are known as:

- ***The traditional.*** This approach to quality measurement is very much related to prestige and having the 'best' business product in your field. This means you would want to be the market leader for the area. It is likely that all the measures used by you would relate to the product of the business. However, in health and social care, our 'product' is people, so this approach to quality is arguably unsuitable for our use.
- ***The scientific.*** This approach is more about meeting the standards set by the service 'expert'. In other words, you would be keen to follow the guidance given, perhaps by social or health care inspectorates, in order to ensure that the service on offer to residents meets the required (often minimum) legal standard.

- **The managerial.** The managerial approach (also known as the 'excellence' approach) is far more interested in what clients or their relatives think about the service. This could be simply to provide better care but it is also likely to have a strong link to the view that if clients like a service they will come back for more or will recommend the service to others.
- **The consumerist.** This approach to achieving quality seeks to empower residents so that they can take part in the overall decision making about the direction the service should take so that their needs are identified and then met.
- **The democratic.** This approach explores quality from the viewpoint of the entire community involved – both service users and other people – who may have a viewpoint even though they do not use the service. It is possibly the most difficult approach for the owner/manager of a small business to access and use effectively.

Try it out

Each of the five approaches listed has advantages and disadvantages. What approach to quality might you want to take in your workplace and why? Might you consider drawing from more than one approach? Select one of the approaches to explore in greater detail, perhaps with a view to you adopting the key features of the approach for your own quality system.

European excellence model

The model often used in self-assessment systems is the European excellence model, which you may find extremely useful as you begin to work within a culture of continuous quality improvement for your organisation. This quality system or framework is currently in use by much of the care sector, the voluntary and community sectors, as well as industry. The model is very similar to the managerial approach explored earlier and is correctly called the European Foundation for Quality Management Excellence Model (EQFM, 1999). This approach (Figure 34) requires you and your staff to have a clear understanding about your clients, which means:

- knowing who they are;
- knowing what they want;
- knowing how to meet their needs;
- having the whole organisation committed to meeting those needs.

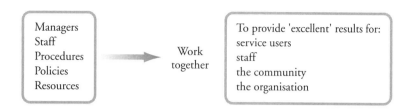

Figure 34. The premise of the excellence model.

The quality assurance arrangements that you put in place should be the catalysts for bringing about the change that leads to 'excellent' results from your service at all times, in all ways.

We need to explore this model further in order to have a sound understanding of the process. The model is a way of explaining to us how a quality assurance system can work on the ground. It should also provide you with ideas for ways in which you can implement the system in your own place of work.

The model can be said to be divided into two halves:

- the 'enabling side';
- the 'results side'.

We can view these as part of a 'whole'. Look at Figure 35 to see a visual representation of the way the model works.

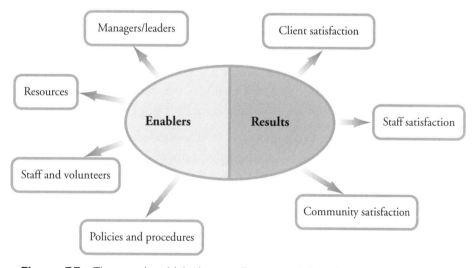

Figure 35. The way in which the excellence model works.

Think it over

Working with others, find out what an 'enabler' is and then think about the 'tools' they use in their enabling role. Are you an 'enabler'? Would you want to develop that aspect of your role as a manager?

We can see from Figure 35 that there are two clear halves to the model, but without a 'joining section' the model does not provide a clear explanation of how excellence is achieved. The missing link is 'learning and innovation' and this feeds between the results half and the enabling half. Thus, we can see the whole picture (Figure 36).

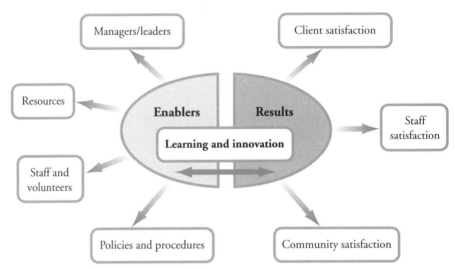

Figure 36. How 'learning and innovation' link the results half and the enabling half of the excellence model.

This model demonstrates how enablers encourage excellent results in quality services through the effective use of policies and procedures, resources, and, of course, staff and others involved in the organisation. For this to be achieved, you must value your staff and the contributions they make, not only in the enabling role, but also as the providers of feedback and information about the results half of the model.

In order to bring about learning and innovation, you need to be open to information from a range of sources about the quality of the service on offer. You also need to take the time to implement ways of 'finding out' what your clients really think of the service and then be prepared to take the necessary action to change the situation if this is what is required. In order to improve service quality, we need to develop a working culture based on:

- honesty;
- trust;
- commitment;
- accurate judgements;
- openness and commitment to change;
- value.

You need to implement ways of 'finding out' what your clients think of the service.

Developing this kind of working culture takes time and hard work. There is a clear need for you, as a leader and manager of change (i.e. a developer of a quality system), to consult with the staff and service users from the very first instance. Management and leadership are the key elements of the enabling role, but without participation and commitment to a strategy that brings about change in quality and procedures, 'ownership' will not occur. The strategy for excellence needs to belong to everyone!

Case study — Exploring quality provision

Janet owns a small residential care home for older people in an area that is over-provisioned. She has recently attended a management training programme that explored the issue of 'quality' provision from both a funder's perspective and that of the organisation. Janet recognises that 'things need to change' if she is to remain competitive and win contracts from her local social service department as a 'preferred provider'.

She feels motivated at the thought of her first task – developing and writing a policy and strategy for the organisation that will identify what the organisation wants to achieve and the approaches it will use to do so. Her second task is to carry out a qualifications audit of the staff and volunteers involved in her organisation to ensure that they have the skills and knowledge required to meet the strategy's aims. She considers the possibility that she will have to offer staff training. Finally, she thinks of the resources and partnerships she will need to enable her business to achieve the targets that she has set in her strategy for the organisation.

Using the excellence model, track through the process that Janet has identified for herself.

- Has she taken the 'best' approach?
- Has she left anything or anyone out?
- Might you take a different approach?

While the excellence model demonstrates a sound way of approaching and developing a quality system, you need to recognise the fact that the criteria by which excellence will be measured still need to be set. The approach to quality is through the generation of strategic and operational objectives. These must define the functions and processes that allow the service to deliver the required outcomes and undergo the process of measurement and then, if appropriate, change.

Evidence collection — Quality improvements

Using the model of excellence to inform debate and discussion, organise and implement a staff development session to assess your organisation's approach and attitude to quality.

Try it out

Find out about Investors in People (IIP) (www.iipuk.co.uk) and ISO 9000 as other options for demonstrating quality standards. What could be the benefits to your organisation of achieving either of these standards?

Defining quality

You will have noticed by now that we have mentioned quality measurement (via assessment or audit) and quality standards several times in the early stages of this unit. It is important that you, as manager, recognise and understand what is meant by 'measuring quality' in an organisation. Which leads us to the nub of the matter: who defines quality anyway?

The particular definition of quality used will depend on the viewpoints and opinions of the people involved. For example, government ministers are likely to have a totally different idea about what constitutes quality in a residential care home from the people who actually live and work there. It is also likely that the owner of the care home will also have a different view about quality from the staff and residents.

Gavin is the owner of a care home for older people with dementia. He was a scaffolder by trade but he and his wife purchased the care home four years ago, when it looked like a booming business.

He is holding a management meeting with the registered manager of the home (a nurse) and two senior staff members to explore the issue of 'quality of life' for the residents. Gavin feels that quality of life for residents could be significantly improved by putting in new window casings, as many residents have complained of being cold in their bedrooms; it would also cut down on heating bills. However, the nurse manager feels that more benefit could be gained from the employment of a 'creative activities' therapist to stimulate the memories of the residents. No one can agree and money is tight.

- Who do you agree with, or would you have a different opinion?
- Who defines 'quality' in your organisation?
- What is the possible impact of this?
- What difference might be made by the involvement of others in setting the quality agenda?

You understand ways of assessing and dealing with the implications of results obtained from quality monitoring

For many managers, dealing with the outcomes of an assessment or quality audit is not easy! You should recognise that, in the first instance, extremely good performance in all areas is highly unlikely. You need to be realistic and see the audit as an exercise that will identify those areas of weakness that need to be addressed in order of priority.

Remember that your audit is a starting point, a benchmark that will allow you to develop a continuous quality improvement cycle. It is also a tool for opening up discussion with team members and others in the organisation and, as such, is useful for the implementation of staff development, training and appraisal systems.

Once you have collected your audit data using a questionnaire, interview or some other method, you will need to assess the results. In other words, make a judgement about your findings. We have already discussed options such as scoring or creating a visual image but often your findings will reflect something you already knew or were aware of. Your data can be confirmation on which to base discussions with authority figures.

The greatest difficulty for a care manager often lies with bringing about change in practice and procedures. This can be most difficult when there are conflicts of opinion with business owners or senior managers. However, improving quality is the main purpose of monitoring and, with the backing of the National Standards, should be achievable in most cases.

Where current practice is found to be dangerous, action needs to be taken urgently and changes implemented. Finding unacceptable practice and not taking action is *not* an acceptable management solution! You and your staff should prioritise actions according to both need and the availability of resources.

You recognise ways of including and motivating people in continuous quality improvement

Throughout this unit we have discussed the importance of including others in the continuous quality improvement process. In some cases this may have looked to be simple but in reality it is often difficult. Service users may be too confused or frail to participate, while others may have learning disabilities that restrict their contributions. The problems do not stop there! In many cases it can be the staff and owners of care establishments who are the barriers to progress and change.

There will be occasions when your staff management skills are called into action. For example, it may be that staff need to be reminded of the standards to which they should be working. This may mean a review of their responsibilities and duties. On the other hand, there may be occasions when your own action needs to be reviewed. Perhaps audit intentions and processes need to be discussed at a team meeting and staff asked to volunteer their assistance, rather than audit becoming something that is imposed from a 'great height'. We know that if someone volunteers to help or provide information there is usually some level of ownership of the task, which ensures the job gets done and perhaps more willingly than would be the case otherwise.

Ruksana has decided to carry out a quality assessment of health and safety procedures in her small nursing and residential care home. She has drafted a questionnaire to help in the identification of potential risks for each room in the establishment. Her own work time is already committed to staff appraisals this month, so she has asked her senior social carer, Rebecca, to carry out the audit, using the questionnaire.

She later overhears Rebecca say to a colleague: 'I have more than enough to do without going into every room to collect useless information, so I will just tick the boxes – no one will ever know the difference anyway. I need to get on with my real work.'

Consider the situation Ruksana has found herself in.

- How would you handle the situation?
- What action could you take to make sure that this kind of situation does not arise?

You recognise your role in promoting continuous quality improvement

Bringing about change can be an unpleasant experience for all involved. Most people like their working arrangements 'just as they are' and may well resent changes to routines and working practices. The theory behind the change process acknowledges that people progress through several stages in the change process. These can be:

- shock and denial;
- depression and loss of confidence;
- letting go of the 'old';
- acceptance.

Think it over

Working with others, make notes of the strategies you would employ to assist an employee who is going through each stage of the change process: denial, depression, letting go and acceptance.

At each stage of the change process, people have different reactions. Your role, as manager, is to assist progress as painlessly as possible, for example, by keeping people informed and allowing them to discuss their fears and anxieties. In general, however, your role should be about:

- planning for the changes comprehensively;
- giving the change a high profile;

- providing effective leadership;
- using a shared approach;
- valuing all staff contributions;
- giving your staff confidence in themselves and in you;
- dealing with any negative attitudes positively;
- dealing with the needs and wants of clients and staff;
- resourcing the changes effectively.

"Well done you two-
you've really helped
Joe to settle in quickly".

As manager, you should value the contributions of your staff.

Evidence collection — Implementing policy

Reflect upon the policy you have developed as part of this unit. Identify any changes to staff routines and attitudes that the implementation of the policy will bring about. Plan how you are going to support your staff while the policy is implemented. Identify the action you can take before and after the policy becomes 'mandatory'.

Make notes of your planned action and the results you expect to obtain. Respecting confidentiality should mean you can use these notes in your portfolio of evidence. Find out more about the theory of change and use the information to support staff while you are developing a continuous quality improvement programme.

Promoting continuous quality improvement

Once you have brought about change and developed your quality assessment systems and procedures, your work continues. Just like the quality assessment process, the cycle must be maintained. Your role is to ensure that your organisation maintains the quality of the service and continues to improve over time. This could be through a range of measures but will most likely include the following:

- *Monitoring trends in the provision of health and social care*. Making sure you are aware of government requirements is one way of staying ahead of the competition. For example, we have already mentioned the Intermediate Care Service that is currently being rolled out across the country. Are you involved with this? If so, how? Have you identified the measures you will need to adopt for your business to stay at the cutting edge of service provision? Additionally, are you aware of the quality agenda and how it might affect you and your organisation in the future if you fail to 'measure up'?
- *Informing others of change*. This could be the action you take with your own staff or it could be further reaching. For example, do you have a duty to keep an owner of the business informed as to current trends within health care? If you are expected to inform a board of governors, how are you going to carry out this aspect of your duties? (Consider the scenario in the case study about Marie below.)
- *Making recommendations for change*. Suggesting changes to the owners of the care establishments is not always an easy task. There are occasions when the owners of care organisations have no real understanding of business needs. The establishment of the new National Minimum Standards will to an extent deal with some of these difficulties. However, having others accept and then resource a series of changes may not be simple. A good starting point is to make sure that you always use an evidence-based approach. In other words, make sure that you are armed with all the facts and details of the needs for change. For example, who is driving the change? Why is change required and how will the business and service users benefit?
- *Monitoring the improvements*. Here we go, straight back into the quality system of self-assessment, progression and improvements.

No matter how you look at quality improvement, you should always find yourself coming full circle. That is:

- Set the targets and goals for your organisation.
- Collect evidence of progression and achievement towards the targets.
- Analyse the evidence to give an understanding of the quality of the service.
- Develop action plans to deal with weaknesses.
- Develop action plans to disseminate information on strengths.
- Develop action plans to set the new goals and targets.

Case study — Implementing change

Marie manages three residential care homes for people with severe forms of dementia. The homes are all owned by a small consortium of general practitioners in the area. She has just realised that the formation of the new mental health trust for her locality has the potential to affect the service she is managing. She has called a meeting of the general practitioners. She has sent them all an agenda of the items that she wants to discuss and has requested any additional items for the agenda from them (in case they have any relevant information to add). She has prepared a short presentation of her thoughts and a brief written report for discussion at the meeting.

- How might this meeting support Marie and the owners of the care homes?
- What are the likely outcomes of an action such as this?

Keys to good management practice

Quality assurance

An effective quality assurance system should be integrated into everyday activity. It must:

- be rigorous;
- be effective;
- raise overall performance;
- inform all aspects of business planning;
- meet the needs of all the stakeholders (clients, funders, owners, etc.);
- involve everyone at all stages;
- have commitment from the 'top'.

C15 Develop and Sustain Arrangements for Joint Working Between Workers and Agencies

This unit introduces you to the concept of joint working and collaboration in the health and social care services. In other words, it seeks to enable you to develop the knowledge and understanding required to secure a variety of services through a range of organisations and agencies to meet your clients' needs. This approach to care has become a high priority for a government that firmly believes that a multi-agency, collaborative approach offers the best outcomes for service users. The traditional boundaries that have prevented high-quality, all-round care are no longer acceptable in a strategic approach based on joint working initiatives. You, as a manager, need to appreciate the importance of joint working at all levels of health and social care and to secure success in this method of working.

The elements are:

- Evaluate the potential for joint working with other workers and agencies.
- Establish and sustain working relationships with other workers and agencies.
- Contribute to joint working with other workers and agencies.

Learning outcomes

- You understand the background to joint working in health and social care.
- You recognise agencies and workers with the potential to contribute to joint working.
- You identify ways of evaluating the potential of your own and other agencies to contribute to joint working.
- You understand the issues involved in establishing a good working relationship.
- You recognise ways of maintaining a good working relationship with other organisations.
- You understand ways of monitoring and reviewing the success of joint working.
- You recognise ways of improving joint working.

You understand the background to joint working in health and social care

Joint working is often seen as an integral part of health and social care. It is usually something managers do as a matter of course. However, if you think about the skills and experience that are required to work successfully with others, you will realise that joint working is something that has to be practised to be successful.

When we discuss joint working in this unit we are referring to the work you undertake with others. This could be a member of your team, someone from an external agency that is providing a specialised service to your clients, or another manager with whom you work. Even the work you undertake through care planning for clients and the roles you have alongside social services can be classed as a joint approach to client welfare.

Think it over

Think about a normal working day. How many different people do you work with? What is your role and what is their role in each case? Would you describe the activity as joint working?

The background to joint working in health and social care

Joint working is not a new concept within the field of health care. When the welfare state was set up in 1948 it was designed on a tripartite basis: the services were organised into three strands, namely hospital services, community services and local authority services. As you can imagine, resources and energy were required to ensure that people being referred from one service 'strand' to another did not fall into the gap between them. Unfortunately, this method of working was not always as successful as it might have been.

During the reforms of the 1990s, and particularly as a result of the NHS and Community Care Act 1990 (which for social care was not implemented until 1993), other divisions in the way health care and social care were organised occurred through the contracting system known as the internal market. The commissioning of services was separated from the actual delivery of care. Furthermore, the finance for the care system was transferred from central government to the local authorities. This required a sound understanding from all involved of the funding and organisational system in order to create effective ways of joint working, especially if inter-agency working was to be successfully achieved.

At the same time, social services departments were charged with a responsibility to produce and publish community care plans that outlined the future of care services in their locality, so that others could contribute as was felt appropriate. These care plans were produced in consultation with health authorities, local authorities, service users and other relevant bodies.

Care plan

As the NHS and Community Care Act 1990 is the forerunner to the current system of health and social care, it is useful to have an understanding of its main points in relation to your service provision. Obtain a summary of the Act and make notes of the relevant sections for your organisation.

The present system of health care is managed by the Secretary of State for Health. Policy is planned and set centrally and then implemented locally. Each health authority takes the lead in a three-year health improvement programme that contains strategies and action plans for improving the health of the local population. These plans are produced in conjunction with local authorities, care trusts, primary care trusts, the public and service users.

It should be clear, then, that joint working is set to become (if it has not already done so) the natural way of working. Already we see that community care planning and delivery are carried out jointly between a range of agencies and it is not unusual to see the following 'services' at the centre of joint working strategies:

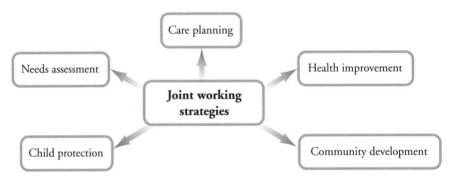

Figure 37. 'Services' involved in joint working strategies.

The benefits of joint working

There are benefits to both the client and the organisation (as well as individuals within the organisation) of working in a joint way; for example, less conflict between services should ensure smooth transitions for people moving from one type of care to another. There are also benefits to the welfare state as a whole of more integrated forms of working; examples include less 'reinventing of the wheel', more effective planning and budgeting, and better use of staff knowledge and resources. For you, as a manager of care provision, similar benefits to joint working can also be assumed.

Working with another person, identify activities that could be undertaken jointly by your organisation and another service to improve the quality of life of your clients. Then discuss the benefits to you as a manager and your organisation as a whole of those joint working activities.

Case study

Bill Patterson has been hospitalised for the last three months after a severe stroke. He has spent one month in a rehabilitation centre and is due to return home at the end of the week. He cannot wait. He knows that he will need a great deal of support, as will his wife. A nice man from social services seems to have got everything sorted out!

- How might this example of joint working between health care and social care have improved quality of life for Bill and his wife?
- What would be the care manager's role in the continuing care of Bill?
- What other agencies and organisations might also be involved in his day-to-day care?
- What could you offer to Bill and his family in terms of additional support?

You recognise agencies and workers with the potential to contribute to joint working

There is the potential for joint working at all levels of the health and social care system. Indeed, as we have already noted, there is a legislative requirement for action to be planned and taken jointly in several aspects of the care system. *Partnership in Action* was published in 1998 as a discussion document about joint working between health and social services. As the Secretary of State says in the document: 'We want to see health and social services working much more closely together to protect those in need' (i.e. the frail elderly, the mentally ill and those who care for themselves in the no-man's-land between health and social services).

Joint working has been identified as having three potential applications:

1 *strategic planning* – agencies sharing their intentions, plans and budgets;
2 *commissioning* – common understanding of clients' needs;
3 *service delivery* – clients receiving a coherent package of care.

For the manager in service delivery, obviously knowledge and understanding of the last is essential, but also a working knowledge of the other two is useful.

It is important for you to recognise that joint working can occur in many different ways and with a wide range of partners. For example, any or all of the following organisations have the potential to become partners in care planning or delivery:

- the public sector (or statutory agencies);
- the independent sector;
- voluntary and charitable organisations;
- the public (through self-help groups and volunteers);
- key staff from other agencies;
- internal staff and work teams.

You should recognise where your organisation fits into the network of local and national services and agencies available to support your residents. You could use a chart such as the one shown in Figure 38 to identify your place in the network.

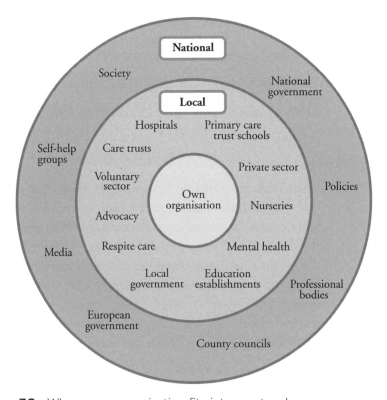

Figure 38. Where your organisation fits into a network.

Produce a network chart showing the services available in your own area. If you include contact details you will also have a useful directory at your fingertips when you need it! Highlight those services and organisations that you have direct contact with for whatever reason.

Case study — The context of joint working

Ahmed works for social services in Anytown. He has just finished collating all the survey data he has collected from statutory, voluntary and independent services about the current care services available in his locality. He plans to use the data to inform the next meeting of the social services committee, which is currently reviewing 'needs' within the area. However, he feels sure that his information could prove useful to other health-related bodies as well.

Once the committee has agreed the level of service required, Sharon will meet with organisations that have been identified as possible sources of service provision. She will aim to agree a contract for specified work and will then take the necessary action to implement the agreement.

Hilda is the manager of Uptown House and she has just agreed to provide 12 places for people with learning disabilities in her new residential and day care home.

- Identify the level each individual is working at (commissioning, strategic planning or service delivery). Remember that people can be working at more than one level at a time.
- What possible effects could Ahmed and Sharon's role have on your organisation?
- How could each individual contribute to the work of other organisations and agencies in terms of joint working?

The independent sector is also known as the 'private sector'. Indeed, you may be working in the independent sector yourself. If you are the owner of your business or if you manage a business on behalf of another company or individual, then the chances are you are working in the independent sector.

Over the last 20 years or so, the contributions from the independent sector to health and social care have been enormous. Residential care homes for older people are now dotted everywhere about the country. We have also seen a huge rise in the number of domestic care agencies being established in areas of greatest need. This is likely to be in response to the government's initiative to enable people to remain in their own homes for as long as possible. We are also seeing private hospitals increasing in number and in the range of services they offer.

Case study — Volunteers

Pauline is extremely creative. She is able to produce almost anything from fabric. She is well known for the puppets and teddy bears that she can make. She enjoys spending her free time in a residential care home for people with learning disabilities. Here she encourages and supports the residents with their own creative activities. The cushions, quilts and other items are sold once a year in a very successful fundraising event. The proceeds are used to enhance the quality of life of the residents.

- What kind of a difference to residents and organisation does the contribution of Pauline make?
- What does Pauline get out of it?
- What does the organisation get out of Pauline?

How you value and use the potential contributions agencies, organisations and individuals have to make to your service will to a great extent depend on the beliefs and values that you hold. For example, not every manager would appreciate the support of someone like Pauline. Some might feel that the service should be funded by a statutory agency and not left to the efforts of people like Pauline.

When selecting agencies and individuals to work alongside (or when they are selecting you!), several other questions should be considered:

- Is the service based nearby? A more distant service will be less convenient and joint working may give rise to substantial travel costs.
- Does the service have the expertise you require? How do you know this?
- Does the service have the capacity to meet your requirements?

Whom you will work with may, to a great extent, already be decided for you through legislation, or existing relationships. However, this does not mean that you cannot implement change if you feel improvements to your service can be obtained by using a different service provider.

How do you bring about change and decide who would make a good joint working partner for your organisation? Use the chart shown to evaluate the potential for joint working with other workers and agencies. You will need to ensure that the information you collect is accurate and up to date.

Services required to meet client/organisational need	Available in-house?	Possible service provider	Expertise available	Costs

Once you have filled in the basic details for each service, you should attach a detailed report on the potential for partnership working. Your report should also cover access and location issues, suggested methods of working together and possible areas for conflict. Finish your report with recommendations for action.

You identify ways of evaluating the potential of your own and other agencies to contribute to joint working

Evaluating your own organisational view of joint working

A good start to exploring the issue of joint working is perhaps to reflect on your own organisation and to some extent your own attitudes towards joint working. What is the culture in your organisation that affects the thinking related to joint working? Schein (1992) defines culture as:

> A pattern of shared assumptions that a group learns as it solves its problems of external adaptation and internal integration, that has worked well enough to be considered valid and, therefore, to be taught to new members as the correct way to think and feel in relation to those problems.

Organisational culture will affect the views related to joint working. For example, does your organisation have a view that all the services required to meet clients' needs and wants should be provided in-house? Or would your organisation be willing to pass some work to other agencies?

Make notes about how your organisation views joint working. For example, what are the attitudes of you and your staff. What arrangements are already in place? Who are your existing partners and what services do they offer? How do you feel about the joint working partnerships? (Be honest!)

Consider whether the approach adopted by your organisation will meet the requirements of a government that advocates joint working as the way forward. If not, what are you going to do about it? If it does, how can it be strengthened?

Working with another person, discuss the purpose of a joint working policy for your organisation. Consider the following:

- Do you have a policy?
- Do you need a policy?
- What might be the benefits to your own and other organisations of having such a policy?

Changing the culture of an organisation is not a quick or simple task – it takes time and skill. If your organisation has never fully developed joint working as an effective strategy, you are likely to face resistance to change from your staff as you attempt to introduce new ways of working. Recognising the sources of resistance can help you to develop effective strategies for dealing with it. Common sources of resistance to change are:

- habit;
- worry about pay and conditions;
- commitment to the organisation.

- job security;
- worry about loss of personal status;

Each source needs to be dealt with sensitively and confidentially.

The introduction of new ways of working is likely to face resistance.

Most managers will have heard of a SWOT analysis, which is a method for ascertaining the Strengths, Weaknesses, Opportunities and Threats (SWOT) of an organisation. It is most often used internally as a way of examining the key areas in your organisation. The headings are designed to allow you to reflect upon the service you are currently delivering to your funders and residents.

Case study — SWOT analysis

Mario has just completed a SWOT analysis of his home care service for frail older people. As he looks at the results he finds that his 'weaknesses' offer him the opportunity to increase his 'strengths'.

Strengths	*Weaknesses*
Willing to overcome threats	Knowledge of requirements
Central location of service	Staff training
Emergency policy	Qualifications of staff
Obtaining social service contracts	Meeting deadlines
Management structure	Communication with other services
Joint working strategy in place	One client group
Motivated to improve the service	Customer care
Opportunities	*Threats*
Improved customer care	Need more joint working
Expand client group	Other providers in the area
Improve staff qualifications	Removal of social service contract
Bigger contract from social services	NVQ training requirements
Research requirements	Changes in demand

Using Mario's example, carry out a SWOT analysis for your own organisation in terms of joint working. This should enable you to identify whether you need to change your current working practices and if so in what way. Make a list of the possible effects of any joint working identified on the residents, staff and the organisation.

It is important to recognise that in any joint working relationship both sides must see benefits. Your SWOT analysis for joint working should have identified possible benefits to you and your organisation under the 'opportunities' section. Without perceived benefits to either the clients or the organisations involved, there is not likely to be a great deal of drive towards joint working!

Another approach to service planning that could include the identification of a need for joint working makes use of the self-assessment process (see Unit F3, page 336 for more details).

Reference to a cycle such as the one shown in Figure 39 can help you plan your provision, by prompting you to identify both future needs and methods of working to meet those needs.

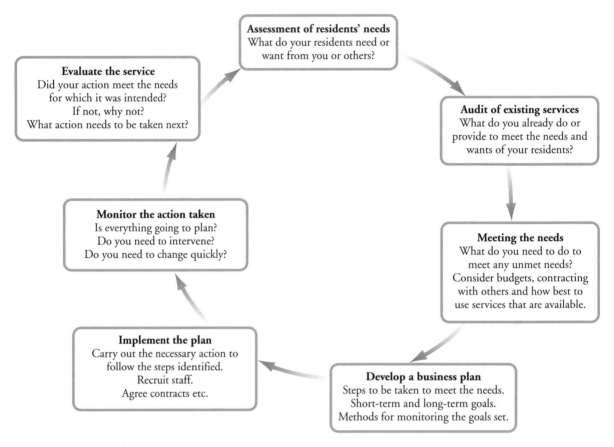

Figure 39. Planning provision through the self-assessment cycle.

Evaluating the potential of other agencies to contribute to joint working

It is possible to try a SWOT analysis for those agencies and organisations that you are considering a joint working arrangement with. However, you would then need to accept the limitations of insufficient information about the organisation that you are considering as a partner. You may have only hearsay or your personal observations on which to make a judgement. Both may be biased!

On the other hand, you could use a range of secondary sources to help you make your decision. For example, all or some of the suggestions listed below could be used to provide a robust information base for your final decision:

- the database of the Social Care Institute for Excellence, which gives guidance on best practice for practitioners;
- annual reports from the agency or organisation being considered for joint working;
- inspection reports on the agency, which are in the public domain;
- users' views of the service;
- staff knowledge about other organisations (do not underestimate this).

Whatever method you choose to find out about the potential of a joint working relationship, you will need to consider the following.

Values, aims and objectives

- Do the values, aims and objectives of the organisation under consideration match your own, or are they in conflict?
- What policies and practices are in place, and do you agree with them?
- How is cooperation with others viewed by both organisations?
- What is in it for them?
- What is in it for you?
- Will their involvement enhance your own reputation or will you lose face by being associated with a failing organisation?

Expertise available

- Does the potential partner organisation actually have the expertise you want?
- What is its reputation?
- Is the expertise readily available?
- Does it have sufficient staff to meet the extra demand imposed by the proposed joint work?

Ease of access to services and managers

- Is the service local?
- Are the policies and services offered user-friendly?
- How accessible and responsive is the management team?
- How accessible and responsive are the staff?

Costs and benefits

- What will the joint working cost in terms of finance and time?
- Is the extra work on your part worth the outcome?
- What might be the hidden extras (positive and negative)?

Try it out

Identify an organisation or service that could contribute towards your own service provision. Use the headings listed to explore whether you would want them to act as a partner in meeting residents' needs, and if so in what way.

You understand the issues involved in establishing a good working relationship

There are several aspects to joint working that have the potential to make or break a relationship before it has even begun. They include:

- understanding everybody's requirements;
- appropriate approaches;
- sound communication skills;
- successful negotiation skills;
- ways of influencing others.

We will explore each of these in more detail.

Understanding everybody's requirements

Identifying a suitable organisation or service as a partner for joint working is only the beginning of the process of joint working. The establishment of good working relationships is probably the most problematic aspect of partnerships. However, with hard work and commitment, they are not impossible to achieve.

A sound starting point for creating a good working relationship is to have a shared understanding of any legislative requirements involved in the service delivery process. For you, as a manager, this means that you should understand the key issues involved in the provision of the service. Keeping yourself up to date is not easy. However, it is a requirement of any leader or manager, no matter what the business, as there is a chance the business will fail if it gets left behind.

Case study — Understanding requirements

David is the manager of a small residential care setting for young people. He has already been inspected by social services, who have identified several areas for action by the management. The inspector is concerned about the lack of written policies for the care organisation and David has been informed that there must be a staff development and training policy in place by the next re-inspection or further action will be taken by social services. The inspector is feeling exasperated by David's continuing negative attitude; 'Why can't he sort himself out?' thinks the inspector. David cannot fathom why social services care about staff training. He thinks, 'As long as my clients are happy it shouldn't matter'.

- Why do you think social services are keen to see a staff training policy in David's place of work?
- How will David's relationship with social services be affected should he fail to take action?
- How could the situation be made more manageable?

If you cannot answer these questions, you will need to obtain a copy of the Care Standards Act and read it.

Appropriate approaches

An aid to successful joint working is the recognition that there are some approaches to another agency or individual that are doomed to failure from the outset or, conversely, that are linked to success.

Examples of the latter are:

- making contact with the right person in the other agency;
- having the right person make contact on behalf of your organisation.

Failure at either of these two points will result in missed opportunities. How many times have you put the telephone down after a conversation that left you wondering who the other person was and what was wanted of you?

Ideally, approaches to another organisation should be carried out between two people of equal status. There is no point delegating a request for input into your service to a junior care assistant. It is unlikely that an assistant will be able to respond appropriately to any questions or issues raised by the potential partner. This can lead to frustration and a lack of clarity on both sides. When in doubt, make the approach yourself or make sure that your negotiator is fully briefed about expectations.

Sound communication skills

Communication skills are primarily about three things:

- establishing good relationships;
- clarity of speech and voice;
- active listening.

People are more likely to be cooperative if they perceive they are being listened to, especially if different needs, values and expectations are involved. More than 80% of our working lives is spent listening!

Try it out

Check you own listening skills.

- Do you give time to listening or do you rush and jump in?
- Do you resist distractions?
- Do you value all contributions?
- Do you keep an open mind?
- Do you avoid assumptions and stereotypical thoughts?
- Do you manage your emotions and control your reactions?
- Are you patient?
- Do you minimise interruptions?

These are the qualities traditionally associated with a good listener.

Successful negotiation skills

Negotiation should be a structured attempt by two or more parties to solve a potential difficulty or area of conflict. Matters of mutual interest should be discussed, ideally without a win/lose perspective. The discussions need to have a mutually beneficial outcome and most importantly contribute towards the meeting of clients' needs.

Negotiation needs to have a mutually beneficial outcome that meets the clients' needs.

Communication is an essential element of sound negotiating skills. When good communication is combined with your authority, credibility and access to information, successful outcomes should be assured, assuming everything else is in place (e.g. the request being made is appropriate for all involved).

Other negotiating skills include:

- understanding the other organisation's issues and viewpoints;
- having a clear rationale for the service being requested;
- ensuring a shared understanding of the intended outcomes.

Personal skills involved in negotiation

- Planning and preparation.
- Knowledge of the issue.
- Active listening.
- Avoiding assumptions and stereotypical attitudes.
- Contingency planning.
- Being open to change.

Make a list of your own strengths and weaknesses in relation to negotiation skills and then ask someone else in a management role to comment on your negotiating skills. Does her or his vision fit with yours?

Ways of influencing others

Having the ability to influence someone else is an essential skill for the manager who is trying to effect a joint working relationship. Influence may be the only thing that will affect the final decision of whether someone wants to work alongside certain staff members within the organisation.

In order to have credibility, you need to have a professional approach to your work and the authority to take decisions about action and resources. In addition, you also need to find out what is important to listeners, what they want, and how their priorities fit with those of your organisation. They may have a preferred time and method for contact. For example, many managers dislike Monday meetings, and many more may prefer to be contacted by email.

Case study

Matt is keen to persuade Katy, an excellent creative activity tutor, to offer two sessions per week in his care home for people who have learning and physical disabilities. He knows she is very busy and often has prior arrangements. He has emailed his request, giving full details of the time required, the type of activity he would value, the rate of pay and the dates that can be available. He has offered Katy the opportunity to try one session before she makes a final decision. He has explained the facilities available, and given general information about the residents to help her make an initial decision.

- What are the key points that may well influence Katy's decision?
- How would you persuade another individual to provide an oversubscribed service in your care setting?

You recognise ways of maintaining a good working relationship with other organisations

Maintaining sound working relationships is not easy in your own place of work, so consider how much more difficult it is to achieve when two external organisations come together for joint working. However, it is widely accepted that having a shared understanding of the requirements of the roles and responsibilities involved will reduce the opportunities for conflict. Suggestions for maintaining sound working relationships therefore include:

- clear allocation of responsibilities;
- dealing with conflict as soon as it arises;
- the use of contracts and formal agreements;
- open and honest transactions;
- respect and value;
- dealing with stereotypical assumptions;
- realistic goals;
- following the principles of good team working.

Clear allocation of responsibilities

It is amazing how many organisations seem happy to use no more than a verbal agreement for the provision of a service. This is especially the case in smaller care settings. However, all you have to do is read the local and national press to find examples of where this kind of agreement has gone very wrong.

Being clear about responsibilities – that is, who does what, when, where and how – is an essential element of maintaining good working relationships. This is not always easy to formalise, especially if managers already know the person or organisation involved.

Try it out

Discuss with another person ways in which you could formalise a working relationship. Include a discussion of the dangers of using only a verbal agreement for the provision of a service or joint working arrangements.

Dealing with conflict

To deal with conflict requires many recognised leadership skills – for example, a personality that inspires confidence in others, the willpower to see things through to completion, sound knowledge, understanding and initiative.

When conflict occurs, you must (if possible) prevent staff and clients feeling as if they are being persecuted. Fairness to staff and service users when handling complaints should achieve this. Additionally, you can follow guidelines to help you avoid the minefield that often surrounds dealing with conflict:

- recognise the conflict and the form it has taken and the people involved;
- acknowledge the issues between the parties;
- share your knowledge of the issue with others involved;
- respect their opinions;
- know the relevant policies and objectives related to the area of conflict;
- know the direction joint working needs to take;
- be prepared to act in the best interests of the majority;
- be prepared to take unpleasant decisions;
- get the balance right between sanctions and incentives;
- be willing to take action.

The use of contracts and formal agreements

If you want to use contracts and formal agreements (always a good idea!) as the basis for your joint working, there are several questions that you need to ask yourself first.

- Is the policy or contract going to be in a written form that outlines the requirements of all the parties involved?
- Is a code of conduct required?
- Are the policy objectives and outcomes developed and understood by all? (How do you know?)
- Has a forum been identified for the discussion of progress towards meeting the objectives?
- Is there an effective communication channel for all levels and areas?
- Will everybody involved receive appropriate training?
- Who will take overall responsibility for the achievement of objectives?
- How will achievement be monitored?
- When and how will evaluation be carried out?

Think it over

Think about a joint working initiative already established in your own workplace. It could be a combined care package for a resident that involves both health and social care or it could be a volunteer scheme that aims to contribute to the quality of life of clients or something else appropriate to your organisation. Using the questions on the use of contracts and formal agreements as a guide, evaluate the likely success (or otherwise) of the joint working initiative. How could you strengthen the teamwork process?

Respect, value and stereotypical assumptions

The only way to ensure the maintenance of good working relationships is through respect for and value of others' contributions. This may involve issues of confidentiality and the avoidance of stereotypical assumptions. Consider the case study on respect and value which also deals with stereotypical assumptions.

Monica is 67 years old and has been retired for seven years. She has recently decided to contribute to the well-being of others through voluntary work. She has approached Dave, the manager of a care home for younger disabled adults, to ask if she can contribute to activity and holiday planning for the residents.

'No,' thought Dave, 'The residents won't want more holidays in a nice, safe, holiday camp environment.' 'No, I don't think so,' was his reply.

As Monica was leaving she stopped to talk to a carer she knew. Dave overheard Monica telling her that she had had such great ideas for activity holidays for the residents. She would have enjoyed encouraging them to participate in some of her favourite pastimes, such as canoeing, rock climbing, orienteering, trekking and camping. 'I didn't even get the chance to tell him my ideas,' she said.

- What might be the results of Dave's stereotypical thoughts in relation to Monica?
- How has this had the potential to affect the relationship between himself and other volunteers and his staff?
- How could the situation have been improved?

Realistic goals

When entering into an agreement with any other agency or individual, it is important to recognise and accept the limitations of your own organisation. Avoid making plans that overstretch the service or that are unlikely to be achieved for other reasons. The planning process must ensure that all commitments on both sides are SMART (see page 333).

Following the principles of good team working

A team can consist of large numbers of people but it has been argued that the most effective team size is between seven and ten. The relationships between team members have the potential to affect the team's overall success. So has your relationship with the team as a whole and the individuals making up that team!

Think it over

Think about the teams you manage. What is your relationship like with them and theirs with you? How do the individuals work together? What are their relationships like? Are they effective as a team? If not, why not?

In all cases, an essential element of successful team working is a shared understanding of the task to be completed. Your role in this case is often one of arranging training and development to ensure that all the members of the team have the necessary skills and knowledge for the job to be done.

An essential element of a successful team is shared understanding.

Knowledge of Belbin's framework for exploring the kind of roles that people are involved with in teamwork is useful. Meredith Belbin's research was first published in book form in 1981. The book, entitled *Management Teams – Why They Succeed or Fail*, explored team building and team roles in great detail. The roles he identified as being most often found in teams are as follows.

- The *innovator* is creative and imaginative.
- The *coordinator* is someone who can pull things together, and is mature, confident and good at organising others' work and at chairing meetings.
- The *shaper* is someone who challenges the things that do not work, and is dynamic and thrives on pressure.
- The *company worker* is an individual who follows plans and company policy as agreed.
- The *completer/finisher* is a person who sees things through to the finish on time, and is often painstaking and conscientious at work.
- The *resource investigator* is someone who researches outside ideas, and is usually an extrovert with plenty of outside contacts.
- The *team worker* is a person who encourages teamwork, and is often diplomatic and cooperative.
- The *monitor/evaluator* is someone who reviews how things are going, and is often a strategic planner and can judge progress (or otherwise) accurately.

While there are advantages and disadvantages to each style of working, overall it would be useful for you to work with the preferred style of your team member to ensure that you get the best from them.

You should value the skills and resources that staff members and external workers bring to their work. Do not be afraid to praise or to celebrate success with your team. Communication is also an essential aspect of teamwork. Team members need to feel valued and in touch with what is happening to the organisation and their own specific job roles. Ensuring that this takes place is one of your duties.

Keys to good management practice

Effective teamwork

- Acknowledge the strengths and needs of each person.
- Be adaptable and flexible.
- Agree working methods.
- Manage time effectively.
- Foster respect and value for each other.

- Share responsibilities.
- Allow time for planning.
- Be professional at all times.
- Give public acknowledgement of achievements.

Try it out

Think about the people in your staff teams. Can you link the roles identified by Belbin to individual people? What kind of difference does their approach make to the team? Are they being used in the best way for the team and your organisation? Find out more about Belbin's work and the potential it has for you as a manager.

You understand ways of monitoring and reviewing the success of joint working

Monitoring and reviewing the success of joint working are essentially quality control activities: they are about achieving high quality and then ensuring the maintenance of that quality. They are also about ensuring that all those involved with joint working are happy with their roles, as well as the processes and intended outcomes.

The monitoring of an activity involves the systematic collection of information, which could then be stored on a database. All too often, however, in the care sector monitoring can be taken to mean 'keeping an eye on' something. This is no longer acceptable practice.

Monitoring and reviewing should be part of an overall quality system that is designed to ensure best practice. You will find Unit F3 particularly helpful at this point.

A word associated with both the monitoring and reviewing of service provision is 'evaluation'. Evaluation should be a four-stage process that encompasses:

Evaluation should make good use of:

- monitoring (systematic collection of data);
- assessment (measurement against set criteria);
- appraisal (currently used to assess the performance of staff).

Each stage of the evaluation process should be used to monitor and review action taken in joint working arrangements.

Analysis and assessment are fundamental to monitoring and reviewing, and these are discussed further below.

Analysis

It is important to use a range of sources when collecting data for analysis but care should be taken to ensure there is 'no paralysis through analysis'. In other words, do not take on too much, especially during the formative stages of evaluation! The information collected will be either quantitative (e.g. achievement of objectives, cost of the activity, resources used) or qualitative (e.g. feelings and attitudes of those involved, experiences, relationships established). It is always a good idea to plan how and what you will analyse at the planning stage of your joint working relationships.

Assessment

Monitoring activities should take three forms:

- initial assessment (where we are now and where we want to be);
- formative assessments (identifies achievement to date and areas for further action);
- summative assessments (summing up of achievement).

Initial assessment

This should have taken place right at the beginning of the joint working process. In many cases the need for joint working will have been identified before the first meeting of intended partners takes place. Once people are together, agreements can be made about the where you are now, where you want to be and by when. This could be the start of the contracting process.

Formative assessments

Formative assessments usually take place regularly throughout the activity. It is a way of monitoring the progress of joint working and allowing for change when necessary. Agreeing to a formative assessment is an essential aspect of joint working. You should agree times and dates for it. For example, when the contract is drawn up it should include 'review points'. This helps to prevent conflict, as everyone knows when and where review will take place (and no one should feel victimised if things are going wrong!).

Summative assessments

Summative assessments take place on completion of the joint working arrangement. There should be a systematic review of all that has happened and all that has been achieved. A final report should be written and recommendations for future action made, based on the findings of the summative review.

Try it out

Using formative and summative approaches, collect qualitative and quantitative data relating to the success or otherwise of existing joint working activities in your organisation. Prepare a report of progress and achievements, including recommendations for any changes to working arrangements.

You recognise ways of improving joint working

One of the most valuable ways of improving joint working is learning through experience. This can be the experience of your own organisation or that of another. For example, Health Action Zones were created to work in partnership with other organisations and were given a remit of using innovative ways to improve the health of disadvantaged populations. Since their inception many lessons have been learned. For instance, we know that partnership working takes commitment from the top, time and effort and dedicated resources. The work of the zones has resulted in a Partnership Toolkit, which can be further explored by visiting the website www.hda-online.org.uk.

When seeking to improve ways and methods of joint working, you will need to start with yourself and your organisation. You are unlikely to have any control over the way others behave and think. Therefore, if necessary, change your own performance and model best practice – that in itself can (and often does) improve joint working relationships.

You can also work towards ensuring that your staff follow the agreements made in any contracts. Joint working is about shared responsibility, which should mean:

- abiding by agreements and arrangements;
- negotiating change when and if it is required;
- providing a suitable level of service to all concerned;
- supporting co-workers in an appropriate manner;
- always maintaining a professional approach and attitude;
- being willing and open to change and suggestions for new ways of working;
- ensuring the client is at the centre of all you do.

Joint working offers many opportunities to both your own and other organisations; making the most of them is up to you.

Evidence collection — Joint working

Using data collected through work on this and other units in the NVQ, prepare a report for management on ways in which joint working could be improved by your own organisation. Your report should include the following headings:

- introduction to the report (purpose, etc.);
- the approach to joint working;
- networks available;
- attitudes and values;
- existing arrangements;
- advantages and disadvantages;
- areas for improvement;
- suggested improvements;
- time scale for change;
- recommendations for action.

Joint working

- Be prepared – know what is required.
- Know your clients' needs and wants.
- Know your partner organisation's needs, wants, values and beliefs.
- Be flexible and adaptable.
- Have good communication skills.
- Ensure you have good negotiation skills.
- Always use written policies and procedures.
- Follow the guidelines.
- Monitor and review progress, and do not be afraid to ask for change.
- Evaluate and make recommendations for future action.

Links between Registered Manager Award and NVQ 4 Care

NVQ 4 Care

Mandatory Units

Code	Title	Available in Care Management in Practice
O3	Develop, maintain and evaluate systems and structures to promote the rights, responsibilities and diversity of people	✓
SC15	Develop and sustain arrangements for joint working between workers and agencies	✓

Option Units

Code	Title	Available in Care Management in Practice
MCI/B3	Manage the use of financial resources	✓
MCI/C8	Select personnel for activities	✓
MCI/C13	Manage the performance of teams and individuals	✓
MCI/D4	Provide information to support decision making	✓

Further reading

Books

Belbin, M. (1996) *Management Teams*, Oxford: Butterworth Heinemann

Bradshaw, J. (1972) The Concept of Social Need, *New Society*, 19, pp 640–643.

Braye, S. and Preston-Shoot, M. (1995) *Empowering Practice in Social Care*, Milton Keynes: Open University Press

Deal, T. and Kennedy, A. (1985) *Corporate Cultures*, Penguin, 1985

Dobson, A. (1996) *Managing Meetings*, How To Books Ltd

Forsyth, P. (1996) *Making Meetings Work*, Guernsey Press

Hodgson, P. and Hodgson, J. (1992) *Effective Meetings*, The Sunday Times Business Skills, Century Business

Kitwood, T. (1997) *Dementia Reconsidered,* Milton Keynes: Open University Press

Maslow, A. (1987) *Motivation and Personality*, (3rd edition), Harlow: Longman

McMahon, T. (1990) *Big Meetings, Big Results*, NTC Publishing Group

Mullins, L. J. (1998) *Management and Organisational Behaviour*, London: FT/Prentice Hall

Schein, E. (1992) *Organizational Culture and Leadership*, Chichester: John Wiley & Sons

Useful documents

Care Homes for Older People: National Minimum Standards. London: Stationery Office, 2002

Children Act 1989, London: HMSO, 1989

Home Life: A Code of Practice for Residential Care. London: Centre for Policy on Ageing, 1984

Modernising health and social services: National priorities guidance 1999/00–2001/02. London: Department of Health, 1998

No secrets: Guidance on developing and implementing multi-agency policies and procedures to protect vulnerable adults from abuse. London: Department of Health, 1999

Partnership in Action: New opportunities for joint working between health and social services London: Department of Health, 1998

Promoting independence, preventative strategies and support for adults.
Local Authority Circular (99) 14 London: Department of Health

The Caldicott Committee: Report on the review of patient identifiable information. London: Department of Health, 1997

Valuing People: A New Strategy for Learning Disability for the 21st Century. London: Department of Health, 2001

Useful websites

Care and Health magazine **www.careandhealth.com**

Care Homes for Older People: National Minimum Standards **www.doh.gov.uk/ncsc**

Care Standards Act (HMSO) **www.hmso.gov.uk/acts/acts2000/20000014.htm**

Department of Health **www.doh.gov.uk**

Health Development Agency **www.hda-online.org.uk**

Information Commissioner (Data Protection) **www.dataprotection.gov.uk/**

Investors in People **www.iipuk.co.uk**

National Care Homes Association **www.ncha.gb.com**

National Care Manager's Association **www.ncma.co.uk**

National Care Standards Commission **www.carestandards.org.uk**

NHS **www.nhs.uk**

Nursing and Midwifery Council **www.nmc-uk.org**

Social Care Association **www.socialcareassoc.com**

TOPSS **www.topss.org.uk**

World Health Organization **www.who.int**

Index

Note: Page numbers in italics refer to charts and diagrams.